American PIONEER WRITERS

American

PIONEER

WRITERS

WILLA CATHER
GERTRUDE ATHERTON
BRET HARTE
GUSTAVE AIMARD

Gallery Books
an imprint of W.H. Smith Publishers, Inc.
112 Madison Avenue
New York, New York 10016

This volume first published in 1991 by

Reed International Books Limited
Michelin House, 81 Fulham Road,
London SW3 6RB

This volume published in 1991 by Gallery Books
an imprint of W.H. Smith Publishers Inc.,
112 Madison Avenue, New York 10016

ISBN 0 8317 0317 2

Printed in Czechoslovakia

CONTENTS

O PIONEERS!

by Willa Cather

PART I

THE WILD LAND

PRAIRIE SPRING

EVENING and the flat land,
Rich and sombre and always silent;
The miles of fresh-plowed soil,
Heavy and black, full of strength and harshness;
The growing wheat, the growing weeds,
The toiling horses, the tired men;
The long empty roads,
Sullen fires of sunset, fading,
The eternal, unresponsive sky.
Against all this, Youth
Flaming like the wild roses,
Singing like the larks over the plowed fields,
Flashing like a star out of the twilight;
Youth with its insupportable sweetness,
Its fierce necessity,
Its sharp desire,
Singing and singing,
Out of the lips of silence,
Out of the earthy dusk.

CHAPTER 1

ONE January day, thirty years ago, the little town of Hanover, anchored on a windy Nebraska tableland, was trying not to be blown away. A mist of fine snowflakes was curling and eddying about the cluster of low drab buildings huddled on the gray prairie, under a gray sky. The dwelling-houses were set about haphazard on the tough prairie sod; some of them looked as if they had been moved in overnight, and others as if they were straying off by themselves, headed straight for the open plain. None of them had any appearance of permanence, and the howling wind blew under them as well as over them. The main street was a deeply rutted road, now frozen hard, which ran from the squat red railway station and the grain 'elevator' at the north end of the town to the lumber yard and the horse pond at the south end. On either side of this road straggled two uneven rows of wooden buildings; the general merchandise stores, the two banks, the drug store, the feed store, the saloon, the post-office. The board sidewalks were gray with trampled snow, but at two o'clock in the afternoon the shopkeepers, having come back from dinner, were keeping well behind their frosty windows. The children were all in school, and there was nobody abroad in the streets but a few rough-looking countrymen in coarse overcoats, with their long caps pulled down to their noses. Some of them had brought their wives to town, and now and then a red or a plaid shawl flashed out of one store into the shelter of another. At the hitch-bars along the street a few heavy work horses, harnessed to farm wagons, shivered under their blankets. About the station everything was quiet, for there would not be another train in until night.

On the sidewalk in front of one of the stores sat a little Swede boy, crying bitterly. He was about five years old. His black cloth coat was much too big for him and made him look like a little old man. His shrunken brown flannel dress had been washed many times and left a long stretch of stocking between the hem of his skirt and the tops of his clumsy, copper-toed shoes. His cap was pulled down over his ears; his nose and his chubby cheeks were chapped and red with cold. He cried quietly, and the few people who hurried by did not notice him. He was afraid to stop any one, afraid to go into the store and ask for help, so he sat wringing his long sleeves and looking up a telegraph pole beside him, whimpering, 'My kitten, oh, my kitten! Her will fweeze!' At the top of the pole crouched a shivering gray kitten, mewing faintly and clinging desperately to the wood with her claws. The boy had been left at the store while his sister went to the doctor's office, and in her absence a dog had chased his kitten up the pole. The little creature had never been so high before, and she was too frightened to move. Her master was sunk in despair. He was a little country boy, and this village was to him a very strange and perplexing place, where people wore fine clothes and had hard hearts. He always felt shy and awkward here, and wanted to hide behind things for fear some one might laugh at him. Just now, he was too unhappy to care who laughed. At last he seemed to see a ray of hope: his sister was coming, and he got up and ran toward her in his heavy shoes.

His sister was a tall, strong girl, and she walked rapidly and resolutely, as if she knew exactly where she was going and what she was going to do next. She wore a man's long ulster (not as if it were an affliction, but as if it were very comfortable and belonged to her; carried it like a young soldier), and a round plush cap, tied down with a thick veil. She had a serious, thoughtful face, and her clear, deep blue eyes were fixed intently on the distance, without seeming to see anything, as if she were in trouble. She did not notice the little boy until he pulled her by the coat. Then she stopped short and stooped down to wipe his wet face.

'Why, Emil! I told you to stay in the store and not to come out. What is the matter with you?'

'My kitten, sister, my kitten! A man put her out, and a dog chased her up there.' His forefinger, projecting from the sleeve of his coat, pointed up to the wretched little creature on the pole.

'Oh, Emil! Didn't I tell you she'd get us into trouble of some kind, if you brought her? What made you tease me so? But there, I ought to have known better myself.' She went to the foot of the pole and held out her arms, crying, 'Kitty, kitty, kitty,' but the kitten only mewed and faintly waved its tail. Alexandra turned away decidedly. 'No, she won't come down. Somebody will have to go up after her. I saw the Linstrums' wagon in town. I'll go and see if I can find Carl.

11

Maybe he can do something. Only you must stop crying, or I won't go a step. Where's your comforter? Did you leave it in the store? Never mind. Hold still, till I put this on you.'

She unwound the brown veil from her head and tied it about his throat. A shabby little traveling man, who was just then coming out of the store on his way to the saloon, stopped and gazed stupidly at the shining mass of hair she bared when she took off her veil; two thick braids, pinned about her head in the German way, with a fringe of reddish-yellow curls blowing out from under her cap. He took his cigar out of his mouth and held the wet end between the fingers of his woolen glove. 'My God, girl, what a head of hair!' he exclaimed, quite innocently and foolishly. She stabbed him with a glance of Amazonian fierceness and drew in her lower lip—most unnecessary severity. It gave the little clothing drummer such a start that he actually let his cigar fall to the sidewalk and went off weakly in the teeth of the wind to the saloon. His hand was still unsteady when he took his glass from the bartender. His feeble flirtatious instincts had been crushed before, but never so mercilessly. He felt cheap and ill-used, as if some one had taken advantage of him. When a drummer had been knocking about in little drab towns and crawling across the wintry country in dirty smoking cars, was he to be blamed if, when he chanced upon a fine human creature, he suddenly wished himself more of a man?

While the little drummer was drinking to recover his nerve, Alexandra hurried to the drug store as the most likely place to find Carl Linstrum. There he was, turning over a portfolio of chromo 'studies' which the druggist sold to the Hanover women who did china painting. Alexandra explained her predicament, and the boy followed her to the corner, where Emil still sat by the pole.

'I'll have to go up after her, Alexandra. I think at the depot they have some spikes I can strap on my feet. Wait a minute.' Carl thrust his hands into his pockets, lowered his head, and darted up the street

12

rt; here and there a windmill gaunt against the
ching in a hollow. But the great fact was the land
l to overwhelm the little beginnings of human
ed in its sombre wastes. It was from facing this
he boy's mouth had become so bitter; because he
too weak to make any mark here, that the land
alone, to preserve its own fierce strength, its
nd of beauty, its uninterrupted mournfulness.
d along over the frozen road. The two friends had
other than usual, as if the cold had somehow
r hearts.

Oscar go to the Blue to cut wood today?' Carl

ost sorry I let them go, it's turned so cold. But
e wood gets low.' She stopped and put her hand to
rushing back her hair. 'I don't know what is to
rl, if father has to die. I don't dare to think about it. I
all go with him and let the grass grow back over

o reply. Just ahead of them was the Norwegian
re the grass had, indeed, grown back over everything,
, hiding even the wire fence. Carl realized that he
helpful companion, but there was nothing he could

Alexandra went on, steadying her voice a little, 'the
g and work hard, but we've always depended so on
on't see how we can go ahead. I almost feel as if there
to go ahead for.'
r father know?'
nk he does. He lies and counts on his fingers all day. I
ying to count up what he is leaving for us. It's a comfort
my chickens are laying right on through the cold weather

against the north wind. He was a tall boy of fifteen, slight and narrow-chested. When he came back with the spikes, Alexandra asked him what he had done with his overcoat.

'I left it in the drug store. I couldn't climb in it, anyhow. Catch me if I fall, Emil,' he called back as he began his ascent. Alexandra watched him anxiously; the cold was bitter enough on the ground. The kitten would not budge an inch. Carl had to go to the very top of the pole, and then had some difficulty in tearing her from her hold. When he reached the ground, he handed the cat to her tearful little master. 'Now go into the store with her, Emil, and get warm.' He opened the door for the child. 'Wait a minute, Alexandra. Why can't I drive for you as far as our place? It's getting colder every minute. Have you seen the doctor?'

'Yes. He is coming over tomorrow. But he says father can't get better; can't get well.' The girl's lip trembled. She looked fixedly up the bleak street as if she were gathering her strength to face something, as if she were trying with all her might to grasp a situation which, no matter how painful, must be met and dealt with somehow. The wind flapped the skirts of her heavy coat about her.

Carl did not say anything, but she felt his sympathy. He, too, was lonely. He was a thin, frail boy, with brooding dark eyes, very quiet in all his movements. There was a delicate pallor in his thin face, and his mouth was too sensitive for a boy's. The lips had already a little curl of bitterness and skepticism. The two friends stood for a few moments on the windy street corner, not speaking a word, as two travelers, who have lost their way, sometimes stand and admit their perplexity in silence. When Carl turned away he said, 'I'll see to your team.' Alexandra went into the store to have her purchases packed in the eggboxes, and to get warm before she set out on her long cold drive.

When she looked for Emil, she found him sitting on a step of the staircase that led up to the clothing and carpet department. He was playing with a little Bohemian girl, Marie Tovesky, who was tying her handkerchief over the kitten's head for a bonnet. Marie was a stranger in the country, having come from Omaha with her mother to visit her uncle, Joe Tovesky. She was a dark child, with brown curly hair, like a brunette doll's, a coaxing little red mouth, and round, yellow-brown eyes. Every one noticed her eyes; the brown iris had golden glints that made them look like gold-stone, or, in softer lights, like that Colorado mineral called tiger-eye.

The country children thereabouts wore their dresses to their shoe-tops, but this city child was dressed in what was then called the 'Kate Greenaway' manner, and her red cashmere frock, gathered full from the yoke, came almost to the floor. This, with her poke bonnet, gave her the look of a quaint little woman. She had a white fur tippet about her neck and made no fussy objections when Emil fingered it admiringly. Alexandra had not the heart to take him away from so pretty a playfellow, and she let them tease the kitten together until Joe Tovesky came in noisily and picked up his little niece, setting her on his shoulder for every one to see. His children were all boys, and he adored this little creature. His cronies formed a circle about him, admiring and teasing the little girl, who took their jokes with great good nature. They were all delighted with her, for they seldom saw so pretty and carefully nurtured a child. They told her that she must choose one of them for a sweetheart, and each began pressing his suit and offering her bribes; candy, and little pigs, and spotted calves. She looked archly into the big, brown, mustached faces, smelling of spirits and tobacco, then she ran her tiny forefinger delicately over Joe's bristly chin and said, 'Here is my sweetheart.'

The Bohemians roared with laughter, and Marie's uncle hugged her until she cried, 'Please don't, Uncle Joe! You hurt me.' Each of Joe's friends gave her a bag of candy, and she kissed them all around, though she did not like country candy very well. Perhaps that was why she bethought herself of Emil. 'Let me down, Uncle Joe,' she

said, 'I want to g
She walked graci
who formed a new
in his sister's skirt

The farm peopl
women were check
shawls about their
with what money th
and gloves and blu
drinking raw alcohol,
to fortify one effectual
after each pull at the
noise in the place, and t
language as it reeked of

Carl came in, wearin
with a brass handle. 'C
team, and the wagon is re
down in the straw in the
boy sleepy, but he still clu

'You were awful good t
When I get big I'll climb a
murmured drowsily. Before
and his cat were both fast as

Although it was only four o
road led southwest, toward
glimmered in the leaden sky.
faces that were turned mutely
who seemed to be looking with
future; upon the sombre eyes of
looking into the past. The little t
it had never been, had fallen beh
stern frozen country received thei

were few and far apa
sky, a sod house crou
itself, which seemed
society that struggl
vast hardness that t
felt that men were
wanted to be let
peculiar, savage ki

The wagon jolt
less to say to eac
penetrated to thei

'Did Lou and
asked.

'Yes. I'm alm
mother frets if th
her forehead, b
become of us, Ca
wish we could
everything.'

Carl made
graveyard, whe
shaggy and re
was not a very

say.

'Of course,
boys are stro
father that I
were nothing

'Does you

'Yes, I th
think he is tr
to him that

and bringing in a little money. I wish we could keep his mind off such things, but I don't have much time to be with him now.'

'I wonder if he'd like to have me bring my magic lantern over some evening?'

Alexandra turned her face toward him. 'Oh, Carl! Have you got it?'

'Yes. It's back there in the straw. Didn't you notice the box I was carrying? I tried it all morning in the drugstore cellar, and it worked ever so well, makes fine big pictures.'

'What are they about?'

'Oh, hunting pictures in Germany, and Robinson Crusoe and funny pictures about cannibals. I'm going to paint some slides for it on glass, out of the Hans Andersen book.'

Alexandra seemed actually cheered. There is often a good deal of the child left in people who have had to grow up too soon. 'Do bring it over, Carl. I can hardly wait to see it, and I'm sure it will please father. Are the pictures colored? Then I know he'll like them. He likes the calendars I get him in town. I wish I could get more. You must leave me here, mustn't you? It's been nice to have company.'

Carl stopped the horses and looked dubiously up at the black sky. 'It's pretty dark. Of course the horses will take you home, but I think I'd better light your lantern, in case you should need it.'

He gave her the reins and climbed back into the wagon-box, where he crouched down and made a tent of his overcoat. After a dozen trials he succeeded in lighting the lantern, which he placed in front of Alexandra, half covering it with a blanket so that the light would not shine in her eyes. 'Now, wait until I find my box. Yes, here it is. Goodnight, Alexandra. Try not to worry.' Carl sprang to the ground and ran off across the fields toward the Linstrum homestead. 'Hoo, hoo-o-o-o!' he called back as he disappeared over a ridge and dropped into a sand gully. The wind answered him like an echo, 'Hoo, hoo-o-o-o-o-o!' Alexandra drove off alone. The rattle of her wagon was lost in the howling of the wind, but her lantern, held firmly between her feet, made a moving point of light along the highway, going deeper and deeper into the dark country.

CHAPTER 2

On one of the ridges of that wintry waste stood the low log house in which John Bergson was dying. The Bergson homestead was easier to find than many another, because it overlooked Norway Creek, a shallow, muddy stream that sometimes flowed, and sometimes stood still, at the bottom of a winding ravine with steep, shelving sides overgrown with brush and cottonwoods and dwarf ash. This creek gave a sort of identity to the farms that bordered upon it. Of all the bewildering things about a new country, the absence of human landmarks is one of the most depressing and disheartening. The houses on the Divide were small and were usually tucked away in low places; you did not see them until you came directly upon them. Most of them were built of the sod itself, and were only the unescapable ground in another form. The roads were but faint tracks in the grass, and the fields were scarcely noticeable. The record of the plow was insignificant, like the feeble scratches on stone left by prehistoric races, so indeterminate that they may, after all, be only the markings of glaciers, and not a record of human strivings.

In eleven long years John Bergson had made but little impression upon the wild land he had come to tame. It was still a wild thing that had its ugly moods; and no one knew when they were likely to come, or why. Mischance hung over it. Its Genius was unfriendly to man. The sick man was feeling this as he lay looking out of the window, after the doctor had left him, on the day following Alexandra's trip to town. There it lay outside his door, the same land, the same lead-colored miles. He knew every ridge and draw and gully between him and the horizon. To the south, his plowed fields; to the east, the sod stables, the cattle corral, the pond,—and then the grass.

Bergson went over in his mind the things that had held him back. One winter his cattle had perished in a blizzard. The next summer one of his plow horses broke its leg in a prairie-dog hole and had to be shot. Another summer he lost his hogs from cholera, and a valuable stallion died from a rattlesnake bite. Time and again his crops had failed. He had lost two children, boys, that came between Lou and Emil, and there had been the cost of sickness and death. Now, when he had at last struggled out of debt, he was going to die himself. He was only forty-six, and had, of course, counted upon more time.

Bergson had spent his first five years on the Divide getting into debt, and the last six getting out. He had paid off his mortgages and had ended pretty much where he began, with the land. He owned exactly six hundred and forty acres of what stretched outside his door; his own original homestead and timber claim, making three hundred and twenty acres, and the half-section adjoining, the homestead of a younger brother who had given up the fight, gone back to Chicago to work in a fancy bakery and distinguish himself in a Swedish athletic club. So far John had not attempted to cultivate the second half-section, but used it for pasture land, and one of his sons rode herd there in open weather.

John Bergson had the Old World belief that land, in itself, is desirable. But this land was an enigma. It was like a horse that no one knows how to break to harness, that runs wild and kicks things to pieces. He had an idea that no one understood how to farm it properly, and this he often discussed with Alexandra. Their neighbors, certainly, knew even less about farming than he did. Many of them had never worked on a farm until they took up their homesteads. They had been *handwerkers* at home; tailors, lock-smiths, joiners, cigar-makers, etc. Bergson himself had worked in a shipyard.

For weeks, John Bergson had been thinking about these things.

His bed stood in the sitting-room, next to the kitchen. Through the day, while the baking and washing and ironing were going on, the father lay and looked up at the roof beams that he himself had hewn, or out at the cattle in the corral. He counted the cattle over and over. It diverted him to speculate as to how much weight each of the steers would probably put on by spring. He often called his daughter in to talk to her about this. Before Alexandra was twelve years old she had begun to be a help to him, and as she grew older he had come to depend more and more upon her resourcefulness and good judgment. His boys were willing enough to work, but when he talked with them they usually irritated him. It was Alexandra who read the papers and followed the markets, and who learned by the mistakes of their neighbors. It was Alexandra who could always tell about what it had cost to fatten each steer, and who could guess the weight of a hog before it went on the scales closer than John Bergson himself. Lou and Oscar were industrious, but he could never teach them to use their heads about their work.

Alexandra, her father often said to himself, was like her grandfather; which was his way of saying that she was intelligent. John Bergson's father had been a shipbuilder, a man of considerable force and of some fortune. Late in life he married a second time, a Stockholm woman of questionable character, much younger than he, who goaded him into every sort of extravagance. On the shipbuilder's part, this marriage was an infatuation, the despairing folly of a powerful man who cannot bear to grow old. In a few years his unprincipled wife warped the probity of a lifetime. He speculated, lost his own fortune and funds entrusted to him by poor seafaring men, and died disgraced, leaving his children nothing. But when all was said, he had come up from the sea himself, had built up a proud little business with no capital but his own skill and foresight, and had proved himself a man. In his daughter, John Bergson recognized the strength of will, and the simple direct way of thinking things out, that had characterized his father in his better days. He would much rather, of course, have seen this likeness in one of his sons, but it was not a question of choice. As he lay there day after day he had to accept the situation as it was, and to be thankful that there was one among his children to whom he could entrust the future of his family and the possibilities of his hard-won land.

The winter twilight was fading. The sick man heard his wife strike a match in the kitchen, and the light of a lamp glimmered through the cracks of the door. It seemed like a light shining far away. He turned painfully in his bed and looked at his white hands, with all the work gone out of them. He was ready to give up, he felt. He did not know how it had come about, but he was quite willing to go deep under his fields and rest, where the plow could not find him. He was tired of making mistakes. He was content to leave the tangle to other hands; he thought of his Alexandra's strong ones.

'*Dotter*,' he called feebly, '*dotter!*' He heard her quick step and saw her tall figure appear in the doorway, with the light of the lamp behind her. He felt her youth and strength, how easily she moved and stooped and lifted. But he would not have had it again if he could, not he! He knew the end too well to wish to begin again. He knew where it all went to, what it all became.

His daughter came and lifted him up on his pillows. She called him by an old Swedish name that she used to call him when she was little and took his dinner to him in the shipyard.

'Tell the boys to come here, daughter. I want to speak to them.'

'They are feeding the horses, father. They have just come back from the Blue. Shall I call them?'

He sighed. 'No, no. Wait until they come in. Alexandra, you will have to do the best you can for your brothers. Everything will come on you.'

'I will do all I can, father.'

'Don't let them get discouraged and go off like Uncle Otto. I want them to keep the land.'

'We will, father. We will never lose the land.'

There was a sound of heavy feet in the kitchen. Alexandra went to the door and beckoned to her brothers, two strapping boys of seventeen and nineteen. They came in and stood at the foot of the bed. Their father looked at them searchingly, though it was too dark to see their faces; they were just the same boys, he told himself, he had not been mistaken in them. The square head and heavy shoulders belonged to Oscar, the elder. The younger boy was quicker, but vacillating.

'Boys,' said the father wearily, 'I want you to keep the land together and to be guided by your sister. I have talked to her since I have been sick, and she knows all my wishes. I want no quarrels among my children, and so long as there is one house there must be one head. Alexandra is the oldest, and she knows my wishes. She will do the best she can. If she makes mistakes, she will not make so many as I have made. When you marry, and want a house of your own, the land will be divided fairly, according to the courts. But for the next few years you will have it hard, and you must all keep together. Alexandra will manage the best she can.'

Oscar, who was usually the last to speak, replied because he was the older, 'Yes, father. It would be so anyway, without your speaking. We will work the place together.'

'And you will be guided by your sister, boys, and be good brothers to her, and good sons to your mother? That is good. And Alexandra must not work in the fields any more. There is no necessity now. Hire a man when you need help. She can make much more with her eggs and butter than the wages of a man. It was one of my mistakes that I did not find that out sooner. Try to break a little more land every year; sod corn is good for fodder. Keep turning the land, and always put up more hay than you need. Don't grudge your mother a little time for plowing her garden and setting out fruit trees, even if it comes in a busy season. She has been a good mother to you, and she has always missed the old country.'

When they went back to the kitchen the boys sat down silently at the table. Throughout the meal they looked down at their places and did not lift their red eyes. They did not eat much, although they had been working in the cold all day, and there was a rabbit stewed in gravy for supper, and prune pies.

John Bergson had married beneath him, but he had married a good housewife. Mrs Bergson was a fair-skinned, corpulent woman, heavy and placid like her son, Oscar, but there was something comfortable about her; perhaps it was her own love of comfort. For eleven years she had worthily striven to maintain some semblance of household order amid conditions that made order very difficult. Habit was very strong with Mrs Bergson, and her unremitting efforts to repeat the routine of her old life among new surroundings had done a great deal to keep the family from disintegrating morally and getting careless in their ways. The Bergsons had a log house, for instance, only because Mrs Bergson would not live in a sod house. She missed the fish diet of her own country, and twice every summer she sent the boys to the river, twenty miles to the southward to fish for channel cat. When the children were little she used to load them all into the wagon, the baby in its crib, and go fishing herself.

Alexandra often said that if her mother were cast upon a desert island, she would thank God for her deliverance, make a garden, and find something to preserve. Preserving was almost a mania with Mrs Bergson. Stout as she was, she roamed the scrubby banks of Norway Creek looking for fox grapes and goose plums, like a wild creature in search of prey. She made a yellow jam of the insipid ground cherries that grew on the prairie, flavoring it with lemon peel; and she made a sticky dark conserve of garden tomatoes. She had experimented even with the rank buffalo pea, and she could not see a fine bronze cluster of them without shaking her head and murmuring, 'What a pity!'

When there was nothing more to preserve, she began to pickle. The amount of sugar she used in these processes was sometimes a serious drain upon the family resources. She was a good mother, but she was glad when her children were old enough not to be in her way in the kitchen. She had never quite forgiven John Bergson for bringing her to the end of the earth; but, now that she was there, she wanted to be let alone to reconstruct her old life in so far as that was possible. She could still take some comfort in the world if she had bacon in the cave, glass jars on the shelves, and sheets in the press. She disapproved of all her neighbors because of their slovenly house-keeping, and the women thought her very proud. Once when Mrs Bergson, on her way to Norway Creek, stopped to see old Mrs Lee, the old woman hid in the haymow 'for fear Mis' Bergson would catch her barefoot.''

CHAPTER 3

ONE Sunday afternoon in July, six months after John Bergson's death, Carl was sitting in the doorway of the Linstrum kitchen, dreaming over an illustrated paper, when he heard the rattle of a wagon along the hill road. Looking up he recognized the Bergsons' team, with two seats in the wagon, which meant they were off for a pleasure excursion. Oscar and Lou, on the front seat, wore their cloth hats and coats, never worn except on Sundays, and Emil, on the second seat with Alexandra, sat proudly in his new trousers, made from a pair of his father's, and a pink-striped shirt, with a wide ruffled collar. Oscar stopped the horses and waved to Carl, who caught up his hat and ran through the melon patch to join them.

'Want to go with us?' Lou called. 'We're going to Crazy Ivar's to buy a hammock.'

'Sure.' Carl ran up panting, and clambering over the wheel sat down beside Emil. 'I've always wanted to see Ivar's pond. They say it's the biggest in all the country. Aren't you afraid to go to Ivar's in that new shirt, Emil? He might want it and take it right off your back.'

Emil grinned. 'I'd be awful scared to go,' he admitted, 'if you big boys weren't along to take care of me. Did you ever hear him howl, Carl? People say sometimes he runs about the country howling at night because he is afraid the Lord will destroy him. Mother thinks he must have done something awful wicked.'

Lou looked back and winked at Carl. 'What would you do, Emil, if you was out on the prairie by yourself and seen him coming?'

Emil stared. 'Maybe I could hide in a badger hole,' he suggested doubtfully.

'But suppose there wasn't any badger hole,' Lou persisted. 'Would you run?'

'No, I'd be too scared to run,' Emil admitted mournfully, twisting his fingers. 'I guess I'd sit right down on the ground and say my prayers.'

The big boys laughed, and Oscar brandished his whip over the broad backs of the horses.

'He wouldn't hurt you, Emil,' said Carl persuasively. 'He came to doctor our mare when she ate green corn and swelled up most as big as the water tank. He petted her just like you do your cats. I couldn't understand much he said, for he don't talk any English, but he kept patting her and groaning as if he had the pain himself, and saying, "There now, sister, that's easier, that's better!"'

Lou and Oscar laughed, and Emil giggled delightedly and looked up at his sister.

'I don't think he knows anything at all about doctoring,' said Oscar scornfully. 'They say when horses have distemper he takes the medicine himself, and then prays over the horses.'

Alexandra spoke up. 'That's what the Crows said, but he cured their horses, all the same. Some days his mind is cloudy, like. But if

25

you can get him on a clear day, you can learn a great deal from him. He understands animals. Didn't I see him take the horn off the Berquist's cow when she had torn it loose and went crazy? She was tearing all over the place, knocking herself against things. And at last she ran out on the roof of the old dugout and her legs went through and there she stuck, bellowing. Ivar came running with his white bag, and the moment he got to her she was quiet and let him saw her horn off and daub the place with tar.'

Emil had been watching his sister, his face reflecting the sufferings of the cow. 'And then didn't it hurt her any more?' he asked.

Alexandra patted him. 'No, not any more. And in two days they could use her milk again.'

The road to Ivar's homestead was a very poor one. He had settled in the rough country across the county line, where no one lived but some Russians,—half a dozen families who dwelt together in one long house, divided off like barracks. Ivar had explained his choice by saying that the fewer neighbors he had, the fewer temptations. Nevertheless, when one considered that his chief business was horse-doctoring, it seemed rather short-sighted of him to live in the most inaccessible place he could find. The Bergson wagon lurched along over the rough hummocks and grass banks, followed the bottom of winding draws, or skirted the margin of wide lagoons, where the golden coreopsis grew up out of the clear water and the wild ducks rose with a whirr of wings.

Lou looked after them helplessly. 'I wish I'd brought my gun, anyway, Alexandra,' he said fretfully. 'I could have hidden it under the straw in the bottom of the wagon.'

'Then we'd have had to lie to Ivar. Besides, they say he can smell dead birds. And if he knew, we wouldn't get anything out of him, not even a hammock. I want to talk to him, and he won't talk sense if he's angry. It makes him foolish.'

Lou sniffed. 'Whoever heard of him talking sense, anyhow! I'd rather have ducks for supper than Crazy Ivar's tongue.'

Emil was alarmed. 'Oh, but, Lou, you don't want to make him mad! He might howl!'

They all laughed again, and Oscar urged the horses up the crumbling side of a clay bank. They had left the lagoons and the red grass behind them. In Crazy Ivar's country the grass was short and gray, the draws deeper than they were in the Bergsons' neighborhood, and the land was all broken up into hillocks and clay ridges. The wild flowers disappeared, and only in the bottom of the draws and gullies grew a few of the very toughest and hardiest: shoestring and ironweed, and snow-on-the-mountain.

'Look, look, Emil, there's Ivar's big pond!' Alexandra pointed to a shining sheet of water that lay at the bottom of a shallow draw. At one end of the pond was an earthen dam, planted with green willow bushes, and above it a door and a single window were set into the hillside. You would not have seen them at all but for the reflection of the sunlight upon the four panes of window-glass. And that was all you saw. Not a shed, not a corral, not a well, not even a path broken in the curly grass. But for the piece of rusty stovepipe sticking up through the sod, you could have walked over the roof of Ivar's dwelling without dreaming that you were near a human habitation. Ivar had lived for three years in the clay bank, without defiling the face of nature any more than the coyote that had lived there before him had done.

When the Bergsons drove over the hill, Ivar was sitting in the doorway of his house, reading the Norwegian Bible. He was a queerly shaped old man, with a thick, powerful body set on short bow-legs. His shaggy white hair, falling in a thick mane about his ruddy cheeks, made him look older than he was. He was barefoot, but he wore a clean shirt of unbleached cotton, open at the neck. He always put on a clean shirt when Sunday morning came round, though he never went to church. He had a peculiar religion of his own and could not get on with any of the denominations. Often he did not see anybody from one week's end to another. He kept a calendar, and every morning he checked off a day, so that he was never in any doubt as to which day of the week it was. Ivar hired himself out in threshing and corn-husking time, and he doctored sick animals when he was sent for. When he was at home, he made hammocks out of twine and committed chapters of the Bible to memory.

Ivar found contentment in the solitude he had sought out for himself. He disliked the litter of human dwellings: the broken food, the bits of broken china, the old wash boilers and tea kettles thrown into the sunflower patch. He preferred the cleanness and tidiness of the wild sod. He always said that the badgers had cleaner houses than people, and that when he took a housekeeper her name would be Mrs Badger. He best expressed his preference for his wild homestead by saying that his Bible seemed truer to him there. If one stood in the doorway of his cave, and looked off at the rough land, the smiling sky, the curly grass white in the hot sunlight; if one listened to the rapturous song of the lark, the drumming of the quail, the burr of the locust against that vast silence, one understood what Ivar meant.

On this Sunday afternoon his face shone with happiness. He closed the book on his knee, keeping the place with his horny finger, and repeated softly:—

He sendeth the springs into the valleys, which run among the hills;
They give drink to every beast of the field; the wild asses quench their thirst.
The trees of the Lord are full of sap; the cedars of Lebanon which he hath
    planted;
Where the birds **make their** nests: as for the stork, the fir trees are her house.
The high hills are a **refuge** for the wild goats; and the rocks for the conies.

Before he opened his Bible again, Ivar heard the Bergsons' wagon approaching, and he sprang up and ran toward it.

'No guns, no guns!' he shouted, waving his arms distractedly.

'No, Ivar, no guns,' Alexandra called reassuringly.

He dropped his arms and went up to the wagon, smiling amiably and looking at them out of his pale blue eyes.

'We want to buy a hammock, if you have one,' Alexandra explained, 'and my little brother, here, wants to see your big pond, where so many birds come.'

Ivar smiled foolishly, and began rubbing the horses' noses and feeling about their mouths behind the bits. 'Not many birds just now. A few ducks this morning; and some snipe come to drink. But there was a crane last week. She spent one night and came back the next evening. I don't know why. It is not her season, of course. Many of them go over in the fall. Then the pond is full of strange voices every night.'

Alexandra translated for Carl, who looked thoughtful. 'Ask him, Alexandra, if it is true that a sea gull came here once. I have heard so.'

She had some difficulty in making the old man understand.

He looked puzzled at first, then smote his hands together as he remembered. 'Oh, yes, yes! A big white bird with long wings and pink feet. My! what a voice she had! She came in the afternoon and kept flying about the pond and screaming until dark. She was in trouble of some sort, but I could not understand her. She was going over to the other ocean, maybe, and did not know how far it was. She was afraid of never getting there. She was more mournful than our birds here; she cried in the night. She saw the light from my window and darted up to it. Maybe she thought my house was a boat, she was such a wild thing. Next morning, when the sun rose, I went out to take her food, but she flew up into the sky and went on her way.' Ivar ran his fingers through his thick hair. 'I have many strange birds stop with me here. They come from very far away and are great company. I hope you boys never shoot wild birds?'

Lou and Oscar grinned, and Ivar shook his bushy head. 'Yes, I know boys are thoughtless. But these wild things are God's birds. He watches over them and counts them, as we do our cattle; Christ says so in the New Testament.'

'Now, Ivar,' Lou asked, 'may we water our horses at your pond and give them some feed? It's a bad road to your place.'

'Yes, yes, it is.' The old man scrambled about and began to loose the tugs. 'A bad road, eh, girls? And the bay with a colt at home!'

Oscar brushed the old man aside. 'We'll take care of the horses, Ivar. You'll be finding some disease on them. Alexandra wants to see your hammocks.'

Ivar led Alexandra and Emil to his little cave house. He had but one room, neatly plastered and whitewashed, and there was a wooden floor. There was a kitchen stove, a table covered with oilcloth, two chairs, a clock, a calendar, a few books on the window-shelf; nothing more. But the place was as clean as a cupboard.

'But where do you sleep, Ivar?' Emil asked, looking about.

Ivar unslung a hammock from a hook on the wall; in it was rolled a buffalo robe. 'There, my son. A hammock is a good bed, and in winter I wrap up in this skin. Where I go to work, the beds are not half so easy as this.'

By this time Emil had lost all his timidity. He thought a cave a very superior kind of house. There was something pleasantly unusual about it and about Ivar. 'Do the birds know you will be kind to them, Ivar? Is that why so many come?' he asked.

Ivar sat down on the floor and tucked his feet under him. 'See, little brother, they have come from a long way, and they are very tired. From up there where they are flying, our country looks dark and flat. They must have water to drink and to bathe in before they can go on with their journey. They look this way and that, and far below them they see something shining, like a piece of glass set in the dark earth. That is my pond. They come to it and are not disturbed. Maybe I sprinkle a little corn. They tell the other birds, and next year more come this way. They have their roads up there, as we have down here.'

Emil rubbed his knees thoughtfully. 'And is that true, Ivar, about the head ducks falling back when they are tired, and the hind ones taking their place?'

'Yes. The point of the wedge gets the worst of it; they cut the wind. They can only stand it there a little while—half an hour, maybe. Then they fall back and the wedge splits a little, while the rear ones come up the middle to the front. Then it closes up and they fly on, with a new edge. They are always changing like that, up in the air. Never any confusion; just like soldiers who have been drilled.'

Alexandra had selected her hammock by the time the boys came up from the pond. They would not come in, but sat in the shade of the bank outside while Alexandra and Ivar talked about the birds and about his housekeeping, and why he never ate meat, fresh or salt.

Alexandra was sitting on one of the wooden chairs, her arms resting on the table. Ivar was sitting on the floor at her feet. 'Ivar,' she said suddenly, beginning to trace the pattern on the oilcloth with her forefinger, 'I came today more because I wanted to talk to you than because I wanted to buy a hammock.'

'Yes?' The old man scraped his bare feet on the plank floor.

'We have a big bunch of hogs, Ivar. I wouldn't sell in the spring, when everybody advised me to, and now so many people are losing their hogs that I am frightened. What can be done?'

Ivar's little eyes began to shine. They lost their vagueness.

'You feed them swill and such stuff? Of course! And sour milk? Oh, yes! And keep them in a stinking pen? I tell you, sister, the hogs of this country are put upon! They become unclean, like the hogs in the Bible. If you kept your chickens like that, what would happen? You have a little sorghum patch, maybe? Put a fence around it, and turn the hogs in. Build a shed to give them shade, a thatch on poles. Let the boys haul water to them in barrels, clean water, and plenty. Get them off the old stinking ground, and do not let them go back

31

there until winter. Give them only grain and clean feed, such as you would give horses or cattle. Hogs do not like to be filthy.'

The boys outside the door had been listening. Lou nudged his brother. 'Come, the horses are done eating. Let's hitch up and get out of here. He'll fill her full of notions. She'll be for having the pigs sleep with us, next.'

Oscar grunted and got up. Carl, who could not understand what Ivar said, saw that the two boys were displeased. They did not mind hard work, but they hated experiments and could never see the use of taking pains. Even Lou, who was more elastic than his older brother, disliked to do anything different from their neighbors. He felt that it made them conspicuous and gave people a chance to talk about them.

Once they were on the homeward road, the boys forgot their ill-humor and joked about Ivar and his birds. Alexandra did not propose any reforms in the care of the pigs, and they hoped she had forgotten Ivar's talk. They agreed that he was crazier than ever, and would never be able to prove up on his land because he worked it so little. Alexandra privately resolved that she would have a talk with Ivar about this and stir him up. The boys persuaded Carl to stay for supper and go swimming in the pasture pond after dark.

That evening, after she had washed the supper dishes, Alexandra sat down on the kitchen doorstep, while her mother was mixing the bread. It was a still, deep-breathing summer night, full of the smell of the hay fields. Sounds of laughter and splashing came up from the pasture, and when the moon rose rapidly above the bare rim of the prairie, the pond glittered like polished metal, and she could see the flash of white bodies as the boys ran about the edge, or jumped into the water. Alexandra watched the shimmering pool dreamily, but eventually her eyes went back to the sorghum patch south of the barn, where she was planning to make her new pig corral.

CHAPTER 4

FOR the first three years after John Bergson's death, the affairs of his family prospered. Then came the hard times that brought every one on the Divide to the brink of despair; three years of drouth and failure, the last struggle of a wild soil against the encroaching plowshare. The first of these fruitless summers the Bergson boys bore courageously. The failure of the corn crop made labor cheap. Lou and Oscar hired two men and put in bigger crops than ever before. They lost everything they spent. The whole country was discouraged. Farmers who were already in debt had to give up their land. A few foreclosures demoralized the county. The settlers sat about on the wooden sidewalks in the little town and told each other that the country was never meant for men to live in; the thing to do was to get back to Iowa, to Illinois, to any place that had been proved habitable. The Bergson boys, certainly would have been happier with their uncle Otto, in the bakery shop in Chicago. Like most of their neighbors, they were meant to follow in paths already marked out for them, not to break trails in a new country. A steady job, a few holidays, nothing to think about, and they would have been very happy. It was no fault of theirs that they had been dragged into the wilderness when they were little boys. A pioneer should have imagination, should be able to enjoy the idea of things more than the things themselves.

The second of these barren summers was passing. One September afternoon Alexandra had gone over to the garden across the draw to dig sweet potatoes—they had been thriving upon the weather that was fatal to everything else. But when Carl Linstrum came up the garden rows to find her, she was not working. She was standing lost in thought, leaning upon her pitchfork, her sunbonnet lying beside her on the ground. The dry garden patch smelled of drying vines and was strewn with yellow seed-cucumbers and pumpkins and citrons. At one end, next the rhubarb, grew feathery asparagus, with red berries. Down the middle of the garden was a row of gooseberry and currant bushes. A few tough zenias and marigolds and a row of scarlet sage bore witness to the buckets of water that Mrs Bergson had carried there after sundown, against the prohibition of her sons. Carl came quietly and slowly up the garden path, looking intently at Alexandra. She did not hear him. She was standing perfectly still, with that serious ease so characteristic of her. Her thick, reddish braids, twisted about her head, fairly burned in the sunlight. The air was cool enough to make the warm sun pleasant on one's back and shoulders, and so clear that the eye could follow a hawk up and up, into the blazing blue depths of the sky. Even Carl, never a very cheerful boy, and considerably darkened by these last two bitter years, loved the country on days like this, felt something strong and young and wild come out of it, that laughed at care.

'Alexandra,' he said as he approached her, 'I want to talk to you. Let's sit down by the gooseberry bushes.' He picked up her sack of potatoes and they crossed the garden. 'Boys gone to town?' he asked as he sank down on the warm, sun-baked earth. 'Well, we have made up our minds at last, Alexandra. We are really going away.'

She looked at him as if she were a little frightened. 'Really, Carl? Is it settled?'

'Yes, father has heard from St Louis, and they will give him back his old job in the cigar factory. He must be there by the first of November. They are taking on new men then. We will sell the place for whatever we can get, and auction the stock. We haven't enough to ship. I am going to learn engraving with a German engraver there, and then try to get work in Chicago.'

Alexandra's hands dropped in her lap. Her eyes became dreamy and filled with tears.

Carl's sensitive lower lip trembled. He scratched in the soft earth beside him with a stick. 'That's all I hate about it, Alexandra,' he said slowly. 'You've stood by us through so much and helped father out so many times, and now it seems as if we were running off and leaving you to face the worst of it. But it isn't as if we could really ever be of any help to you. We are only one more drag, one more thing you look out for and feel responsible for. Father was never meant for a farmer, you know that. And I hate it. We'd only get in deeper and deeper.'

'Yes, yes, Carl, I know. You are wasting your life here. You are able to do much better things. You are nearly nineteen now, and I wouldn't have you stay. I've always hoped you would get away. But I can't help feeling scared when I think how I will miss you—more than you will ever know.' She brushed the tears from her cheeks, not trying to hide them.

'But, Alexandra,' he said sadly and wistfully, 'I've never been any real help to you, beyond sometimes trying to keep the boys in a good humor.'

Alexandra smiled and shook her head. 'Oh, it's not that. Nothing like that. It's by understanding me, and the boys, and mother, that you've helped me. I expect that is the only way one person ever really can help another. I think you are about the only one that ever helped me. Somehow it will take more courage to bear your going than everything that has happened before.'

Carl looked at the ground. 'You see, we've all depended so on you,' he said, 'even father. He makes me laugh. When anything comes up he always says, "I wonder what the Bergsons are going to do about that? I guess I'll go and ask her." I'll never forget that time, when we first came here, and our horse had the colic, and I ran over to your place—your father was away, and you came home with me and showed father how to let the wind out of the horse. You were only a little girl then, but you knew ever so much more about farm work than poor father. You remember how homesick I used to get, and what long talks we used to have coming from school? We've

35

someway always felt alike about things.'

'Yes, that's it; we've liked the same things and we've liked them together, without anybody else knowing. And we've had good times, hunting for Christmas trees and going for ducks and making our plum wine together every year. We've never either of us had any other close friend. And now—' Alexandra wiped her eyes with the corner of her apron, 'and now I must remember that you are going where you will have many friends, and will find the work you were meant to do. But you'll write to me, Carl? That will mean a great deal to me here.'

'I'll write as long as I live,' cried the boy impetuously. 'And I'll be working for you as much as for myself, Alexandra. I want to do something you'll like and be proud of. I'm a fool here, but I know I can do something!' He sat up and frowned at the red grass.

Alexandra sighed. 'How discouraged the boys will be when they hear. They always come home from town discouraged, anyway. So many people are trying to leave the country, and they talk to our boys and make them low-spirited. I'm afraid they are beginning to feel hard toward me because I won't listen to any talk about going. Sometimes I feel like I'm getting tired of standing up for this country.'

'I won't tell the boys yet, if you'd rather not.'

'Oh, I'll tell them myself, tonight, when they come home. They'll be talking wild, anyway, and no good comes of keeping bad news. It's all harder on them than it is on me. Lou wants to get married, poor boy, and he can't until times are better. See, there goes the sun, Carl. I must be getting back. Mother will want her potatoes. It's chilly already, the moment the light goes.'

Alexandra rose and looked about. A golden afterglow throbbed in the west, but the country already looked empty and mournful. A dark moving mass came over the western hill, the Lee boy was bringing in the herd from the other half-section. Emil ran from the windmill to open the corral gate. From the log house, on the little rise across the draw, the smoke was curling. The cattle lowed and bellowed. In the sky the pale half-moon was slowly silvering. Alexandra and Carl walked together down the potato rows. 'I have to keep telling myself what is going to happen,' she said softly. 'Since you have been here, ten years now, I have never really been lonely. But I can remember what it was like before. Now I shall have nobody but Emil. But he is my boy, and he is tender-hearted.'

That night, when the boys were called to supper, they sat down moodily. They had worn their coats to town, but they ate in their striped shirts and suspenders. They were grown men now, and, as Alexandra said, for the last few years they had been growing more and more like themselves. Lou was still the slighter of the two, the quicker and more intelligent, but apt to go off at half-cock. He had a lively blue eye, a thin, fair skin (always burned red to the neckband of his shirt in summer), stiff, yellow hair that would not lie down on his head, and a bristly little yellow mustache, of which he was very proud. Oscar could not grow a mustache; his pale face was as bare as an egg, and his white eyebrows gave it an empty look. He was a man of powerful body and unusual endurance; the sort of man you could attach to a corn-sheller as you would an engine. He would turn it all day, without hurrying, without slowing down. But he was as indolent of mind as he was unsparing of his body. His love of routine amounted to a vice. He worked like an insect, always doing the same thing over in the same way, regardless of whether it was best or no. He felt that there was a sovereign virtue in mere bodily toil, and he rather liked to do things in the hardest way. If a field had once been in corn, he couldn't bear to put it into wheat. He liked to begin his corn-planting at the same time every year, whether the season were backward or forward. He seemed to feel that by his own irreproachable regularity he would clear himself of blame and reprove the weather. When the wheat crop failed, he threshed the straw at a dead loss to demonstrate how little grain there was, and thus prove his case against Providence.

Lou, on the other hand, was fussy and flighty; always planned to get through two days' work in one, and often got only the least important things done. He liked to keep the place up, but he never got round to doing odd jobs until he had to neglect more pressing work to attend to them. In the middle of the wheat harvest, when the grain was over-ripe and every hand was needed, he would stop to mend fences or to patch the harness; then dash down to the field and overwork and be laid up in bed for a week. The two boys balanced each other, and they pulled well together. They had been good friends since they were children. One seldom went anywhere, even to town, without the other.

Tonight, after they sat down to supper, Oscar kept looking at Lou as if he expected him to say something, and Lou blinked his eyes and frowned at his plate. It was Alexandra herself who at last opened the discussion.

'The Linstrums,' she said calmly, as she put another plate of hot biscuit on the table, 'are going back to St Louis. The old man is going to work in the cigar factory again.'

At this Lou plunged in. 'You see, Alexandra, everybody who can crawl out is going away. There's no use of us trying to stick it out, just to be stubborn. There's something in knowing when to quit.'

'Where do you want to go Lou?'

'Any place where things will grow,' said Oscar grimly.

Lou reached for a potato. 'Chris Arnson has traded his half-section for a place down on the river.'

'Who did he trade with?'

'Charley Fuller, in town.'

'Fuller the real estate man? You see, Lou, that Fuller has a head on him. He's buying and trading for every bit of land he can get up here. It'll make him a rich man, some day.'

'He's rich now, that's why he can take a chance.'

'Why can't we? We'll live longer than he will. Some day the land itself will be worth more than all we can ever raise on it.'

Lou laughed. 'It could be worth that, and still not be worth much. Why, Alexandra, you don't know what you're talking about. Our place wouldn't bring now what it would six years ago. The fellows that settled up here just made a mistake. Now they're beginning to see this high land wasn't never meant to grow nothing on, and everybody who ain't fixed to graze cattle is trying to crawl out. It's too high to farm up here. All the Americans are skinning out. That man Percy Adams, north of town, told me that he was going to let Fuller take his land and stuff for four hundred dollars and a ticket to Chicago.'

'There's Fuller again!' Alexandra exclaimed. 'I wish that man would take me for a partner. He's feathering his nest! If only poor people could learn a little from rich people! But all these fellows who are running off are bad farmers, like poor Mr Linstrum. They couldn't get ahead even in good years, and they all got into debt while father was getting out. I think we ought to hold on as long as we can on father's account. He was so set on keeping this land. He must have seen harder times than this, here. How was it in the early days, mother?'

Mrs Bergson was weeping quietly. These family discussions always depressed her, and made her remember all that she had been torn away from. 'I don't see why the boys are always taking on about going away,' she said, wiping her eyes. 'I don't want to move again; out to some raw place, maybe, where we'd be worse off than we are here, and all to do over again. I won't move! If the rest of you go, I will ask some of the neighbors to take me in, and stay and be buried by father. I'm not going to leave him by himself on the prairie, for cattle to run over.' She began to cry more bitterly.

The boys looked angry. Alexandra put a soothing hand on her

mother's shoulder. 'There's no question of that, mother. You don't have to go if you don't want to. A third of the place belongs to you by American law, and we can't sell without your consent. We only want you to advise us. How did it use to be when you and father first came? Was it really as bad as this, or not?'

'Oh, worse! Much worse,' moaned Mrs Bergson. 'Drouth, chince-bugs, hail, everything! My garden all cut to pieces like sauerkraut. No grapes on the creek, no nothing. The people all lived just like coyotes.'

Oscar got up and tramped out of the kitchen. Lou followed him. They felt that Alexandra had taken an unfair advantage in turning their mother loose on them. The next morning they were silent and reserved. They did not offer to take the women to church, but went down to the barn immediately after breakfast and stayed there all day. When Carl Linstrum came over in the afternoon, Alexandra winked to him and pointed toward the barn. He understood her and went down to play cards with the boys. They believed that a very wicked thing to do on Sunday, and it relieved their feelings.

Alexandra stayed in the house. On Sunday afternoon Mrs Bergson always took a nap, and Alexandra read. During the week she read only the newspaper, but on Sunday, and in the long evenings of winter, she read a good deal; read a few things over a great many times. She knew long portions of the *Frithjof Saga* by heart, and, like most Swedes who read at all, she was fond of Longfellow's verse,— the ballads and the 'Golden Legend' and 'The Spanish Student.' Today she sat in the wooden rockingchair with the Swedish Bible open on her knees, but she was not reading. She was looking thoughtfully away at the point where the upland road disappeared over the rim of the prairie. Her body was in an attitude of perfect repose, such as it was apt to take when she was thinking earnestly. Her mind was slow, truthful, steadfast. She had not the least spark of cleverness.

All afternoon the sitting-room was full of quiet and sunlight. Emil was making rabbit traps in the kitchen shed. The hens were clucking and scratching brown holes in the flower beds, and the wind was teasing the prince's feather by the door.

That evening Carl came in with the boys to supper.

'Emil,' said Alexandra, when they were all seated at the table, 'how would you like to go traveling? Because I am going to take a trip, and you can go with me if you want to.'

The boys looked up in amazement; they were always afraid of Alexandra's schemes. Carl was interested.

'I've been thinking, boys,' she went on, 'that maybe I am too set against making a change. I'm going to take Brigham and the buckboard tomorrow and drive down to the river country and spend a few days looking over what they've got down there. If I find anything good, you boys can go down and make a trade.'

'Nobody down there will trade for anything up here,' said Oscar gloomily.

'That's just what I want to find out. Maybe they are just as discontented down there as we are up here. Things away from home often look better than they are. You know what your Hans Andersen book says, Carl, about the Swedes liking to buy Danish bread and the Danes liking to buy Swedish bread, because people always think the bread of another country is better than their own. Anyway, I've heard so much about the river farms, I won't be satisfied till I've seen for myself.'

Lou fidgeted. 'Look out! Don't agree to anything. Don't let them fool you.'

Lou was apt to be fooled himself. He had not yet learned to keep away from the shell-game wagons that followed the circus.

After supper Lou put on a necktie and went across the fields to court Annie Lee, and Carl and Oscar sat down to a game of checkers, while Alexandra read *The Swiss Family Robinson* aloud to her mother and Emil. It was not long before the two boys at the table neglected their game to listen. They were all big children together, and they found the adventures of the family in the tree house so absorbing that they gave them their undivided attention.

CHAPTER 5

ALEXANDRA and Emil spent five days down among the river farms, driving up and down the valley. Alexandra talked to the men about their crops and to the women about their poultry. She spent a whole day with one young farmer who had been away at school, and who was experimenting with a new kind of clover hay. She learned a great deal. As they drove along, she and Emil talked and planned. At last, on the sixth day, Alexandra turned Brigham's head northward and left the river behind.

'There's nothing in it for us down there, Emil. There are a few fine farms, but they are owned by the rich men in town, and couldn't be bought. Most of the land is rough and hilly. They can always scrape along down there, but they can never do anything big. Down there they have a little certainty, but up with us there is a big chance. We must have faith in the high land, Emil. I want to hold on harder than ever, and when you're a man you'll thank me.' She urged Brigham forward.

When the road began to climb the first long swells of the Divide, Alexandra hummed an old Swedish hymn, and Emil wondered why his sister looked so happy. Her face was so radiant that he felt shy about asking her. For the first time, perhaps, since that land emerged from the waters of geologic ages, a human face was set toward it with love and yearning. It seemed beautiful to her, rich and strong and glorious. Her eyes drank in the breadth of it, until her tears blinded her. Then the Genius of the Divide, the great, free spirit which breathes across it, must have bent lower than it ever bent to a human will before. The history of every country begins in the heart of a man or a woman.

Alexandra reached home in the afternoon. That evening she held a family council and told her brothers all that she had seen and heard.

'I want you boys to go down yourselves and look it over. Nothing will convince you like seeing with your own eyes. The river land was settled before this, and so they are a few years ahead of us, and have learned more about farming. The land sells for three times as much as this, but in five years we will double it. The rich men down there own all the best land, and they are buying all they can get. The thing to do is to sell our cattle and what little old corn we have, and buy the Linstrum place. Then the next thing to do is to take out two loans on our half-sections, and buy Peter Crow's place; raise every dollar we can, and buy every acre we can.'

'Mortgage the homestead again?' Lou cried. He sprang up and began to wind the clock furiously. 'I won't slave to pay off another mortgage. I'll never do it. You'd just as soon kill us all, Alexandra, to carry out some scheme!'

Oscar rubbed his high, pale forehead. 'How do you propose to pay off your mortgages?'

Alexandra looked from one to the other and bit her lip. They had never seen her so nervous. 'See here,' she brought out at last. 'We borrow the money for six years. Well, with the money we buy a half-section from Linstrum and a half from Crow, and a quarter from Struble, maybe. That will give us upwards of fourteen hundred acres, won't it? You won't have to pay off your mortgages for six years. By that time, any of this land will be worth thirty dollars an acre—it will be worth fifty, but we'll say thirty; then you can sell a garden patch anywhere, and pay off a debt of sixteen hundred dollars. It's not the principal I'm worried about, it's the interest and taxes. We'll have to strain to meet the payments. But as sure as we are sitting here tonight, we can sit down here ten years from now

43

independent landowners, not struggling farmers any longer. The chance that father was always looking for has come.'

Lou was pacing the floor. 'But how do you *know* that land is going to go up enough to pay the mortages and—'

'And make us rich besides?' Alexandra put in firmly. 'I can't explain that, Lou, You'll have to take my word for it. I *know*, that's all. When you drive about over the country you can feel it coming.'

Oscar had been sitting with his head lowered, his hands hanging between his knees. 'But we can't work so much land,' he said dully, as if he were talking to himself. 'We can't even try. It would just lie there and we'd work ourselves to death.' He sighed, and laid his calloused fist on the table.

Alexandra's eyes filled with tears. She put her hand on his shoulder. 'You poor boy, you won't have to work it. The men in town who are buying up other people's land don't try to farm it. They are the men to watch, in a new country. Let's try to do like the shrewd ones, and not like these stupid fellows. I don't want you boys always to have to work like this. I want you to be independent, and Emil to go to school.'

Lou held his head as if it were splitting. 'Everybody will say we are crazy. It must be crazy, or everybody would be doing it.'

'If they were, we wouldn't have much chance. No, Lou, I was talking about that with the smart young man who is raising the new kind of clover. He says the right thing is usually just what everybody don't do. Why are we better fixed than any of our neighbors? Because father had more brains. Our people were better people than these in the old country. We ought to do more than they do, and see further ahead. Yes, mother, I'm going to clear the table now.'

Alexandra rose. The boys went to the stable to see to the stock, and they were gone a long while. When they came back Lou played on his *dragharmonika* and Oscar sat figuring at his father's secretary all evening. They said nothing more about Alexandra's project, but she felt sure now that they would consent to it. Just before bedtime Oscar went out for a pail of water. When he did not come back, Alexandra threw a shawl over her head and ran down the path to the windmill. She found him sitting there with his head in his hands, and she sat down beside him.

'Don't do anything you don't want to do, Oscar,' she whispered. She waited a moment, but he did not stir. 'I won't say any more about it, if you'd rather not. What makes you so discouraged?'

'I dread signing my name to them pieces of paper,' he said slowly. 'All the time I was a boy we had a mortgage hanging over us.'

'Then don't sign one. I don't want you to, if you feel that way.'

Oscar shook his head. 'No, I can see there's a chance that way. I've thought a good while there might be. We're in so deep now, we might as well go deeper. But it's hard work pulling out of debt. Like pulling a threshing machine out of the mud; breaks your back. Me and Lou's worked hard, and I can't see it's got us ahead much.'

'Nobody knows about that as well as I do, Oscar. That's why I want to try an easier way. I don't want you to have to grub for every dollar.'

'Yes, I know what you mean. Maybe it'll come out right. But signing papers is signing papers. There ain't no maybe about that.' He took his pail and trudged up the path to the house.

Alexandra drew her shawl closer about her and stood leaning against the frame of the mill, looking at the stars which glittered so keenly through the frosty autumn air. She always loved to watch them, to think of their vastness and distance, and of their ordered march. It fortified her to reflect upon the great operations of nature, and when she thought of the law that lay behind them, she felt a sense of personal security. That night she had a new consciousness of the country, felt almost a new relation to it. Even her talk with the boys had not taken away the feeling that had overwhelmed her when she drove back to the Divide that afternoon. She had never known before how much the country meant to her. The chirping of the insects down in the long grass had been like the sweetest music. She had felt as if her heart were hiding down there, somewhere, with the quail and the plover and all the little wild things that crooned or buzzed in the sun. Under the long shaggy ridges, she felt the future stirring.

PART II

NEIGHBORING FIELDS

CHAPTER 1

It is sixteen years since John Bergson died. His wife now lies beside him, and the white shaft that marks their graves gleams across the wheatfields. Could he rise from beneath it, he would not know the country under which he has been asleep. The shaggy coat of the prairie, which they lifted to make him a bed, has vanished forever. From the Norwegian graveyard one looks out over a vast checkerboard, marked off in squares of wheat and corn; light and dark, dark and light. Telephone wires hum along the white roads, which always run at right angles. From the graveyard gate one can count a dozen gayly painted farmhouses; the gilded weather-vanes on the big red barns wink at each other across the green and brown and yellow fields. The light steel windmills tremble throughout their frames and tug at their moorings, as they vibrate in the wind that often blows from one week's end to another across that high, active, resolute stretch of country.

The Divide is now thickly populated. The rich soil yields heavy harvests; the dry, bracing climate and the smoothness of the land make labor easy for men and beasts. There are few scenes more gratifying than a spring plowing in that country, where the furrows of a single field often lie a mile in length, and the brown earth, with such a strong, clean smell, and such a power of growth and fertility in it, yields itself eagerly to the plow; rolls away from the shear, not even dimming the brightness of the metal, with a soft, deep sigh of happiness. The wheat-cutting sometimes goes on all night as well as all day, and in good seasons there are scarcely men and horses enough to do the harvesting. The grain is so heavy that it bends toward the blade and cuts like velvet.

There is something frank and joyous and young in the open face of the country. It gives itself ungrudgingly to the moods of the season, holding nothing back. Like the plains of Lombardy, it seems to rise a little to meet the sun. The air and the earth are curiously mated and intermingled, as if the one were the breath of the other. You feel in the atmosphere the same tonic, puissant quality that is in the tilth, the same strength and resoluteness.

One June morning a young man stood at the gate of the Norwegian graveyard, sharpening his scythe in strokes unconsciously timed to the tune he was whistling. He wore a flannel cap and duck trousers, and the sleeves of his white flannel shirt were rolled back to the elbow. When he was satisfied with the edge of his blade, he slipped the whetstone into his hip pocket and began to swing his scythe, still whistling, but softly, out of respect to the quiet folk about him. Unconscious respect, probably, for he seemed intent upon his own thoughts, and, like the Gladiator's, they were far away. He was a splendid figure of a boy, tall and straight as a young pine tree, with a handsome head, and stormy gray eyes, deeply set under a serious brow. The space between his two front teeth, which were unusually far apart, gave him the proficiency in whistling for which he was distinguished at college. (He also played the cornet in the University band.)

When the grass required his close attention, or when he had to stoop to cut about a headstone, he paused in his lively air,—the 'Jewel' song,—taking it up where he had left it when his scythe swung free again. He was not thinking about the tired pioneers over whom his blade glittered. The old wild country, the struggle in which his sister was destined to succeed while so many men broke their hearts and died, he can scarcely remember. That is all among the dim things of childhood and has been forgotten in the brighter pattern life weaves today, in the bright facts of being captain of the track team, and holding the interstate record for the high jump, in the all-suffusing brightness of being twenty-one. Yet sometimes, in the pauses of his work, the young man frowned and looked at the ground with an intentness which suggested that even twenty-one might have its problems.

When he had been mowing the better part of an hour, he heard the rattle of a light cart on the road behind him. Supposing that it was his sister coming back from one of her farms, he kept on with his work. The cart stopped at the gate and a merry contralto voice called, 'Almost through, Emil?' He dropped his scythe and went toward the fence, wiping his face and neck with his handkerchief. In the cart sat a young woman who wore driving gauntlets and a wide shade hat, trimmed with red poppies. Her face, too, was rather like a poppy, round and brown, with rich color in her cheeks and lips, and her dancing yellow-brown eyes bubbled with gayety. The wind was flapping her big hat and teasing a curl of her chestnut-colored hair. She shook her head at the tall youth.

'What time did you get over here? That's not much of a job for an athlete. Here I've been to town and back. Alexandra lets you sleep late. Oh, I know! Lou's wife was telling me about the way she spoils you. I was going to give you a lift, if you were done.' She gathered up her reins.

'But I will be, in a minute. Please wait for me, Marie,' Emil coaxed. 'Alexandra sent me to mow our lot, but I've done half a dozen others, you see. Just wait till I finish off the Kourdnas'. By the way, they were Bohemians. Why aren't they up in the Catholic graveyard?'

'Free-thinkers,' replied the young woman laconically.

'Lots of the Bohemian boys at the University are,' said Emil, taking up his scythe again. 'What did you ever burn John Huss for, anyway? It's made an awful row. They still jaw about it in history classes.'

'We'd do it right over again, most of us,' said the young woman hotly. 'Don't they ever teach you in your history classes that you'd all be heathen Turks if it hadn't been for the Bohemians?'

Emil had fallen to mowing. 'Oh, there's no denying you're a spunky little bunch, you Czechs,' he called back over his shoulder.

Marie Shabata settled herself in her seat and watched the rhythmical movement of the young man's long arms, swinging her foot as if in time to some air that was going through her mind. The minutes passed. Emil mowed vigorously and Marie sat sunning herself and watching the long grass fall. She sat with the ease that belongs to persons of an essentially happy nature, who can find a comfortable spot almost anywhere; who are supple, and quick in adapting themselves to circumstances. After a final swish, Emil snapped the gate and sprang into the cart, holding his scythe well out over the wheel. 'There,' he sighed. 'I gave old man Lee a cut or so, too. Lou's wife needn't talk. I never see Lou's scythe over here.'

Marie clucked to her horse. 'Oh, you know Annie!' She looked at the young man's bare arms. 'How brown you've got since you came home. I wish I had an athlete to mow my orchard. I get wet to my knees when I go down to pick cherries.'

'You can have one, any time you want him. Better wait until after it rains.' Emil squinted off at the horizon as if he were looking for clouds.

'Will you? Oh, there's a good boy!' She turned her head to him with a quick, bright smile. He felt it rather than saw it. Indeed, he had looked away with the purpose of not seeing it. 'I've been up looking at Angélique's wedding clothes,' Marie went on, 'and I'm so excited I can hardly wait until Sunday. Amédée will be a handsome bridegroom. Is anybody but you going to stand up with him? Well, then it will be a handsome wedding party.' She made a droll face at Emil, who flushed. 'Frank,' Marie continued, flicking her horse, 'is cranky at me because I loaned his saddle to Jan Smirka, and I'm terribly afraid he won't take me to the dance in the evening. Maybe the supper will tempt him. All Angélique's folks are baking for it, and all Amédée's twenty cousins. There will be barrels of beer. If once I get Frank to the supper, I'll see that I stay for the dance. And by the way, Emil, you mustn't dance with me but once or twice. You must dance with all the French girls. It hurts their feelings if you don't. They think you're proud because you've been away to school or something.'

Emil sniffed. 'How do you know they think that?'

'Well, you didn't dance with them much at Raoul Marcel's party, and I could tell how they took it by the way they looked at you—and at me.'

'All right,' said Emil shortly, studying the glittering blade of his scythe.

They drove westward toward Norway Creek, and toward a big white house that stood on a hill, several miles across the fields. There were so many sheds and outbuildings grouped about it that the place looked not unlike a tiny village. A stranger, approaching it, could not help noticing the beauty and fruitfulness of the outlying fields. There was something individual about the great farm, a most unusual trimness and care for detail. On either side of the road, for a mile before you reached the foot of the hill, stood tall osage orange hedges, their glossy green marking off the yellow fields. South of the hill, in a low, sheltered swale, surrounded by a mulberry hedge, was the orchard, its fruit trees knee-deep in timothy grass. Any one thereabouts would have told you that this was one of the richest farms on the Divide, and that the farmer was a woman, Alexandra Bergson.

If you go up the hill and enter Alexandra's big house, you will find that it is curiously unfinished and uneven in comfort. One room is papered, carpeted, over-furnished; the next is almost bare. The pleasantest rooms in the house are the kitchen—where Alexandra's three young Swedish girls chatter and cook and pickle and preserve all summer long—and the sitting-room, in which Alexandra has brought together the old homely furniture that the Bergsons used in their first log house, the family portraits, and the few things her mother brought from Sweden.

When you go out of the house into the flower garden, there you feel again the order and fine arrangement manifest all over the great farm; in the fencing and hedging, in the windbreaks and sheds, in the symmetrical pasture ponds, planted with scrub willows to give shade to the cattle in fly-time. There is even a white row of beehives in the orchard, under the walnut trees. You feel that, properly, Alexandra's house is the big out-of-doors, and that it is in the soil that she expresses herself best.

CHAPTER 2

EMIL reached home a little past noon, and when he went into the kitchen Alexandra was already seated at the head of the long table, having dinner with her men, as she always did unless there were visitors. He slipped into his empty place at his sister's right. The three pretty young Swedish girls who did Alexandra's housework were cutting pies, refilling coffee-cups, placing platters of bread and meat and potatoes upon the red tablecloth, and continually getting in each other's way between the table and the stove. To be sure they always wasted a good deal of time getting in each other's way and giggling at each other's mistakes. But, as Alexandra had pointedly told her sisters-in-law, it was to hear them giggle that she kept three young things in her kitchen; the work she could do herself, if it were necessary. These girls, with their long letters from home, their finery, and their love-affairs, afforded her a great deal of entertainment, and they were company for her when Emil was away at school.

Of the youngest girl, Signa, who has a pretty figure, mottled pink cheeks, and yellow hair, Alexandra is very fond, though she keeps a sharp eye upon her. Signa is apt to be skittish at mealtime, when the men are about, and to spill the coffee or upset the cream. It is supposed that Nelse Jensen, one of the six men at the dinner-table, is courting Signa, though he has been so careful not to commit himself that no one in the house, least of all Signa, can tell just how far the matter has progressed. Nelse watches her glumly as she waits upon the tble, and in the evening he sits on a bench behind the stove with his *dragharmonika*, playing mournful airs and watching her as she goes about her work. When Alexandra asked Signa whether she thought Nelse was in earnest, the poor child hid her hands under her apron and murmured, 'I don't know, ma'm. But he scolds me about everything, like as if he wanted to have me!'

At Alexandra's left sat a very old man, barefoot and wearing a long blue blouse, open at the neck. His shaggy head is scarcely whiter than it was sixteen years ago, but his little blue eyes have become pale and watery, and his ruddy face is withered, like an apple that has clung all winter to the tree. When Ivar lost his land through mismanagement a dozen years ago, Alexandra took him in, and he has been a member of her household ever since. He is too old to work in the fields, but he hitches and unhitches the work-teams and looks after the health of the stock. Sometimes of a winter evening Alexandra calls him into the sitting-room to read the Bible aloud to her, for he still reads very well. He dislikes human habitations, so Alexandra has fitted him up a room in the barn, where he is very comfortable, being near the horses and, as he says, further from temptations. No one has ever found out what his temptations are. In cold weather he sits by the kitchen fire and makes hammocks or mends harness until it is time to go to bed. Then he says his prayers at great length behind the stove, puts on his buffalo-skin coat and goes out to his room in the barn.

Alexandra herself has changed very little. Her figure is fuller, and she has more color. She seems sunnier and more vigorous than she did as a young girl. But she still has the same calmness and deliberation of manner, the same clear eyes, and she still wears her hair in two braids wound round her head. It is so curly that fiery ends escape from the braids and make her head look like one of the big double sunflowers that fringe her vegetable garden. Her face is always tanned in summer, for her sunbonnet is oftener on her arm than on her head. But where her collar falls away from her neck, or where her sleeves are pushed back from her wrist, the skin is of such smoothness and whiteness as none but Swedish women ever possess; skin with the freshness of the snow itself.

Alexandra did not talk much at the table, but she encouraged her men to talk, and she always listened attentively, even when they seemed to be talking foolishly.

Today Barney Flinn, the big red-headed Irishman who had been with Alexandra for five years and who was actually her foreman, though he had no such title, was grumbling about the new silo she had put up that spring. It happened to be the first silo on the Divide, and Alexandra's neighbors and her men were skeptical about it. 'To be sure, if the thing don't work, we'll have plenty of feed without it, indeed,' Barney conceded.

Nelse Jensen, Signa's gloomy suitor, had his word. 'Lou, he says he wouldn't have no silo on his place if you'd give it to him. He says the feed outen it gives the stock the bloat. He heard of somebody lost four head of horses, feedin' 'em that stuff.'

Alexandra looked down the table from one to another. 'Well, the only way we can find out is to try. Lou and I have different notions about feeding stock, and that's a good thing. It's bad if all the members of a family think alike. They never get anywhere. Lou can learn by my mistakes and I can learn by his. Isn't that fair, Barney?'

The Irishman laughed. He had no love for Lou, who was always uppish with him and who said that Alexandra paid her hands too much. 'I've no thought but to give the thing an honest try, mum. 'Twould be only right, after puttin' so much expense into it. Maybe Emil will come out an' have a look at it wid me.' He pushed back his chair, took his hat from the nail, and marched out with Emil, who, with his university ideas, was supposed to have instigated the silo. The other hands followed them, all except old Ivar. He had been depressed throughout the meal and had paid no heed to the talk of the men, even when they mentioned cornstalk bloat, upon which he was sure to have opinions.

'Did you want to speak to me, Ivar?' Alexandra asked as she rose from the table. 'Come into the sitting-room.'

The old man followed Alexandra, but when she motioned him to a chair he shook his head. She took up her workbasket and waited for him to speak. He stood looking at the carpet, his bushy head bowed, his hands clasped in front of him. Ivar's bandy legs seemed to have grown shorter with years, and they were completely misfitted to his broad, thick body and heavy shoulders.

'Well, Ivar, what is it?' Alexandra asked after she had waited longer than usual.

Ivar had never learned to speak English and his Norwegian was quaint and grave, like the speech of the more old-fashioned people. He always addressed Alexandra in terms of the deepest respect, hoping to set a good example to the kitchen girls, whom he thought too familiar in their manners.

'Mistress,' he began faintly, without raising his eyes, 'the folk have been looking coldly at me of late. You know there has been talk.'

'Talk about what, Ivar?'

'About sending me away; to the asylum.'

Alexandra put down her sewing-basket. 'Nobody has come to me with such talk,' she said decidedly. 'Why need you listen? You know I would never consent to such a thing.'

Ivar lifted his shaggy head and looked at her out of his little eyes. 'They say that you cannot prevent it if the folk complain of me, if your brothers complain to the authorities. They say that your brothers are afraid—God forbid!—that I may do you some injury when my spells are on me. Mistress, how can any one think that?—that I could bite the hand that fed me!' The tears trickled down on the old man's beard.

Alexandra frowned. 'Ivar, I wonder at you, that you should come bothering me with such nonsense. I am still running my own house, and other people have nothing to do with either you or me. So long as I am suited with you, there is nothing to be said.'

Ivar pulled a red handkerchief out of the breast of his blouse and wiped his eyes and beard. 'But I should not wish you to keep me if, as they say, it is against your interests, and if it is hard for you to get hands because I am here.'

Alexandra made an impatient gesture, but the old man put out his hand and went on earnestly:—

'Listen, mistress, it is right that you should take these things into account. You know that my spells come from God, and that I would not harm any living creature. You believe that every one should worship God in the way revealed to him. But that is not the way of this country. The way here is for all to do alike. I am despised because I do not wear shoes, because I do not cut my hair, and because I have visions. At home, in the old country, there were many like me, who had been touched by God, or who had seen things in the graveyard at night and were different afterward. We thought nothing of it, and let them alone. But here, if a man is different in his feet or in his head, they put him in the asylum. Look at Peter Kralik; when he was a boy, drinking out of a creek, he swallowed a snake, and always after that he could eat only such food as the creature liked, for when he ate anything else, it became enraged and gnawed him. When he felt it whipping about in him, he drank alcohol to stupefy it and get some ease for himself. He could work as good as any man, and his head was clear, but they locked him up for being different in his stomach. That is the way; they have built the asylum for people who are different, and they will not even let us live in the holes with the badgers. Only your great prosperity has protected me so far. If you had had ill-fortune, they would have taken me to Hastings long ago.'

As Ivar talked, his gloom lifted. Alexandra had found that she could often break his fasts and long penances by talking to him and letting him pour out the thoughts that troubled him. Sympathy always cleared his mind, and ridicule was poison to him.

"There is a great deal in what you say, Ivar. Like as not they will be wanting to take me to Hastings because I have built a silo; and then I may take you with me. But at present I need you here. Only don't come to me again telling me what people say. Let people go on talking as they like, and we will go on living as we think best. You have been with me now for twelve years, and I have gone to you for advice oftener than I have ever gone to any one. That ought to satisfy you.'

Ivar bowed humbly. 'Yes, mistress, I shall not trouble you with their talk again. And as for my feet, I have observed your wishes all these years, though you have never questioned me; washing them every night, even in winter.'

Alexandra laughed. 'Oh, never mind about your feet, Ivar. We can remember when half our neighbors went barefoot in summer. I expect old Mrs Lee would love to slip her shoes off now sometimes, if she dared. I'm glad I'm not Lou's mother-in-law.'

Ivar looked about mysteriously and lowered his voice almost to a whisper. 'You know what they have over at Lou's house? A great

56

white tub, like the stone water-troughs in the old country, to wash themselves in. When you sent me over with the strawberries, they were all in town but the old woman Lee and the baby. She took me in and showed me the thing, and she told me it was impossible to wash yourself clean in it, because, in so much water, you could not make a strong suds. So when they fill it up and send her in there, she pretends, and makes a splashing noise. Then, when they are all asleep, she washes herself in a little wooden tub she keeps under her bed.'

Alexandra shook with laughter. 'Poor old Mrs Lee! They won't let her wear nightcaps, either. Never mind; when she comes to visit me, she can do all the old things in the old way, and have as much beer as she wants. We'll start an asylum for old-time people, Ivar.'

Ivar folded his big handkerchief carefully and thrust it back into his blouse. 'This is always the way, mistress. I come to you sorrowing, and you send me away with a light heart. And will you be so good as to tell the Irishman that he is not to work the brown gelding until the sore on its shoulder is healed?'

'That I will. Now go and put Emil's mare to the cart. I am going to drive up to the north quarter to meet the man from town who is to buy my alfalfa hay.'

CHAPTER 3

ALEXANDRA was to hear more of Ivar's case, however. On Sunday her married brothers came to dinner. She had asked them for that day because Emil, who hated family parties, would be absent, dancing at Amédée Chevalier's wedding, up in the French country. The table was set for company in the dining-room, where highly varnished wood and colored glass and useless pieces of china were conspicuous enough to satisfy the standards of the new prosperity. Alexandra had put herself into the hands of the Hanover furniture dealer, and he had conscientiously done his best to make her dining-room look like his display window. She said frankly that she knew nothing about such things, and she was willing to be governed by the general conviction that the more useless and utterly unusable objects were, the greater their virtue as ornament. That seemed reasonable enough. Since she liked plain things herself, it was all the more necessary to have jars and punchbowls and candlesticks in the company rooms for people who did appreciate them. Her guests liked to see about them these reassuring emblems of prosperity.

The family party was complete except for Emil, and Oscar's wife who, in the country phrase, 'was not going anywhere just now.' Oscar sat at the foot of the table and his four tow-headed little boys, aged from twelve to five, were ranged at one side. Neither Oscar nor Lou has changed much; they have simply, as Alexandra said of them long ago, grown to be more and more like themselves. Lou now looks the older of the two; his face is thin and shrewd and wrinkled about the eyes, while Oscar's is thick and dull. For all his dullness, however, Oscar makes more money than his brother, which adds to Lou's sharpness and uneasiness and tempts him to make a show. The trouble with Lou is that he is tricky, and his neighbors have found out that, as Ivar says, he has not a fox's face for nothing. Politics being the natural field for such talents, he neglects his farm to attend conventions and to run for county offices.

Lou's wife formerly Annie Lee, has grown to look curiously like her husband. Her face has become longer, sharper, more aggressive. She wears her yellow hair in a high pompadour, and is bedecked with rings and chains and 'beauty pins.' Her tight, high-heeled shoes give her an awkward walk, and she is always more or less preoccupied with her clothes. As she sat at the table, she kept telling her youngest daughter to 'be careful now, and not drop anything on mother.'

The conversation at the table was all in English. Oscar's wife, from the malaria district of Missouri, was ashamed of marrying a foreigner, and his boys do not understand a word of Swedish. Annie and Lou sometimes speak Swedish at home, but Annie is almost as much afraid of being 'caught' at it as ever her mother was of being caught barefoot. Oscar still has a thick accent, but Lou speaks like anybody from Iowa.

'When I was in Hastings to attend the convention,' he was saying, 'I saw the superintendent of the asylum, and I was telling him about Ivar's symptoms. He says Ivar's case is one of the most dangerous kind, and it's a wonder he hadn't done something violent before this.'

Alexandra laughed good-humoredly. 'Oh, nonsense, Lou! The doctors would have us all crazy if they could. Ivar's queer, certainly, but he has more sense than half the hands I hire.'

Lou flew at his fried chicken. 'Oh, I guess the doctor knows his business, Alexandra. He was very much surprised when I told him how you'd put up with Ivar. He says he's likely to set fire to the barn any night, or to take after you and the girls with an axe.'

Little Signa, who was waiting on the table, giggled and fled to the kitchen. Alexandra's eyes twinkled. 'That was too much for Signa, Lou. We all know that Ivar's perfectly harmless. The girls would as soon expect me to chase them with an axe.'

Lou flushed and signaled to his wife. 'All the same, the neighbors will be having a say about it before long. He may burn anybody's barn. It's only necessary for one property-owner in the township to make complaint, and he'll be taken up by force. You'd better send him yourself and not have any hard feelings.'

Alexandra helped one of her little nephews to gravy. 'Well, Lou, if any of the neighbors try that, I'll have myself appointed Ivar's guardian and take the case to court, that's all. I am perfectly satisfied with him.'

'Pass the preserves, Lou,' said Annie in a warning tone. She had reasons for not wishing her husband to cross Alexandra too openly.

'But don't you sort of hate to have people see him around here, Alexandra?' she went on with persuasive smoothness.' 'He *is* a disgraceful object, and you're fixed up so nice now. It sort of makes people distant with you, when they never know when they'll hear him scratching about. My girls are afraid as death of him, aren't you, Milly, dear?'

Milly was fifteen, fat and jolly and pompadoured, with a creamy complexion, square white teeth, and a short upper lip. She looked like her grandmother Bergson, and had her comfortable and comfort-loving nature. She grinned at her aunt, with whom she was a great deal more at ease than she was with her mother. Alexandra winked a reply.

'Milly needn't be afraid of Ivar. She's an especial favorite of his. In my opinion Ivar has just as much right to his own way of dressing and thinking as we have. But I'll see that he doesn't bother other people. I'll keep him at home, so don't trouble any more about him, Lou. I've been wanting to ask you about your new bathtub. How does it work?'

Annie came to the fore to give Lou time to recover himself. 'Oh, it works something grand! I can't keep him out of it. He washes himself all over three times a week now, and uses all the hot water. I think it's weakening to stay in as long as he does. You ought to have one, Alexandra.'

'I'm thinking of it. I might have one put in the barn for Ivar, if it will ease people's minds. But before I get a bathtub, I'm going to get a piano for Milly.'

Oscar, at the end of the table, looked up from his plate. 'What does Milly want of a pianny? What's the matter with her organ? She can make some use of that, and play in church.'

Annie looked flustered. She had begged Alexandra not to say anything about this plan before Oscar, who was apt to be jealous of what his sister did for Lou's children. Alexandra did not get on with

Oscar's wife at all. 'Milly can play in church just the same, and she'll still play on the organ. But practising on it so much spoils her touch. Her teacher says so,' Annie brought out with spirit.

Oscar rolled his eyes. 'Well, Milly must have got on pretty good if she's got past the organ. I know plenty of grown folks that ain't,' he said bluntly.

Annie threw up her chin. 'She has got on good, and she's going to play for her commencement when she graduates in town next year.'

'Yes,' said Alexandra firmly, 'I think Milly deserves a piano. All the girls around her have been taking lessons for years, but Milly is the only one of them who can ever play anything when you ask her. I'll tell you when I first thought I would like to give you a piano, Milly, and that was when you learned that book of old Swedish songs that your grandfather used to sing. He had a sweet tenor voice, and when he was a young man he loved to sing. I can remember hearing him singing with the sailors down in the shipyard, when I was no bigger than Stella here,' pointing to Annie's younger daughter.

Milly and Stella both looked through the door into the sitting-room, where a crayon portrait of John Bergson hung on the wall. Alexandra had had it made from a little photograph, taken for his friends just before he left Sweden; a slender man of thirty-five, with soft hair curling about his high forehead, a drooping mustache, and wondering, sad eyes that looked forward into the distance, as if they already beheld the New World.

After dinner Lou and Oscar went to the orchard to pick cherries— they had neither of them had the patience to grow an orchard of their own—and Annie went down to gossip with Alexandra's kitchen girls while they washed the dishes. She could always find out more about Alexandra's domestic economy from the prattling maids than from Alexandra herself, and what she discovered she used to her own advantage with Lou. On the Divide, farmers' daughters no longer went out into service, so Alexandra got her girls from Sweden, by paying their fare over. They stayed with her until they married, and were replaced by sisters or cousins from the old country.

Alexandra took her three nieces into the flower garden. She was fond of the little girls, especially of Milly, who came to spend a week with her aunt now and then, and read aloud to her from the old books about the house, or listened to stories about the early days on the Divide. While they were walking among the flower beds, a buggy drove up the hill and stopped in front of the gate. A man got out and stood talking to the driver. The little girls were delighted at the advent of a stranger, some one from very far away, they knew by his clothes, his gloves, and the sharp, pointed cut of his dark beard. The girls fell behind their aunt and peeped out at him from among the castor beans. The stranger came up to the gate and stood holding his hat in his hand, smiling, while Alexandra advanced slowly to meet him. As she approached he spoke in a low. pleasant voice.

'Don't you know me, Alexandra? I would have known you anywhere.'

Alexandra shaded her eyes with her hand. Suddenly she took a quick step forward. 'Can it be!' she exclaimed with feeling; 'can it be that it is Carl Linstrum? Why, Carl, it is!' She threw out both her hands and caught his across the gate. 'Sadie, Milly, run tell your father and Uncle Oscar that our old friend Carl Linstrum is here. Be quick! Why, Carl, how did it happen? I can't believe this!' Alexandra shook the tears from her eyes and laughed.

The stranger nodded to his driver, dropped his suitcase inside the fence, and opened the gate. 'Then you are glad to see me, and you can put me up overnight? I couldn't go through this country without stopping off to have a look at you. How little you have changed! Do you know, I was sure it would be like that. You simply couldn't be different. How fine you are!' He stepped back and looked at her admiringly.

Alexandra blushed and laughed again. 'But you yourself, Carl—

with that beard—how could I have known you? You went away a little boy.' She reached for his suitcase and when he intercepted her she threw up her hands. 'You see, I give myself away. I have only women come to visit me, and I do not know how to behave. Where is your trunk?'

'It's in Hanover. I can stay only a few days. I am on my way to the coast.'

They started up the path. 'A few days? After all these years!' Alexandra shook her finger at him. 'See this, you have walked into a trap. You do not get away so easy.' She put her hand affectionately on his shoulder. 'You owe me a visit for the sake of old times. Why must you go to the coast at all?'

'Oh, I must! I am a fortune hunter. From Seattle I go on to Alaska.'

'Alaska?' She looked at him in astonishment. 'Are you going to paint the Indians?'

'Paint?' the young man frowned. 'Oh! I'm not a painter, Alexandra. I'm an engraver. I have nothing to do with painting.'

'But on my parlor wall I have the paintings—'

He interrupted nervously. 'Oh, water-color sketches—done for amusement. I sent them to remind you of me, not because they were good. What a wonderful place you have made of this, Alexandra.' He turned and looked back at the wide, map-like prospect of field and hedge and pasture. 'I would never have believed it could be done. I'm disappointed in my own eye, in my imagination.'

At this moment Lou and Oscar came up the hill from the orchard. They did not quicken their pace when they saw Carl; indeed, they did not openly look in his direction. They advanced distrustfully, and as if they wished the distance were longer.

Alexandra beckoned to them. 'They think I am trying to fool them. Come, boys, it's Carl Linstrum, our old Carl!'

Lou gave the visitor a quick, sidelong glance and thrust out his hand. 'Glad to see you.' Oscar followed with 'How d'do.' Carl could not tell whether their offishness came from unfriendliness or from embarrassment. He and Alexandra led the way to the porch.

'Carl,' Alexandra explained, 'is on his way to Seattle. He is going to Alaska.'

Oscar studied the visitor's yellow shoes. 'Got business there?' he asked.

Carl laughed. 'Yes, very pressing business. I'm going there to get rich. Engraving's a very interesting profession, but a man never makes any money at it. So I'm going to try the goldfields.'

Alexandra felt that this was a tactful speech, and Lou looked up with some interest. 'Ever done anything in that line before?'

'No, but I'm going to join a friend of mine who went out from New York and has done well. He has offered to break me in.'

'Turrible cold winters, there, I hear,' remarked Oscar. 'I thought people went up there in the spring.'

'They do. But my friend is going to spend the winter in Seattle and I am to stay with him there and learn something about prospecting before we start north next year.'

Lou looked skeptical. 'Let's see, how long have you been away from here?'

'Sixteen years. You ought to remember that, Lou, for you were married just after we went away.'

'Going to stay with us some time?' Oscar asked.

'A few days, if Alexandra can keep me.'

'I expect you'll be wanting to see your old place,' Lou observed more cordially. 'You won't hardly know it. But there's a few chunks of your old sod house left. Alexandra wouldn't never let Frank Shabata plough over it.'

Annie Lee, who, ever since the visitor was announced, had been touching up her hair and settling her lace and wishing she had worn another dress, now emerged with her three daughters and introduced them. She was greatly impressed by Carl's urban appearance, and in her excitement talked very loud and threw her head about. 'And you ain't married yet? At your age, now! Think of that! You'll have to wait for Milly. Yes. we've got a boy, too. The youngest. He's at home with his grandma. You must come over to see mother and hear Milly play. She's the musician of the family. She does pyrography, too. That's burnt wood, you know. You wouldn't believe what she can do with her poker. Yes, she goes to school in town, and she is the youngest in her class by two years.'

Milly looked uncomfortable and Carl took her hand again. He liked her creamy skin and happy, innocent eyes, and he could see that her mother's way of talking distressed her. 'I'm sure she's a clever little girl,' he murmured, looking at her thoughtfully. 'Let me see— Ah, it's your mother that she looks like, Alexandra. Mrs Bergson must have looked just like this when she was a little girl. Does Milly run about over the country as you and Alexandra used to, Annie?'

Milly's mother protested. 'Oh, my, no! Things has changed since we was girls. Milly has it very different. We are going to rent the place and move into town as soon as the girls are old enough to go out into company. A good many are doing that here now. Lou is going into business.'

Lou grinned. 'That's what she says. You better go get your things on. Ivar's hitching up,' he added, turning to Annie.

Young farmers seldom address their wives by name. It is always 'you,' or 'she.'

Having got his wife out of the way, Lou sat down on the step and began to whittle. 'Well, what do folks in New York think of William Jennings Bryan?' Lou began to bluster, as he always did when he talked politics. 'We gave Wall Street a scare in ninety-six, all right, and we're fixing another to hand them. Silver wasn't the only issue,' he nodded mysteriously. 'There's a good many things got to be changed. The West is going to make itself heard.'

Carl laughed. 'But, surely, it did do that, if nothing else.'

Lou's thin face reddened up to the roots of his bristly hair. 'Oh, we've only begun. We're waking up to a sense of our responsibilities, out here, and we ain't afraid, neither. You fellows back there must be a tame lot. If you had any nerve you'd get together and march down to Wall Street and blow it up. Dynamite it, I mean,' with a threatening nod.

He was so much in earnest that Carl scarcely knew how to answer him. 'That would be a waste of powder. The same business would go on in another street. The street doesn't matter. But what have you fellows out here got to kick about? You have the only safe place there is. Morgan himself couldn't touch you. One only has to drive through this country to see that you're all as rich as barons.'

'We have a good deal more to say than we had when we were poor,' said Lou threateningly. 'We're getting on to a whole lot of things.'

As Ivar drove a double carriage up to the gate, Annie came out in a hat that looked like the model of a battleship. Carl rose and took her down to the carriage, while Lou lingered for a word with his sister.

'What do you suppose he's come for?' he asked, jerking his head toward the gate.

'Why, to pay us a visit. I've been begging him to for years.'

Oscar looked at Alexandra. 'He didn't let you know he was coming?'

'No. Why should he? I told him to come at any time.'

Lou shrugged his shoulders. 'He doesn't seem to have done much for himself. Wandering around this way!'

Oscar spoke solemnly, as from the depths of a cavern. 'He never was much account.'

Alexandra left them and hurried down to the gate where Annie was rattling on to Carl about her new dining-room furniture. 'You must bring Mr Linstrum over real soon, only be sure to telephone me first,' she called back, as Carl helped her into the carriage. Old

Ivar, his white head bare, stood holding the horses. Lou came down the path and climbed into the front seat, took up the reins, and drove off without saying anything further to any one. Oscar picked up his youngest boy and trudged off down the road, the other three trotting after him. Carl, holding the gate open for Alexandra, began to laugh. 'Up and coming on the Divide, eh, Alexandra?' he cried gayly.

CHAPTER 4

CARL had changed, Alexandra felt, much less than one might have expected. He had not become a trim, self-satisfied city man. There was still something homely and wayward and definitely personal about him. Even his clothes, his Norfolk coat and his very high collars, were a little unconventional. He seemed to shrink into himself as he used to do; to hold himself away from things, as if he were afraid of being hurt. In short, he was more self-conscious than a man of thirty-five is expected to be. He looked older than his years and not very strong. His black hair, which still hung in a triangle over his pale forehead, was thin at the crown, and there were fine, relentless lines about his eyes. His back, with its high, sharp shoulders, looked like the back of an overworked German professor off on his holiday. His face was intelligent, sensitive, unhappy.

That evening after supper, Carl and Alexandra were sitting by the clump of castor beans in the middle of the flower garden. The gravel paths glittered in the moonlight, and below them the fields lay white and still.

'Do you know, Alexandra,' he was saying, 'I've been thinking how strangely things work out. I've been away engraving other men's pictures, and you've stayed at home and made your own.' He pointed with his cigar toward the sleeping landscape. 'How in the world have you done it? How have your neighbors done it?'

'We hadn't any of us much to do with it, Carl. The land did it. It had its little joke. It pretended to be poor because nobody knew how to work it right; and then, all at once, it worked itself. It woke up out of its sleep and stretched itself, and it was so big, so rich, that we suddenly found we were rich, just from sitting still. As for me, you remember when I began to buy land. For years after that I was always squeezing and borrowing until I was ashamed to show my face in the banks. And then, all at once, men began to come to me offering to lend me money—and I didn't need it! Then I went ahead and built this house. I really built it for Emil. I want you to see Emil, Carl. He is so different from the rest of us!'

'How different?'

'Oh, you'll see! I'm sure it was to have sons like Emil, and to give them a chance, that father left the old country. It's curious, too; on the outside Emil is just like an American boy,—he graduated from the State University in June, you know,—but underneath he is more Swedish than any of us. Sometimes he is so like father that he frightens me; he is so violent in his feelings like that.'

'Is he going to farm here with you?'

'He shall do whatever he wants to,' Alexandra declared warmly. 'He is going to have a chance, a whole chance; that's what I've worked for. Sometimes he talks about studying law, and sometimes, just lately, he's been talking about going out into the sand hills and taking up more land. He has his sad times, like father. But I hope he won't do that. We have land enough, at last!' Alexandra laughed.

'How about Lou and Oscar? They've done well, haven't they?'

'Yes, very well; but they are different, and now that they have farms of their own I do not see so much of them. We divided the land equally when Lou married. They have their own way of doing things, and they do not altogether like my way, I am afraid. Perhaps they think me too independent. But I have had to think for myself a good many years and am not likely to change. On the whole, though, we take as much comfort in each other as most brothers and sisters do. And I am very fond of Lou's oldest daughter.'

'I think I liked the old Lou and Oscar better, and they probably feel the same about me. I even, if you can keep a secret,'—Carl leaned forward and touched her arm, smiling,—'I even think I liked the old country better. This is all very splendid in its way, but there was something about this country when it was a wild old beast that has haunted me all these years. Now, when I come back to all this milk and honey, I feel like the old German song, 'Wo bist du, wo bist du, mein geliebtest Land?'—Do you ever feel like that, I wonder?'

'Yes, sometimes, when I think about father and mother and those who are gone; so many of our old neighbors.' Alexandra paused and looked up thoughtfully at the stars. 'We can remember the graveyard when it was wild prairie, Carl, and now—'

'And now the old story has begun to write itself over there,' said Carl softly. 'Isn't it queer: there are only two or three human stories, and they go on repeating themselves as fiercely as if they had never happened before; like the larks in this country, that have been singing the same five notes over for thousands of years.'

'Oh, yes! The young people, they live so hard. And yet I sometimes envy them. There is my little neighbor, now; the people who bought your old place. I wouldn't have sold it to any one else, but I was always fond of that girl. You must remember her, little Marie Tovesky, from Omaha, who used to visit here? When she was eighteen she ran away from the convent school and got married, crazy child! She came out here a bride, with her father and husband. He had nothing, and the old man was willing to buy them a place and set them up. Your farm took her fancy, and I was glad to have her so near me. I've never been sorry, either. I even try to get along with Frank on her account.'

'Is Frank her husband?'

'Yes. He's one of these wild fellows. Most Bohemians are good-natured, but Frank thinks we don't appreciate him here, I guess.

He's jealous about everything, his farm and his horses and his pretty wife. Everybody likes her, just the same as when she was little. Sometimes I go up to the Catholic church with Emil, and it's funny to see Marie standing there laughing and shaking hands with people, looking so excited and gay, with Frank sulking behind her as if he could eat everybody alive. Frank's not a bad neighbor, but to get on with him you've got to make a fuss over him and act as if you thought he was a very important person all the time, and different from other people. I find it hard to keep that up from one year's end to another.'

'I shouldn't think you'd be very successful at that kind of thing, Alexandra.' Carl seemed to find the idea amusing.

'Well,' said Alexandra firmly, 'I do the best I can, on Marie's account. She has it hard enough, anyway. She's too young and pretty for this sort of life. We're all ever so much older and slower. But she's the kind that won't be downed easily. She'll work all day and go to a Bohemian wedding and dance all night, and drive the hay wagon for a cross man next morning. I could stay by a job, but I never had the go in me that she has, when I was going my best. I'll have to take you over to see her tomorrow.'

Carl dropped the end of his cigar softly among the castor beans and sighed. 'Yes, I suppose I must see the old place. I'm cowardly about things that remind me of myself. It took courage to come at all, Alexandra. I wouldn't have, if I hadn't wanted to see you very, very much.'

Alexandra looked at him with her calm, deliberate eyes. 'Why do you dread things like that, Carl?' she asked earnestly. 'Why are you dissatisfied with yourself?'

Her visitor winced. 'How direct you are, Alexandra! Just like you used to be. Do I give myself away so quickly? Well, you see, for one thing, there's nothing to look forward to in my profession. Wood-engraving is the only thing I care about, and that had gone out before I began. Everything's cheap metal work nowadays, touching up miserable photographs, forcing up poor drawings, and spoiling good ones. I'm absolutely sick of it all.' Carl frowned. 'Alexandra, all the way out from New York I've been planning how I could deceive you and make you think me a very enviable fellow, and here I am telling you the truth the first night. I waste a lot of time pretending to people, and the joke of it is, I don't think I ever deceive any one. There are too many of my kind; people know us on sight.'

Carl paused. Alexandra pushed her hair back from her brow with a puzzled, thoughtful gesture. 'You see,' he went on calmly, 'measured by your standards here, I'm a failure. I couldn't buy even one of your cornfields. I've enjoyed a great many things, but I've got nothing to show for it all.'

'But you show for it yourself, Carl. I'd rather have had your freedom than my land.'

Carl shook his head mournfully. 'Freedom so often means that one isn't needed anywhere. Here you are an individual, you have a background of your own, you would be missed. But off there in the cities there are thousands of rolling stones like me. We are all alike; we have no ties, we know nobody, we own nothing. When one of us dies, they scarcely know where to bury him. Our landlady and the delicatessen man are our mourners, and we leave nothing behind us but a frock-coat and a fiddle, or an easel, or a typewriter, or whatever tool we got our living by. All we have ever managed to do is to pay our rent, the exorbitant rent that one has to pay for a few square feet of space near the heart of things. We have no house, no place, no people of our own. We live in the streets, in the parks, in the theatres. We sit in restaurants and concert halls and look about at the hundreds of our own kind and shudder.'

Alexandra was silent. She sat looking at the silver spot the moon made on the surface of the pond down in the pasture. He knew that she understood what he meant. At last she said slowly, 'And yet I would rather have Emil grow up like that than like his two brothers.

We pay a high rent, too, though we pay differently. We grow hard and heavy here. We don't move lightly and easily as you do, and our minds get stiff. If the world were no wider than my cornfields, if there were not something beside this, I wouldn't feel that it was much worth while to work. No, I would rather have Emil like you than like them. I felt that as soon as you came.'

'I wonder why you feel like that?' Carl mused.

'I don't know. Perhaps I am like Carrie Jensen, the sister of one of my hired men. She had never been out of the cornfields, and a few years ago she got despondent and said life was just the same thing over and over, and she didn't see the use of it. After she had tried to kill herself once or twice, her folks got worried and sent her over to Iowa to visit some relations. Ever since she's come back she's been perfectly cheerful, and she says she's contented to live and work in a world that's so big and interesting. She said that anything as big as the bridges over the Platte and the Missouri reconciled her. And it's what goes on in the world that reconciles me.'

CHAPTER 5

ALEXANDRA did not find time to go to her neighbor's the next day, nor the next. It was a busy season on the farm, with the corn-plowing going on, and even Emil was in the field with a team and cultivator. Carl went about over the farms with Alexandra in the morning, and in the afternoon and evening they found a great deal to talk about. Emil, for all his track practice, did not stand up under farmwork very well, and by night he was too tired to talk or even to practise on his cornet.

On Wednesday morning Carl got up before it was light, and stole downstairs and out of the kitchen door just as old Ivar was making his morning ablutions at the pump. Carl nodded to him and hurried up the draw, past the garden, and into the pasture where the milking cows used to be kept.

The dawn in the east looked like the light from some great fire that was burning under the edge of the world. The color was reflected in the globules of dew that sheathed the short gray pasture grass. Carl walked rapidly until he came to the crest of the second hill, where the Bergson pasture joined the one that had belonged to his father. There he sat down and waited for the sun to rise. It was just there that he and Alexandra used to do their milking together, he on his side of the fence, she on hers. He could remember exactly how she looked when she came over the close-cropped grass, her skirts pinned up, her head bare, a bright tin pail in either hand, and the milky light of the early morning all about her. Even as a boy he used to feel, when he saw her coming with her free step, her upright head and calm shoulders, that she looked as if she had walked straight out of the morning itself. Since then, when he had happened to see the sun come up in the country or on the water, he had often remembered the young Swedish girl and her milking pails.

Carl sat musing until the sun leaped above the prairie, and in the grass about him all the small creatures of day began to tune their tiny instruments. Birds and insects without number began to chirp, to twitter, to snap and whistle, to make all manner of fresh shrill noises. The pasture was flooded with light; every clump of ironweed and snow-on-the-mountain threw a long shadow, and the golden light seemed to be rippling through the curly grass like the tide racing in.

He crossed the fence into the pasture that was now the Shabatas' and continued his walk toward the pond. He had not gone far, however, when he discovered that he was not the only person abroad. In the draw below, his gun in his hands, was Emil, advancing cautiously, with a young woman beside him. They were moving softly, keeping close together, and Carl knew that they expected to find ducks on the pond. At the moment when they came in sight of the bright spot of water, he heard a whir of wings and the ducks shot up into the air. There was a sharp crack from the gun, and five of the birds fell to the ground. Emil and his companion laughed delightedly, and Emil ran to pick them up. When he came back, dangling the ducks by their feet, Marie held her apron and he dropped them into it. As she stood looking down at them, her face changed. She took up one of the birds, a rumpled ball of feathers with the blood dripping slowly from its mouth, and looked at the live color that still burned on its plumage.

As she let it fall, she cried in distress, 'Oh, Emil, why did you?'

'I like that!' the boy exclaimed indignantly. 'Why, Marie, you asked me to come yourself.'

'Yes, yes, I know,' she said tearfully, 'but I didn't think. I hate to see them when they are first shot. They were having such a good time, and we've spoiled it all for them.'

Emil gave a rather sore laugh. 'I should say we had! I'm not going hunting with you any more. You're as bad as Ivar. Here, let me take them.' He snatched the ducks out of her apron.

'Don't be cross, Emil. Only—Ivar's right about wild things. They're too happy to kill. You can tell just how they felt when they flew up. They were scared, but they didn't really think anything could hurt them. No, we won't do that any more.'

'All right,' Emil assented. 'I'm sorry I made you feel bad.' As he looked down into her tearful eyes, there was a curious, sharp young bitterness in his own.

Carl watched them as they moved slowly down the draw. They had not seen him at all. He had not overheard much of their dialogue, but he felt the import of it. It made him, somehow, unreasonably mournful to find two young things abroad in the pasture in the early morning. He decided that he needed his breakfast.

CHAPTER 6

At dinner that day Alexandra said she thought they must really manage to go over to the Shabatas' that afternoon. 'It's not often I let three days go by without seeing Marie. She will think I have forsaken her, now that my old friend has come back.'

After the men had gone back to work, Alexandra put on a white dress and her sun-hat, and she and Carl set forth across the fields. 'You see we have kept up the old path, Carl. It has been so nice for me to feel that there was a friend at the other end of it again.'

Carl smiled a little ruefully. 'All the same, I hope it hasn't been *quite* the same.'

Alexandra looked at him with surprise. 'Why, no, of course not. Not the same. She could not very well take your place, if that's what you mean. I'm friendly with all my neighbors, I hope. But Marie is really a companion, some one I can talk to quite frankly. You wouldn't want me to be more lonely than I have been, would you?'

Carl laughed and pushed back the triangular lock of hair with the edge of his hat. 'Of course I don't. I ought to be thankful that this path hasn't been worn by—well, by friends with more pressing errands than your little Bohemian is likely to have.' He paused to give Alexandra his hand as she stepped over the stile. 'Are you the least bit disappointed in our coming together again?' he asked abruptly. 'Is it the way you hoped it would be?'

Alexandra smiled at this. 'Only better. When I've thought about your coming, I've sometimes been a little afraid of it. You have lived where things move so fast, and everything is slow here; the people slowest of all. Our lives are like the years, all made up of weather and crops and cows. How you hated cows!' She shook her head and laughed to herself.

'I didn't when we milked together. I walked up to the pasture corners this morning. I wonder whether I shall ever be able to tell you all that I was thinking about up there. It's a strange thing, Alexandra; I find it easy to be frank with you about everything under the sun except—yourself!'

'You are afraid of hurting my feelings, perhaps.' Alexandra looked at him thoughtfully.

'No, I'm afraid of giving you a shock. You've seen yourself for so long in the dull minds of the people about you, that if I were to tell you how you seem to me, it would startle you. But you must see that you astonish me. You must feel when people admire you.'

Alexandra blushed and laughed with some confusion. 'I felt that you were pleased with me, if you mean that.'

'And you've felt when other people were pleased with you?' he insisted.

'Well, sometimes. The men in town, at the banks and the county offices, seem glad to see me. I think, myself, it is more pleasant to do business with people who are clean and healthy-looking,' she admitted blandly.

Carl gave a little chuckle as he opened the Shabatas' gate for her. 'Oh, do you?' he asked dryly.

There was no sign of life about the Shabatas' house except a big yellow cat, sunning itself on the kitchen doorstep.

Alexandra took the path that led to the orchard. 'She often sits there and sews. I didn't telephone her we were coming, because I didn't want her to go to work and bake cake and freeze ice-cream. She'll always make a party if you give her the least excuse. Do you recognize the apple trees, Carl?'

Linstrum looked about him. 'I wish I had a dollar for every bucket of water I've carried for those trees. Poor father, he was an easy man, but he was perfectly merciless when it came to watering the orchard.'

'That's one thing I like about Germans; they make an orchard grow if they can't make anything else. I'm so glad these trees belong to some one who takes comfort in them. When I rented this place, the tenants never kept the orchard up, and Emil and I used to come over and take care of it ourselves. It needs mowing now. There she is, down in the corner. Maria-a-a!' she called.

A recumbent figure started up from the grass and came running toward them through the flickering screen of light and shade.

'Look at her! Isn't she like a little brown rabbit?' Alexandra laughed.

Marie ran up panting and threw her arms about Alexandra. 'Oh, I had begun to think you were not coming at all, maybe. I knew you were so busy. Yes, Emil told me about Mr Linstrum being here. Won't you come up to the house?'

'Why not sit down there in your corner? Carl wants to see the orchard. He kept all these trees alive for years, watering them with his own back.'

Marie turned to Carl. 'Then I'm thankful to you, Mr Linstrum. We'd never have bought the place if it hadn't been for this orchard, and then I wouldn't have had Alexandra, either.' She gave Alexandra's arm a little squeeze as she walked beside her. 'How nice your dress smells, Alexandra; you put rosemary leaves in your chest, like I told you.'

She led them to the northwest corner of the orchard, sheltered on one side by a thick mulberry hedge and bordered on the other by a wheatfield, just beginning to yellow. In this corner the ground dipped a little, and the bluegrass, which the weeds had driven out in the upper part of the orchard, grew thick and luxuriant. Wild roses were flaming in the tufts of bunchgrass along the fence. Under a white mulberry tree there was an old wagon-seat. Beside it lay a book and a workbasket.

'You must have the seat, Alexandra. The grass would stain your dress,' the hostess insisted. She dropped down on the ground at Alexandra's side and tucked her feet under her. Carl sat at a little distance from the two women, his back to the wheatfield, and watched them. Alexandra took off her shade-hat and threw it on the ground. Marie picked it up and played with the white ribbons, twisting them about her brown fingers as she talked. They made a pretty picture in the strong sunlight, the leafy pattern surrounding them like a net; the Swedish woman so white and gold, kindly and amused, but armored in calm, and the alert brown one, her full lips parted, points of yellow light dancing in her eyes as she laughed and chattered. Carl had never forgotten little Marie Tovesky's eyes, and he was glad to have an opportunity to study them. The brown iris, he found, was curiously slashed with yellow, the color of sunflower honey, or of old amber. In each eye one of these streaks must have been larger than the others, for the effect was that of two dancing points of light, two little yellow bubbles, such as rise in a glass of champagne. Sometimes they seemed like the sparks from a forge. She seemed so easily excited, to kindle with a fierce little flame if one but breathed upon her. 'What a waste,' Carl reflected. 'She ought to be doing all that for a sweetheart. How awkwardly things come about!'

It was not very long before Marie sprang up out of the grass again. 'Wait a moment. I want to show you something.' She ran away and disappeared behind the low-growing apple trees.

'What a charming creature,' Carl murmured. 'I don't wonder that her husband is jealous. But can't she walk? does she always run?'

Alexandra nodded. 'Always. I don't see many people, but I don't believe there are many like her, anywhere.'

Marie came back with a branch she had broken from an apricot tree, laden with pale-yellow, pink-cheeked fruit. She dropped it beside Carl. 'Did you plant those, too? They are such beautiful little trees.'

Carl fingered the blue-green leaves, porous like blotting-paper and shaped like birch leaves, hung on waxen red stems. 'Yes, I think

I did. Are these the circus trees, Alexandra?'

'Shall I tell her about them?' Alexandra asked. 'Sit down like a good girl, Marie, and don't ruin my poor hat, and I'll tell you a story. A long time ago, when Carl and I were, say, sixteen and twelve, a circus came to Hanover and we went to town in our wagon, with Lou and Oscar, to see the parade. We hadn't money enough to go to the circus. We followed the parade out to the circus grounds and hung around until the show began and the crowd went inside the tent. Then Lou was afraid we looked foolish standing outside in the pasture, so we went back to Hanover feeling very sad. There was a man in the streets selling apricots, and we had never seen any before. He had driven down from somewhere up in the French country, and he was selling them twenty-five cents a peck. We had a little money our fathers had given us for candy, and I bought two pecks and Carl bought one. They cheered us a good deal, and we saved all the seeds and planted them. Up to the time Carl went away, they hadn't borne at all.'

'And now he's come back to eat them,' cried Marie, nodding at Carl. 'That *is* a good story. I can remember you a little, Mr Linstrum. I used to see you in Hanover sometimes, when Uncle Joe took me to town. I remember you because you were always buying pencils and tubes of paint at the drug store. Once, when my uncle left me at the store, you drew a lot of little birds and flowers for me on a piece of wrapping-paper. I kept them for a long while. I thought you were very romantic because you could draw and had such black eyes.'

Carl smiled. 'Yes, I remember that time. Your uncle bought you some kind of a mechanical toy, a Turkish lady sitting on an ottoman and smoking a hookah, wasn't it? And she turned her head backwards and forwards.'

'Oh, yes! Wasn't she splendid! I knew well enough I ought not to tell Uncle Joe I wanted it, for he had just come back from the saloon and was feeling good. You remember how he laughed? She tickled him, too. But when we got home, my aunt scolded him for buying toys when she needed so many things. We wound our lady up every night, and when she began to move her head my aunt used to laugh as hard as any of us. It was a music-box, you know, and the Turkish lady played a tune while she smoked. That was how she made you feel so jolly. As I remember her, she was lovely, and had a gold crescent on her turban.'

Half an hour later, as they were leaving the house, Carl and Alexandra were met in the path by a strapping fellow in overalls and a blue shirt. He was breathing hard, as if he had been running, and was muttering to himself.

Marie ran forward, and, taking him by the arm, gave him a little push toward her guests. 'Frank, this is Mr Linstrum.'

Frank took off his broad straw hat and nodded to Alexandra. When he spoke to Carl, he showed a fine set of white teeth. He was burned a dull red down to his neckband, and there was a heavy three-days' stubble on his face. Even in his agitation he was handsome, but he looked a rash and violent man.

Barely saluting the callers, he turned at once to his wife and began, in an outraged tone, 'I have to leave my team to drive the old woman Hiller's hogs out-a my wheat. I go to take dat old woman to de court if she ain't careful, I tell you!'

His wife spoke soothingly. 'But, Frank, she has only her lame boy to help her. She does the best she can.'

Alexandra looked at the excited man and offered a suggestion. 'Why don't you go over there some afternoon and hog-tight her fences? You'd save time for yourself in the end.'

Frank's neck stiffened. 'Not-a-much, I won't. I keep my hogs home. Other peoples can do like me. See? If that Louis can mend shoes, he can mend fence.'

'Maybe,' said Alexandra placidly; 'but I've found it sometimes pays to mend other people's fences. Goodbye, Marie. Come to see me soon.'

Alexandra walked firmly down the path and Carl followed her.

Frank went into the house and threw himself on the sofa, his face to the wall, his clenched fist on his hip. Marie, having seen her guests off, came in and put her hand coaxingly on his shoulder.

'Poor Frank! You've run until you've made your head ache, now haven't you? Let me make you some coffee.'

'What else am I to do?' he cried hotly in Bohemian. 'Am I to let any old woman's hogs root up my wheat? Is that what I work myself to death for?'

'Don't worry about it, Frank. I'll speak to Mrs Hiller again. But, really, she almost cried last time they got out, she was so sorry.'

Frank bounced over on his other side. 'That's it; you always side with them against me. They all know it. Anybody here feels free to borrow the mower and break it, or turn their hogs in on me. They know you won't care!'

Marie hurried away to make his coffee. When she came back, he was fast asleep. She sat down and looked at him for a long while, very thoughtfully. When the kitchen clock struck six she went out to get supper, closing the door gently behind her. She was always sorry for Frank when he worked himself into one of these rages, and she was sorry to have him rough and quarrelsome with his neighbors. She was perfectly aware that the neighbors had a good deal to put with, and that they bore with Frank for her sake.

CHAPTER 7

MARIE'S father, Albert Tovesky, was one of the more intelligent Bohemians who came West in the early seventies. He settled in Omaha and became a leader and adviser among his people there.

Marie was his youngest child, by a second wife, and was the apple of his eye. She was barely sixteen, and was in the graduating class of the Omaha High School, when Frank Shabata arrived from the old country and set all the Bohemian girls in a flutter. He was easily the buck of the beer-gardens, and on Sunday he was a sight to see, with his silk hat and tucked shirt and blue frock-coat, wearing gloves and carrying a little wisp of a yellow cane. He was tall and fair, with splendid teeth and close-cropped yellow curls, and he wore a slightly disdainful expression, proper for a young man with high connections, whose mother had a big farm in the Elbe valley. There was often an interesting discontent in his blue eyes, and every Bohemian girl he met imagined herself the cause of that unsatisfied expression. He had a way of drawing out his cambric handkerchief slowly, by one corner, from his breast-pocket, that was melancholy and romantic in the extreme. He took a little flight with each of the more eligible Bohemian girls, but it was when he was with little Marie Tovesky that he drew his handkerchief out most slowly, and, after he had lit a fresh cigar, dropped the match most despairingly. Any one could see, with half an eye, that his proud heart was bleeding for somebody.

One Sunday, late in the summer after Marie's graduation, she met Frank at a Bohemian picnic down the river and went rowing with him all the afternoon. When she got home that evening she went straight to her father's room and told him that she was engaged to Shabata. Old Tovesky was having a comfortable pipe before he went to bed. When he heard his daughter's announcement, he first prudently corked his beer bottle and then leaped to his feet and had a turn of temper. He characterized Frank Shabata by a Bohemian expression which is the equivalent of stuffed shirt.

'Why don't he go to work like the rest of us did? His farm in the Elbe valley, indeed! Ain't he got plenty brothers and sisters? It's his mother's farm, and why don't he stay at home and help her? Haven't

I seen his mother out in the morning at five o'clock with her ladle and her big bucket on wheels, putting liquid manure on the cabbages? Don't I know the look of old Eva Shabata's hands? Like an old horse's hoofs they are—and this fellow wearing gloves and rings! Engaged, indeed! You aren't fit to be out of school, and that's what's the matter with you. I will send you off the the Sisters of the Sacred Heart in St Louis, and they will teach you some sense, *I* guess!'

Accordingly, the very next week, Albert Tovesky took his daughter, pale and tearful, down the river to the convent. But the way to make Frank want anything was to tell him he couldn't have it. He managed to have an interview with Marie before she went away, and whereas he had been only half in love with her before, he now persuaded himself that he would not stop at anything. Marie took with her to the convent, under the canvas lining of her trunk, the results of a laborious and satisfying morning on Frank's part; no less than a dozen photographs of himself, taken in a dozen different love-lorn attitudes. There was a little round photograph for her watch-case, photographs for her wall and dresser, and even long narrow ones to be used as bookmarks. More than once the handsome gentleman was torn to pieces before the French class by an indignant nun.

Marie pined in the convent for a year, until her eighteenth birthday was passed. Then she met Frank Shabata in the Union Station in St Louis and ran away with him. Old Tovesky forgave his daughter because there was nothing else to do, and bought her a farm in the country that she had loved so well as a child. Since then her story had been a part of the history of the Divide. She and Frank had been living there for five years when Carl Linstrum came back to pay his long deferred visit to Alexandra. Frank had, on the whole, done better than one might have expected. He had flung himself at the soil with savage energy. Once a year he went to Hastings or to Omaha, on a spree. He stayed away for a week or two, and then came home and worked like a demon. He did work; if he felt sorry for himself, that was his own affair.

CHAPTER 8

ON the evening of the day of Alexandra's call at the Shabatas', a heavy rain set in. Frank sat up until a late hour reading the Sunday newspapers. One of the Goulds was getting a divorce, and Frank took it as a personal affront. In printing the story of the young man's marital troubles, the knowing editor gave a sufficiently colored account of his career, stating the amount of his income and the manner in which he was supposed to spend it. Frank read English slowly, and the more he read about this divorce case, the angrier he grew. At last he threw down the page with a snort. He turned to his farmhand who was reading the other half of the paper.

'By God! if I have that young feller in de hayfield once, I show him someting. Listen here what he do wit his money.' And Frank began the catalogue of the young man's reputed extravagances.

Marie sighed. She thought it hard that the Goulds, for whom she had nothing but good will, should make her so much trouble. She hated to see the Sunday newspapers come into the house. Frank was always reading about the doings of rich people and feeling outraged. He had an inexhaustible stock of stories about their crimes and follies, how they bribed the courts and shot down their butlers with impunity whenever they chose. Frank and Lou Bergson had very similar ideas, and they were two of the political agitators of the county.

The next morning broke clear and brilliant, but Frank said the ground was too wet to plough, so he took the cart and drove over to Sainte-Agnes to spend the day at Moses Marcel's saloon. After he was gone, Marie went out to the back porch to begin her butter-making. A brisk wind had come up and was driving puffy white clouds across the sky. The orchard was sparkling and rippling in the sun. Marie stood looking toward it wistfully, her hand on the lid of the churn, when she heard a sharp ring in the air, the merry sound of the whetstone on the scythe. That invitation decided her. She ran into the house, put on a short skirt and a pair of her husband's boots, caught up a tin pail and started for the orchard. Emil had already begun work and was mowing vigorously. When he saw her coming, he stopped and wiped his brow. His yellow canvas leggings and khaki trousers were splashed to the knees.

'Don't let me disturb you, Emil. I'm going to pick cherries. Isn't everything beautiful after the rain? Oh, but I'm glad to get this place mowed! When I heard it raining in the night, I thought maybe you would come and do it for me today. The wind wakened me. Didn't it blow dreadfully? Just smell the wild roses! They are always so spicy after a rain. We never had so many of them in here before. I suppose it's the wet season. Will you have to cut them, too?'

'If I cut the grass, I will,' Emil said teasingly. 'What's the matter with you? What makes you so flighty?'

'Am I flighty? I suppose that's the wet season, too, then. It's exciting to see everything growing so fast,—and to get the grass cut! Please leave the roses till last, if you must cut them. Oh, I don't mean all of them, I mean that low place down by my tree, where there are so many. Aren't you splashed! Look at the spider webs all over the grass. Goodbye. I'll call you if I see a snake.'

She tripped away and Emil stood looking after her. In a few moments he heard the cherries dropping smartly into the pail, and he began to swing his scythe with that long, even stroke that few American boys ever learn. Marie picked cherries and sang softly to herself, stripping one glittering branch after another, shivering when she caught a shower of raindrops on her neck and hair. And Emil mowed his way slowly down toward the cherry trees.

That summer the rains had been so many and opportune that it was almost more than Shabata and his man could do to keep up with the corn; the orchard was a neglected wilderness. All sorts of weeds and herbs and flowers had grown up there; splotches of wild larkspur, pale green-and-white spikes of hoarhound, plantations of wild cotton, tangles of foxtail and wild wheat. South of the apricot trees, cornering on the wheatfield, was Frank's alfalfa, where myriads of white and yellow butterflies were always fluttering above the purple blossoms. When Emil reached the lower corner by the hedge, Marie was sitting under her white mulberry tree, the pailful of cherries beside her, looking off at the gentle, tireless swelling of the wheat.

'Emil,' she said suddenly—he was mowing quietly about under the tree so as not to disturb her—'what religion did the Swedes have away back, before they were Christians?'

Emil paused and straightened his back. 'I don't know. About like the Germans', wasn't it?'

Marie went on as if she had not heard him. 'The Bohemians, you know, were tree worshipers before the missionaries came. Father says the people in the mountains still do queer things, sometimes,— they believe that trees bring good or bad luck.'

Emil looked superior. 'Do they? Well, which are the lucky trees? I'd like to know.'

'I don't know all of them, but I know lindens are. The old people in the mountains plant lindens to purify the forest, and to do away with the spells that come from the old trees they say have lasted from heathen times. I'm a good Catholic, but I think I could get along with caring for trees, if I hadn't anything else.'

'That's a poor saying,' said Emil, stooping over to wipe his hands in the wet grass.

'Why is it? If I feel that way, I feel that way. I like trees because they seem more resigned to the way they have to live than other things do. I feel as if this tree knows everything I ever think of when I sit here. When I come back to it, I never have to remind it of anything; I begin just where I left off.'

Emil had nothing to say to this. He reached up among the branches and began to pick the sweet, insipid fruit,—long ivory-colored berries, tipped with faint pink, like white coral, that fall to the ground unheeded all summer through. He dropped a handful into her lap.

'Do you like Mr Linstrum?' Marie asked suddenly.

'Yes. Don't you?'

'Oh, ever so much; only he seems kind of staid and school-teachery. But, of course, he is older than Frank, even. I'm sure I don't want to live to be more than thirty, do you? Do you think Alexandra likes him very much?'

'I suppose so. They were old friends.'

'Oh, Emil, you know what I mean!' Marie tossed her head impatiently. 'Does she really care about him? When she used to tell me about him, I always wondered whether she wasn't a little in love with him.'

'Who, Alexandra?' Emil laughed and thrust his hands into his trousers pockets. 'Alexandra's never been in love, you crazy!' He laughed again. 'She wouldn't know how to go about it. The idea!'

Marie shrugged her shoulders. 'Oh, you don't know Alexandra as well as you think you do! If you had any eyes, you would see that she is very fond of him. It would serve you all right if she walked off with Carl. I like him because he appreciates her more than you do.'

Emil frowned. 'What are you talking about, Marie? Alexandra's all right. She and I have always been good friends. What more do you want? I like to talk to Carl about New York and what a fellow can do there.'

'Oh, Emil! Surely you are not thinking of going off there?'

'Why not? I must go somewhere, mustn't I?' The young man took up his scythe and leaned on it. 'Would you rather I went off in the sand hills and lived like Ivar?'

Marie's face fell under his brooding gaze. She looked down at his wet leggings. 'I'm sure Alexandra hopes you will stay on here,' she murmured.

'Then Alexandra will be disappointed,' the young man said roughly. 'What do I want to hang around here for? Alexandra can run the farm all right, without me. I don't want to stand around and look on. I want to be doing something on my own account.'

'That's so,' Marie sighed. 'There are so many, many things you can do. Almost anything you choose.'

'And there are so many, many things I can't do.' Emile echoed her tone sarcastically. 'Sometimes I don't want to do anything at all, and sometimes I want to pull the four corners of the Divide together,'—he threw out his arm and brought it back with a jerk,— 'so, like a table-cloth. I get tired of seeing men and horses going up and down, up and down.'

Marie looked up at his defiant figure and her face clouded. 'I wish you weren't so restless, and didn't get so worked up over things,' she said sadly.

'Thank you,' he returned shortly.

She sighed despondently. 'Everything I say makes you cross, don't it? And you never used to be cross to me.'

Emil took a step nearer and stood frowning down at her bent head. He stood in an attitude of self-defense, his feet well apart, his hands clenched and drawn up at his sides, so that the cords stood out on his bare arms. 'I can't play with you like a little boy any more,' he said slowly. 'That's what you miss, Marie. You'll have to get some other little boy to play with.' He stopped and took a deep breath. Then he went on in a low tone, so intense that it was almost threatening: 'Sometimes you seem to understand perfectly, and then sometimes you pretend you don't. You don't help things any by pretending. It's then that I want to pull the corners of the Divide together. If you *won't* understand, you know, I could make you!'

Marie clasped her hands and started up from her seat. She had grown very pale and her eyes were shining with excitement and distress. 'But, Emil, if I understand, then all our good times are over, we can never do nice things together any more. We shall have to behave like Mr Linstrum. And, anyhow, there's nothing to understand!' She struck the ground with her little foot fiercely. 'That won't last. It will go away, and things will be just as they used to. I wish you were a Catholic. The Church helps people, indeed it does. I pray for you, but that's not the same as if you prayed yourself.'

She spoke rapidly and pleadingly, looked entreatingly into his face. Emil stood defiant, gazing down at her.

'I can't pray to have the things I want,' he said slowly, 'and I won't pray not to have them, not if I'm damned for it.'

Marie turned away, wringing her hands. 'Oh, Emil, you won't try! Then all our good times are over.'

'Yes; over. I never expect to have any more.'

Emil gripped the hand-holds of his scythe and began to mow. Marie took up her cherries and went slowly toward the house, crying bitterly.

CHAPTER 9

ON Sunday afternoon, a month after Carl Linstrum's arrival, he rode with Emil up into the French country to attend a Catholic fair. He sat for most of the afternoon in the basement of the church, where the fair was held, talking to Marie Shabata, or strolled about the gravel terrace, thrown up on the hillside in front of the basement doors, where the French boys were jumping and wrestling and throwing the discus. Some of the boys were in their white baseball suits; they had just come up from a Sunday practice game down in the ballgrounds. Amédée, the newly married, Emil's best friend, was their pitcher, renowed among the country towns for his dash and skill. Amédée was a little fellow, a year younger than Emil and much more boyish in appearance; very lithe and active and neatly made, with a clear brown and white skin, and flashing white teeth. The Sainte-Agnes boys were to play the Hastings nine in a fortnight, and Amédée's lightning balls were the hope of his team. The little Frenchman seemed to get every ounce there was in him behind the ball as it left his hand.

'You'd have made the battery at the University for sure, 'Médée,' Emil said as they were walking from the ballgrounds back to the church on the hill. 'You're pitching better than you did in the spring.'

Amédée grinned. 'Sure! A married man don't lose his head no more.' He slapped Emil on the back as he caught step with him. 'Oh, Emil, you wanna get married right off quick! It's the greatest thing ever!'

Emil laughed. 'How am I going to get married without any girl?'

Amédée took his arm. 'Pooh! There are plenty girls will have you. You wanna get some nice French girl, now. She treat you well; always be jolly. See,'—he began checking off on his fingers,— 'there is Séverine, and Alphosen, and Joséphine, and Hectorine, and Louise, and Malvina—why, I could love any of them girls! Why don't you get after them? Are you stuck up, Emil, or is anything the matter with you? I never did know a boy twenty-two years old before that didn't have no girl. You wanna be a priest, maybe? Not-a for me!' Amédée swaggered. 'I bring many good Catholics into this world, I hope, and that's a way I help the Church.'

Emil looked down and patted him on the shoulder. 'Now you're windy, 'Médée. You Frenchies like to brag.'

But Amédée had the zeal of the newly married, and he was not to be lightly shaken off. 'Honest and true, Emil, don't you want *any* girl? Maybe there's some young lady in Lincoln, now, very grand,'—Amédée waved his hand languidly before his face to denote the fan of heartless beauty,—'and you lost your heart up there. Is that it?'

'Maybe,' said Emil.

But Amédée saw no appropriate glow in his friend's face. 'Bah!' he exclaimed in disgust. 'I tell all the French girls to keep 'way from you. You gotta rock in there,' thumping Emil on the ribs.

When they reached the terrace at the side of the church, Amédée, who was excited by his success on the ballgrounds, challenged Emil to a jumping match, though he knew he would be beaten. They belted themselves up, and Raoul Marcel, the choir tenor and Father Duchesne's pet, and Jean Bordelau, held the string over which they vaulted. All the French boys stood round, cheering and humping themselves up when Emil or Amédée went over the wire, as if they were helping in the lift. Emil stopped at five-feet-five, declaring that he would spoil his appetite for supper if he jumped any more.

Angélique, Amédée's pretty bride, as blonde and fair as her name, who had come out to watch the match, tossed her head at Emil and said:—

"Médée could jump much higher than you if he were as tall. And anyhow, he is much more graceful. He goes over like a bird, and you have to hump yourself all up.'

'Oh, I do, do I?' Emil caught her and kissed her saucy mouth squarely, while she laughed and struggled and called, "Médée! 'Médée!'

'There, you see your 'Médée isn't even big enough to get you away from me. I could run away with you right now and he could only sit down and cry about it. I'll show you whether I have to hump myself!' Laughing and panting, he picked Angélique up in his arms and began running about the rectangle with her. Not until he saw Marie Shabata's tiger eyes flashing from the gloom of the basement doorway did he hand the disheveled bride over to her husband. 'There, go to your graceful; I haven't the heart to take you away from him.'

Angélique clung to her husband and made faces at Emil over the white shoulder of Amédée's ball-shirt. Emil was greatly amused at her air of proprietorship and at Amédée's shameless submission to it. He was delighted with his friend's good fortune. He liked to see and to think about Amédée's sunny, natural, happy love.

He and Amédée had ridden and wrestled and larked together since they were lads of twelve. On Sundays and holidays they were always arm in arm. It seemed strange that now he should have to hide the thing that Amédée was so proud of, that the feeling which gave one of them such happiness should bring the other such despair. It was like that when Alexandra tested her seed-corn in the spring, he mused. From two ears that had grown side by side, the grains of one shot up joyfully into the light, projecting themselves into the future, and the grains from the other lay still in the earth and rotted; and nobody knew why.

CHAPTER 10

WHILE Emil and Carl were amusing themselves at the fair, Alexandra was at home, busy with her account books, which had been neglected of late. She was almost through with her figures when she heard a cart drive up to the gate, and looking out of the window she saw her two older brothers. They had seemed to avoid her ever since Carl Linstrum's arrival, four weeks ago that day, and she hurried to the door to welcome them. She saw at once that they had come with some very definite purpose. They followed her stiffly into the sitting-room. Oscar sat down, but Lou walked over to the window and remained standing, his hands behind him.

'You are by yourself?' he asked, looking toward the doorway into the parlor.

'Yes. Carl and Emil went up to the Catholic fair.'

For a few moments neither of the men spoke.

Then Lou came out sharply. 'How soon does he intend to go away from here?'

'I don't know, Lou. Not for some time, I hope.' Alexandra spoke in an even, quiet tone that often exasperated her brothers. They felt that she was trying to be superior with them.

Oscar spoke up grimly. 'We thought we ought to tell you that people have begun to talk,' he said meaningly.

Alexandra looked at him. 'What about?'

Oscar met her eyes blankly. 'About you, keeping him here so long. It looks bad for him to be hanging on to a woman this way. People think you're getting taken in.'

Alexandra shut her account book firmly. 'Boys,' she said seriously, 'don't let's go on with this. We won't come out anywhere. I can't take advice on such a matter. I know you mean well, but you must not feel responsible for me in things of this sort. If we go on with this talk it will only make hard feeling.'

Lou whipped about from the window. 'You ought to think a little about your family. You're making us all ridiculous.'

'How am I?'

'People are beginning to say you want to marry the fellow.'

'Well, and what is ridiculous about that?'

Lou and Oscar exchanged outraged looks. 'Alexandra! Can't you see he's just a tramp and he's after your money? He wants to be taken care of, he does!'

'Well, suppose I want to take care of him? Whose business is it but my own?'

'Don't you know he'd get hold of your property?'

'He'd get hold of what I wished to give him, certainly.'

Oscar sat up suddenly and Lou clutched at his bristly hair.

'Give him?' Lou shouted. 'Our property, our homestead?'

'I don't know about the homestead,' said Alexandra quietly. 'I know you and Oscar have always expected that it would be left to your children, and I'm not sure but what you're right. But I'll do exactly as I please with the rest of my land, boys.'

'The rest of your land!' cried Lou, growing more excited every minute. 'Didn't all the land come out of the homestead? It was bought with money borrowed on the homestead, and Oscar and me worked ourselves to the bone paying interest on it.'

'Yes, you paid the interest. But when you married we made a division of the land, and you were satisfied. I've made more on my farms since I've been alone than when we all worked together.'

'Everything you've made has come out of the original land that us boys worked for, hasn't it? The farms and all that comes out of them belongs to us as a family.'

Alexandra waved her hand impatiently. 'Come now, Lou. Stick to the facts. You are talking nonsense. Go to the county clerk and ask him who owns my land, and whether my titles are good.'

Lou turned to his brother. 'This is what comes of letting a woman meddle in business,' he said bitterly. 'We ought to have taken things in our own hands years ago. But she liked to run things, and we humored her. We thought you had good sense, Alexandra. We never thought you'd do anything foolish.'

Alexandra rapped impatiently on her desk with her knuckles. 'Listen, Lou, Don't talk wild. You say you ought to have taken things into your own hands years ago. I suppose you mean before you left home. But how could you take hold of what wasn't there?

I've got most of what I have now since we divided the property; I've built it up myself, and it has nothing to do with you.'

Oscar spoke up solemnly. 'The property of a family really belongs to the men of the family, no matter about the title. If anything goes wrong, it's the men that are held responsible.'

'Yes, of course,' Lou broke in. 'Everybody knows that. Oscar and me have always been easy-going and we've never made any fuss. We were willing you should hold the land and have the good of it, but you got no right to part with any of it. We worked in the fields to pay for the land you bought, and whatever's come out of it has got to be kept in the family.'

Oscar reinforced his brother, his mind fixed on the one point he could see. 'The property of a family belongs to the men of the family, because they are held responsible, and because they do the work.'

Alexandra looked from one to the other, her eyes full of indignation. She had been impatient before, but now she was beginning to feel angry. 'And what about my work?' she asked in an unsteady voice.

Lou looked at the carpet. 'Oh, now, Alexandra, you always took it pretty easy! Of course we wanted you to. You liked to manage round, and we always humored you. We realize you were a great deal of help to us. There's no woman anywhere around that knows as much about business as you do, and we've always been proud of that, and thought you were pretty smart. But, of course, the real work always fell on us. Good advice is all right, but it don't get the weeds out of the corn.'

'Maybe not, but it sometimes puts in the crop, and it sometimes keeps the fields for corn to grow in,' said Alexandra dryly. 'Why, Lou, I can remember when you and Oscar wanted to sell this homestead and all the improvements to old preacher Ericson for two thousand dollars. If I'd consented, you'd have gone down to the river and scraped along on poor farms for the rest of your lives. When I put in our first field of alfalfa you both opposed me, just because I first heard about it from a young man who had been to the University. You said I was being taken in then, and all the neighbors said so. You know as well as I do that alfalfa has been the salvation of this country. You all laughed at me when I said our land here was about ready for wheat, and I had to raise three big wheat crops before the neighbors quit putting all their land in corn. Why, I remember you cried, Lou, when we put in the first big wheat-planting, and said everybody was laughing at us.'

Lou turned to Oscar. 'That's the woman of it; if she tells you to put in a crop, she thinks she's put it in. It makes women conceited to meddle in business. I shouldn't think you'd want to remind us how hard you were on us, Alexandra, after the way you baby Emil.'

'Hard on you? I never meant to be hard. Conditions were hard. Maybe I would never have been very soft, anyhow; but I certainly didn't choose to be the kind of girl I was. If you take even a vine and cut it back again and again, it grows hard, like a tree.'

Lou felt that they were wandering from the point, and that in digression Alexandra might unnerve him. He wiped his forehead with a jerk of his handkerchief. 'We never doubted you, Alexandra. We never questioned anything you did. You've always had your own way. But you can't expect us to sit like stumps and see you done out of the property by any loafer who happens along, and making yourself ridiculous into the bargain.'

Oscar rose. 'Yes,' he broke in, 'everybody's laughing to see you get took in; at your age, too. Everybody knows he's nearly five years younger than you, and is after your money. Why, Alexandra, you are forty years old!'

'All that doesn't concern anybody but Carl and me. Go to town and ask your lawyers what you can do to restrain me from disposing of my own property. And I advise you to do what they tell you; for the authority you can exert by law is the only influence you will ever have over me again.' Alexandra rose. 'I think I would rather not have lived to find out what I have today,' she said quietly, closing her desk.

Lou and Oscar looked at each other questioningly. There seemed to be nothing to do but to go, and they walked out.

'You can't do business with women,' Oscar said heavily as he clambered into the cart. 'But anyhow, we've had our say, at last.'

Lou scratched his head. 'Talk of that kind might come too high, you know; but she's apt to be sensible. You hadn't ought to said that about her age, though, Oscar. I'm afraid that hurt her feelings; and the worst thing we can do is to make her sore at us. She'd marry him out of contrariness.'

'I only meant,' said Oscar, 'that she is old enough to know better, and she is. If she was going to marry, she ought to done it long ago, and not go making a fool of herself now.'

Lou looked anxious, nevertheless. 'Of course,' he reflected hopefully and inconsistently, 'Alexandra ain't much like other women-folks. Maybe it won't make her sore. Maybe she'd as soon be forty as not!'

CHAPTER 11

EMIL came home at about half-past seven o'clock that evening. Old Ivar met him at the windmill and took his horse, and the young man went directly into the house. He called to his sister and she answered from her bedroom, behind the sitting-room, saying that she was lying down.

Emil went to her door.

'Can I see you for a minute?' he asked. 'I want to talk to you about something before Carl comes.'

Alexandra rose quickly and came to the door. 'Where is Carl?'

'Lou and Oscar met us and said they wanted to talk to him, so he rode over to Oscar's with them. Are you coming out?' Emil asked impatiently.

'Yes, sit down. I'll be dressed in a moment.'

Alexandra closed her door, and Emil sank down on the old slat lounge and sat with his head in his hands. When his sister came out, he looked up, not knowing whether the interval had been short or long, and he was surprised to see that the room had grown quite dark. That was just as well; it would be easier to talk if he were not under the gaze of those clear, deliberate eyes, that saw so far in some directions and were so blind in others. Alexandra, too, was glad of the dusk. Her face was swollen from crying.

Emil started up and then sat down again. 'Alexandra,' he said slowly, in his deep young baritone, 'I don't want to go away to law school this fall. Let me put it off another year. I want to take a year off and look around. It's awfully easy to rush into a profession you don't really like, and awfully hard to get out of it. Linstrum and I have been talking about that.'

'Very well, Emil. Only don't go off looking for land.' She came up and put her hand on his shoulder. 'I've been wishing you could stay with me this winter.'

'That's just what I don't want to do, Alexandra. I'm restless. I want to go to a new place. I want to go down to the City of Mexico to join one of the University fellows who's at the head of an electrical plant. He wrote me he could give me a little job, enough to pay my way, and I could look around and see what I want to do. I want to go as soon as harvest is over. I guess Lou and Oscar will be sore about it.'

'I suppose they will.' Alexandra sat down on the lounge beside him. 'They are very angry with me, Emil. We have had a quarrel.

They will not come here again.'

Emil scarcely heard what she was saying; he did not notice the sadness of her tone. He was thinking about the reckless life he meant to live in Mexico.

'What about?' he asked absently.

'About Carl Linstrum. They are afraid I am going to marry him, and that some of my property will get away from them.'

Emil shrugged his shoulders. 'What nonsense!' he murmured. 'Just like them.'

Alexandra drew back. 'Why nonsense, Emil?'

'Why, you've never thought of such a thing, have you? They always have to have something to fuss about.'

'Emil,' said his sister slowly, 'you ought not to take things for granted. Do you agree with them that I have no right to change my way of living?'

Emil looked at the outline of his sister's head in the dim light. They were sitting close together and he somehow felt that she could hear his thoughts. He was silent for a moment, and then said in an embarrassed tone, 'Why, no, certainly not. You ought to do whatever you want to. I'll always back you.'

'But it would seem a little bit ridiculous to you if I married Carl?'

Emil fidgeted. The issue seemed to him too far-fetched to warrant discussion. 'Why, no. I should be surprised if you wanted to. I can't see exactly why. But that's none of my business. You ought to do as you please. Certainly you ought not to pay any attention to what the boys say.'

Alexandra sighed. 'I had hoped you might understand, a little, why I do want to. But I suppose that's too much to expect. I've had a pretty lonely life, Emil. Besides Marie, Carl is the only friend I have ever had.'

Emil was awake now; a name in her last sentence roused him. He put out his hand and took his sister's awkwardly. 'You ought to do just as you wish, and I think Carl's a fine fellow. He and I would always get on. I don't believe any of the things the boys say about him, honest I don't. They are suspicious of him because he's intelligent. You know their way. They've been sore at me ever since you let me go away to college. They're always trying to catch me up. If I were you, I wouldn't pay any attention to them. There's nothing to get upset about. Carl's a sensible fellow. He won't mind them.'

'I don't know. If they talk to him the way they did to me, I think he'll go away.'

Emil grew more and more uneasy. 'Think so? Well, Marie said it would serve us all right if you walked off with him.'

'Did she? Bless her little heart! *She* would.' Alexandra's voice broke.

Emil began unlacing his leggings. 'Why don't you talk to her about it? There's Carl, I hear his horse. I guess I'll go upstairs and get my boots off. No, I don't want any supper. We had supper at five o'clock, at the fair.'

Emil was glad to escape and get to his own room. He was a little ashamed for his sister, though he had tried not to show it. He felt that there was something indecorous in her proposal, and she did seem to him somewhat ridiculous. There was trouble enough in the world, he reflected, as he threw himself upon his bed, without people who were forty years old imagining they wanted to get married. In the darkness and silence Emil was not likely to think long about Alexandra. Every image slipped away but one. He had seen Marie in the crowd that afternoon. She sold candy at the fair. *Why* had she ever run away with Frank Shabata, and how could she go on laughing and working and taking an interest in things? Why did she like so many people, and why had she seemed pleased when all the French and Bohemian boys, and the priest himself, crowded round her candy stand? Why did she care about any one but him?

Why could he never, never find the thing he looked for in her playful, affectionate eyes?

Then he fell to imagining that he looked once more and found it there, and what it would be like if she loved him,—she who, as Alexandra said, could give her whole heart. In that dream he could lie for hours, as if in a trance. His spirit went out of his body and crossed the fields to Marie Shabata.

At the University dances the girls had often looked wonderingly at the tall young Swede with the fine head, leaning against the wall and frowning, his arms folded, his eyes fixed on the ceiling or the floor. All the girls were a little afraid of him. He was distinguished-looking, and not the jollying kind. They felt that he was too intense and preoccupied. There was something queer about him. Emil's fraternity rather prided itself upon its dances, and sometimes he did his duty and danced every dance. But whether he was on the floor or brooding in a corner, he was always thinking about Marie Shabata. For two years the storm had been gathering in him.

CHAPTER 12

CARL came into the sitting-room while Alexandra was lighting the lamp. She looked up at him as she adjusted the shade. His sharp shoulders stooped as if he were very tired, his face was pale, and there were bluish shadows under his dark eyes. His anger had burned itself out and left him sick and disgusted.

'You have seen Lou and Oscar?' Alexandra asked.

'Yes.' His eyes avoided hers.

Alexandra took a deep breath. 'And now you are going away. I thought so.'

Carl threw himself into a chair and pushed the dark lock back from his forelock with his white, nervous hand. 'What a hopeless position you are in, Alexandra!' he exclaimed feverishly. 'It is your fate to be always surrounded by little men. And I am no better than the rest. I am too little to face the criticism of even such men as Lou and Oscar. Yes, I am going away; tomorrow. I cannot even ask you to give me a promise until I have something to offer you. I thought, perhaps, I could do that; but I find I can't.'

'What good comes of offering people things they don't need?' Alexandra asked sadly. 'I don't need money. But I have needed you for a great many years. I wonder why I have been permitted to prosper, if it is only to take my friends away from me.'

'I don't deceive myself,' Carl said frankly. 'I know that I am going away on my own account. I must make the usual effort. I must have something to show for myself. To take what you would give me, I should have to be either a very large man or a very small one, and I am only in the middle class.'

Alexandra sighed. 'I have a feeling that if you go away, you will not come back. Something will happen to one of us, or to both. People have to snatch at happiness when they can, in this world. It is always easier to lose than to find. What I have is yours, if you care enough about me to take it.'

Carl rose and looked up at the picture of John Bergson. 'But I can't, my dear, I can't! I will go North at once. Instead of idling about in California all winter, I shall be getting my bearings up there. I won't waste another week. Be patient with me, Alexandra. Give me a year!'

'As you will,' said Alexandra wearily. 'All at once, in a single day, I lose everything; and I do not know why. Emil, too, is going away.'

Carl was still studying John Bergson's face and Alexandra's eyes followed his. 'Yes,' she said, 'if he could have seen all that would come of the task he gave me, he would have been sorry. I hope he does not see me now. I hope that he is among the old people of his blood and country, and that tidings do not reach him from the New World.'

PART III

WINTER MEMORIES

CHAPTER 1

WINTER has settled down over the Divide again; the season in which Nature recuperates, in which she sinks to sleep between the fruitfulness of autumn and the passion of spring. The birds have gone. The teeming life that goes on down in the long grass is exterminated. The prairie-dog keeps his hole. The rabbits run shivering from one frozen garden patch to another and are hard put to it to find frost-bitten cabbage stalks. At night the coyotes roam the wintry waste, howling for food. The variegated fields are all one color now; the pastures, the stubble, the roads, the sky are the same leaden gray. The hedgerows and trees are scarcely perceptible against the bare earth, whose slaty hue they have taken on. The ground is frozen so hard that it bruises the foot to walk in the roads or in the ploughed fields. It is like an iron country, and the spirit is oppressed by its rigor and melancholy. One could easily believe that in that dead landscape the germs of life and fruitfulness were extinct forever.

Alexandra has settled back into her old routine. There are weekly letters from Emil. Lou and Oscar she has not seen since Carl went away. To avoid awkward encounters in the presence of curious spectators, she has stopped going to the Norwegian Church and drives up to the Reform Church at Hanover, or goes with Marie Shabata to the Catholic Church, locally known as 'the French Church.' She has not told Marie about Carl, or her differences with her brothers. She was never very communicative about her own affairs, and when she came to the point, an instinct told her that about such things she and Marie would not understand one another.

Old Mrs Lee had been afraid that family misunderstandings might deprive her of her yearly visit to Alexandra. But on the first day of December Alexandra telephoned Annie that tomorrow she would send Ivar over for her mother, and the next day the old lady arrived with her bundles. For twelve years Mrs Lee had always entered Alexandra's sitting-room with the same exclamation, 'Now we be yust-a like old times!' She enjoyed the liberty Alexandra gave her, and hearing her own language about her all day long. Here she could wear her nightcap and sleep with all her windows shut, listen to Ivar reading the Bible, and here she could run about among the stables in a pair of Emil's old boots. Though she was bent almost double, she was as spry as a gopher. Her face was as brown as if it had been varnished, and as full of wrinkles as a washerwoman's hands. She had three jolly old teeth left in the front of her mouth, and when she grinned she looked very knowing, as if when you found out how to take it, life wasn't half bad. While she and Alexandra patched and pieced and quilted, she talked incessantly about stories she read in a Swedish family paper, telling the plots in great detail; or about her life on a dairy farm in Gottland when she was a girl. Sometimes she forgot which were the printed stories and which were the real stories, it all seemed so far away. She loved to take a little brandy, with hot water and sugar, before she went to bed, and Alexandra always had it ready for her. 'It sends good dreams,' she would say with a twinkle in her eye.

When Mrs Lee had been with Alexandra for a week, Marie Shabata telephoned one morning to say that Frank had gone to town for the day, and she would like them to come over for coffee in the afternoon. Mrs Lee hurried to wash out and iron her new cross-stitched apron, which she had finished only the night before; a checked gingham apron worked with a design ten inches broad across the bottom; a hunting scene, with fir trees and a stag and dogs and huntsmen. Mrs Lee was firm with herself at dinner, and refused a second helping of apple dumplings. 'I ta-ank I save up,' she said with a giggle.

At two o'clock in the afternoon Alexandra's cart drove up to the Shabatas' gate, and Marie saw Mrs Lee's red shawl come bobbing up the path. She ran to the door and pulled the old woman into the house with a hug, helping her to take off her wraps while Alexandra blanketed the horse outside. Mrs Lee had put on her best black satine dress—she abominated woolen stuffs, even in winter—and a crocheted collar, fastened with a big pale gold pin, containing faded daguerreotypes of her father and mother. She had not worn her apron for fear of rumpling it, and now she shook it out and tied it round her waist with a conscious air. Marie drew back and threw up hands, exclaiming, 'Oh, what a beauty! I've never seen this one before, have I, Mrs Lee?'

The old woman giggled and ducked her head. 'No, yust las' night I ma-ake. See dis tread; verra strong, no wa-ash out, no fade. My sister send from Sveden. I yust-a ta-ank you like dis.'

Marie ran to the door again. 'Come in, Alexandra. I have been looking at Mrs Lee's apron. Do stop on your way home and show it to Mrs Hiller. She's crazy about cross-stitch.'

While Alexandra removed her hat and veil, Mrs Lee went out to the kitchen and settled herself in a wooden rocking-chair by the stove, looking with great interest at the table, set for three, with a white cloth, and a pot of pink geraniums in the middle. 'My, a-an't you gotta fine plants; such-a much flower. How you keep from freeze?'

She pointed to the windowshelves, full of blooming fuchsias and geraniums.

'I keep the fire all night, Mrs Lee, and when it's very cold I put them all on the table, in the middle of the room. Other nights I only put newspapers behind them. Frank laughs at me for fussing, but when they don't bloom he says, "What's the matter with the darned things?"—What do you hear from Carl, Alexandra?'

'He got to Dawson before the river froze, and now I suppose I won't hear any more until spring. Before he left California he sent me a box of orange flowers, but they didn't keep very well. I have brought a bunch of Emil's letters for you.' Alexandra came out from the sitting-room and pinched Marie's cheek playfully. 'You don't look as if the weather ever froze you up. Never have colds, do you? That's a good girl. She had dark red cheeks like this when she was a little girl, Mrs Lee. She looked like some queer foreign kind of a doll. I've never forgot the first time I saw you in Mieklejohn's store, Marie, the time father was lying sick. Carl and I were talking about that before he went away.'

'I remember, and Emil had his kitten along. When are you going to send Emil's Christmas box?'

'It ought to have gone before this. I'll have to send it by mail now, to get it there in time.'

Marie pulled a dark purple silk necktie from her workbasket. 'I knit this for him. It's a good color, don't you think? Will you please put it in with your things and tell him it's from me, to wear when he goes serenading.'

Alexandra laughed. 'I don't believe he goes serenading much. He says in one letter that the Mexican ladies are said to be very beautiful, but that don't seem to me very warm praise.'

Marie tossed her head. 'Emil can't fool me. If he's bought a guitar, he goes serenading. Who wouldn't, with all those Spanish girls dropping flowers down from their windows! I'd sing to them every night, wouldn't you, Mrs Lee?'

The old lady chuckled. Her eyes lit up as Marie bent down and opened the oven door. A delicious hot fragrance blew out into the tidy kitchen. 'My, somet'ing smell good!' She turned to Alexandra with a wink, her three yellow teeth making a brave show, 'I ta-ank dat stop my yaw from ache no more!' she said contentedly.

Marie took out a pan of delicate little rolls, stuffed with stewed apricots, and began to dust them over with powdered sugar. 'I hope you'll like these, Mrs Lee; Alexandra does. The Bohemians always like them with their coffee. But if you don't, I have a coffee-cake with nuts and poppy seeds. Alexandra, will you get the cream jug? I put it in the window to keep cool.'

'The Bohemians,' said Alexandra, as they drew up to the table, 'certainly know how to make more kinds of bread than any other people in the world. Old Mrs Hiller told me once at the church supper that she could make seven kinds of fancy bread, but Marie could make a dozen.'

Mrs Lee held up one of the apricot rolls between her brown thumb and forefinger and weighed it critically. 'Yust like-a fedders,' she pronounced with satisfaction. 'My, a-an't dis nice!' she exclaimed as she stirred her coffee. 'I yust ta-ake a liddle yelly now, too, I ta-ank.'

Alexandra and Marie laughed at her forehandedness, and fell to talking of their own affairs. 'I was afraid you had a cold when I talked to you over the telephone the other night, Marie. What was the matter, had you been crying?'

'Maybe I had,' Marie smiled guiltily. 'Frank was out late that night. Don't you get lonely sometimes in the winter, when everybody has gone away?'

'I thought it was something like that. If I hadn't company, I'd have run over to see for myself. If you get downhearted, what will become of the rest of us?' Alexandra asked.

'I don't, very often. There's Mrs Lee without any coffee!'

Later, when Mrs Lee declared that her powers were spent, Marie and Alexandra went upstairs to look for some crochet patterns the old lady wanted to borrow. 'Better put on your coat, Alexandra. It's cold up there, and I have no idea where those patterns are. I may have to look through my old trunks.' Marie caught up a shawl and opened the stair door, running up the steps ahead of her guest. 'While I go through the bureau drawers, you might look in those hat-boxes on the closet shelf, over where Frank's clothes hang. There are a lot of odds and ends in them.'

She began tossing over the contents of the drawers, and Alexandra went into the clothes-closet. Presently she came back, holding a slender elastic yellow stick in her hand.

'What in the world is this, Marie? You don't mean to tell me Frank ever carried such a thing?'

Marie blinked at it with astonishment and sat down on the floor. 'Where did you find it? I didn't know he had kept it. I haven't seen it for years.'

'It really is a cane, then?'

'Yes. One he brought from the old country. He used to carry it when I first knew him. Isn't it foolish? Poor Frank!'

Alexandra twirled the stick in her fingers and laughed. 'He must have looked funny!'

Marie was thoughtful. 'No, he didn't, really. It didn't seem out of place. He used to be awfully gay like that when he was a young man. I guess people always get what's hardest for them, Alexandra.' Marie gathered the shawl closer about her and still looked hard at the cane. 'Frank would be all right in the right place,' she said reflectively. 'He ought to have a different kind of wife, for one thing. Do you know, Alexandra, I could pick out exactly the right sort of woman for Frank—now. The trouble is you almost have to marry a man before you can find out the sort of wife he needs; and usually it's exactly the sort you are not. Then what are you going to do about it?' she asked candidly.

Alexandra confessed she didn't know. 'However,' she added, 'it seems to me that you get along with Frank about as well as any woman I've ever seen or heard of could.'

Marie shook her head, pursing her lips and blowing her warm breath softly out into the frosty air. 'No; I was spoiled at home. I like my own way, and I have a quick tongue. When Frank brags, I say sharp things, and he never forgets. He goes over and over it in his mind; I can feel him. Then I'm too giddy. Frank's wife ought to be timid, and she ought not to care about another living thing in the world but just Frank! I didn't, when I married him, but I suppose I was too young to stay like that.' Marie sighed.

Alexandra had never heard Marie speak so frankly about her husband before, and she felt that it was wiser not to encourage her. No good, she reasoned, ever came from talking about such things, and while Marie was thinking aloud, Alexandra had been steadily searching the hat-boxes. 'Aren't these the patterns, Maria?'

Marie sprang up from the floor. 'Sure enough, we were looking for patterns, weren't we? I'd forgot about everything but Frank's other wife. I'll put that away.'

She poked the cane behind Frank's Sunday clothes, and though she laughed, Alexandra saw there were tears in her eyes.

When they went back to the kitchen, the snow had begun to fall, and Marie's visitors thought they must be getting home. She went out to the cart with them, and tucked the robes about old Mrs Lee while Alexandra took the blanket off her horse. As they drove away, Marie turned and went slowly back to the house. She took up the package of letters Alexandra had brought, but she did not read them. She turned them over and looked at the foreign stamps, and then sat watching the flying snow while the dusk deepened in the kitchen and the stove sent out a red glow.

Marie knew perfectly well that Emil's letters were written more for her than for Alexandra. They were not the sort of letters that a young man writes to his sister. They were both more personal and more painstaking; full of descriptions of the gay life in the old

Mexican capital in the days when the strong hand of Porfirio Diaz was still strong. He told about bull-fights and cock-fights, churches and *fiestas*, the flower-markets and the fountains, the music and dancing, the people of all nations he met in the Italian restaurants on San Francisco Street. In short, they were the kind of letters a young man writes to a woman when he wishes himself and his life to seem interesting to her, when he wishes to enlist her imagination in his behalf.

Marie, when she was alone or when she sat sewing in the evening, often thought about what it must be like down there where Emil was; where there were flowers and street bands everywhere, and carriages rattling up and down, and where there was a little blind boot-black in front of the cathedral who could play any tune you asked for by dropping the lids of blacking-boxes on the stone steps. When everything is done and over for one at twenty-three, it is pleasant to let the mind wander forth and follow a young adventurer who has life before him. 'And if it had not been for me,' she thought, 'Frank might still be free like that, and having a good time making people admire him. Poor Frank, getting married wasn't very good for him either. I'm afraid I do set people against him, as he says. I seem, somehow, to give him away all the time. Perhaps he would try to be agreeable to people again, if I were not around. It seems as if I always make him just as bad as he can be.'

Later in the winter Alexandra looked back upon that afternoon as the last satisfactory visit she had had with Marie. After that day the younger woman seemed to shrink more and more into herself. When she was with Alexandra she was not spontaneous and frank as she used to be. She seemed to be brooding over something, and holding something back. The weather had a good deal to do with their seeing less of each other than usual. There had not been such snowstorms in twenty years, and the path across the fields was drifted deep from Christmas until March. When the two neighbors went to see each other, they had to go round by the wagon-road, which was twice as far. They telephoned each other almost every night, though in January there was a stretch of three weeks when the wires were down, and when the postman did not come at all.

Marie often ran in to see her nearest neighbor, old Mrs Hiller, who was crippled with rheumatism and had only her son, the lame shoemaker, to take care of her; and she went to the French Church, whatever the weather. She was a sincerely devout girl. She prayed for herself and for Frank, and for Emil, among the temptations of that gay, corrupt old city. She found more comfort in the Church that winter than ever before. It seemed to come closer to her, and to fill an emptiness that ached in her heart. She tried to be patient with her husband. He and his hired man usually played California Jack in the evening. Marie sat sewing or crocheting and tried to take a friendly interest in the game, but she was always thinking about the wide fields outside, where the snow was drifting over the fences; and about the orchard, where the snow was falling and packing, crust over crust. When she went out into the dark kitchen to fix her plants for the night, she used to stand by the window and look out at the white fields, or watch the currents of snow whirling over the orchard. She seemed to feel the weight of all the snow that lay down there. The branches had become so hard that they wounded your hand if you but tried to break a twig. And yet, down under the frozen crusts, at the roots of the trees, the secret of life was still safe, warm as the blood in one's heart; and the spring would come again! Oh, it would come again!

CHAPTER 2

IF Alexandra had had much imagination she might have guessed what was going on in Marie's mind, and she would have seen long before what was going on in Emil's. But that, as Emil himself had more than once reflected, was Alexandra's blind side, and her life had not been of the kind to sharpen her vision. Her training had all been toward the end of making her proficient in what she had undertaken to do. Her personal life, her own realization of herself, was almost a subconscious existence; like an underground river that came to the surface only here and there, at intervals months apart, and then sank again to flow on under her own fields. Nevertheless, the underground stream was there, and it was because she had so much personality to put into her enterprises and succeeded in putting it into them so completely, that her affairs prospered better than those of her neighbors.

There were certain days in her life, outwardly uneventful, which Alexandra remembered as peculiarly happy; days when she was close to the flat, fallow world about her, and felt, as it were, in her own body the joyous germination in the soil. There were days, too, which she and Emil had spent together, upon which she loved to look back. There had been such a day when they were down on the river in the dry year, looking over the land. They had made an early start one morning and had driven a long way before noon. When Emil said he was hungry, they drew back from the road, gave Brigham his oats among the bushes, and climbed up to the top of a grassy bluff to eat their lunch under the shade of some little elm trees. The river was clear there, and shallow, since there had been no rain, and it ran in ripples over the sparkling sand. Under the overhanging willows of the opposite bank there was an inlet where the water was deeper and flowed so slowly that it seemed to sleep in the sun. In this little bay a single wild duck was swimming and diving and preening her feathers, disporting herself very happily in the flickering light and shade. They sat for a long time, watching the solitary bird take its pleasure. No living thing had ever seemed to Alexandra as beautiful as that wild duck. Emil must have felt about it as she did, for afterward, when they were at home, he used sometimes to say, 'Sister, you know our duck down there—' Alexandra remembered that day as one of the happiest in her life. Years afterward she thought of the duck as still there, swimming and diving all by herself in the sunlight, a kind of enchanted bird that did not know age or change.

Most of Alexandra's happy memories were as impersonal as this one; yet to her they were very personal. Her mind was a white book, with clear writing about weather and beasts and growing things. Not many people would have cared to read it; only a happy few. She had never been in love, she had never indulged in sentimental reveries. Even as a girl she had looked upon men as work-fellows. She had grown up in serious times.

There was one fancy indeed, which persisted through her girlhood. It most often came to her on Sunday mornings, the one day in the week when she lay late abed listening to the familiar morning sounds; the windmill singing in the brisk breeze, Emil whistling as he blacked his boots down by the kitchen door. Sometimes, as she lay thus luxuriously idle, her eyes closed, she used to have an illusion of being lifted up bodily and carried lightly by some one very strong. It was a man, certainly, who carried her, but he was like no man she knew; he was much larger and stronger and swifter, and he carried her as easily as if she were a sheaf of wheat. She never saw him, but, with eyes closed, she could feel that he was yellow like the sunlight, and there was the smell of ripe cornfields about him. She could feel him approach, bend over her and lift her, and then she could feel herself being carried swiftly off across the fields. After such a reverie she would rise hastily, angry with herself, and go down to the bath-house that was partitioned off the kitchen shed. There she would stand in a tin tub and prosecute her bath with vigor, finishing it by pouring buckets of cold well-water over her gleaming white body which no man on the Divide could have carried very far.

As she grew older, this fancy more often came to her when she was tired than when she was fresh and strong. Sometimes, after she had been in the open all day, overseeing the branding of the cattle or the loading of the pigs, she would come in chilled, take a concoction of spices and warm homemade wine, and go to bed with her body actually aching with fatigue. Then, just before she went to sleep, she had the old sensation of being lifted and carried by a strong being who took from her all her bodily weariness.

PART IV

THE WHITE MULBERRY TREE

CHAPTER 1

THE French Church, properly the Church of Sainte-Agnes, stood upon a hill. The high, narrow, red-brick building, with its tall steeple and steep roof, could be seen for miles across the wheatfields, though the little town of Sainte-Agnes was completely hidden away at the foot of the hill. The church looked powerful and triumphant there on its eminence, so high above the rest of the landscape, with miles of warm color lying at its feet, and by its position and setting it reminded one of some of the churches built long ago in the wheat-lands of middle France.

Late one June afternoon Alexandra Bergson was driving along one of the many roads that led through the rich French farming country to the big church. The sunlight was shining directly in her face, and there was a blaze of light all about the red church on the hill. Beside Alexandra lounged a strikingly exotic figure in a tall Mexican hat, a silk sash, and a black velvet jacket sewn with silver buttons. Emil had returned only the night before, and his sister was so proud of him that she decided at once to take him up to the church supper, and to make him wear the Mexican costume he had brought home in his trunk. 'All the girls who have stands are going to wear fancy costumes,' she argued, 'and some of the boys. Marie is going to tell fortunes, and she sent to Omaha for a Bohemian dress her father brought back from a visit to the old country. If you wear those clothes, they will all be pleased. And you must take your guitar. Everybody ought to do what they can to help along, and we have never done much. We are not a talented family.'

The supper was to be at six o'clock, in the basement of the church, and afterward there would be a fair, with charades and an auction. Alexandra had set out from home early, leaving the house to Signa and Nelse Jensen, who were to be married next week. Signa had shyly asked to have the wedding put off until Emil came home.

Alexandra was well satisfied with her brother. As they drove through the rolling French country toward the westering sun and the stalwart church, she was thinking of that time long ago when she and Emil drove back from the river valley to the still unconquered Divide. Yes, she told herself, it had been worth while; both Emil and the country had become what she had hoped. Out of her father's children there was one who was fit to cope with the world, who had not been tied to the plow, and who had a personality apart from the soil. And that, she reflected, was what she had worked for. She felt well satisfied with her life.

When they reached the church, a score of teams were hitched in front of the basement doors that opened from the hillside upon the sanded terrace, where the boys wrestled and had jumping matches. Amédée Chevalier, a proud father of one week, rushed out and embraced Emil. Amédée was an only son,—hence he was a very rich young man,—but he meant to have twenty children himself, like his uncle Xavier. 'Oh, Emil,' he cried, hugging his old friend rapturously, 'why ain't you been up to see my boy? You come tomorrow, sure? Emil, you wanna get a boy right off! It's the greatest thing ever! No, no, no! Angel not sick at all. Everything just fine. That boy he come into this world laughin', and he been laughin' ever since. You come an' see!' He pounded Emil's ribs to emphasize each announcement.

Emil caught his arms. 'Stop, Amédée. You're knocking the wind out of me. I brought him cups and spoons and blankets and moccasins enough for an orphan asylum. I'm awful glad it's a boy, sure enough!'

The young men crowded round Emil to admire his costume and to tell him in a breath everything that had happened since he went away. Emil had more friends up here in the French country than down on Norway Creek. The French and Bohemian boys were spirited and jolly, liked variety, and were as much predisposed to favor anything new as the Scandinavian boys were to reject it. The Norwegian and Swedish lads were much more self-centred, apt to be egotistical and jealous. They were cautious and reserved with Emil because he had been away to college, and were prepared to take him down if he should try to put on airs with them. The French boys liked a bit of swagger, and they were always delighted to hear about anything new: new clothes, new games, new songs, new dances. Now they carried Emil off to show him the club room they had just fitted up over the post-office, down in the village. They ran down the hill in a drove, all laughing and chattering at once, some in

French, some in English.

Alexandra went into the cool, whitewashed basement where the women were setting the tables. Marie was standing on a chair, building a little tent of shawls where she was to tell fortunes. She sprang down and ran toward Alexandra, stopping short and looking at her in disappointment. Alexandra nodded to her encouragingly.

'Oh, he will be here, Marie. The boys have taken him off to show him something. You won't know him. He is a man now, sure enough. I have no boy left. He smokes terrible-smelling Mexican cigarettes and talks Spanish. How pretty you look, child. Where did you get those beautiful earrings?'

'They belonged to father's mother. He always promised them to me. He sent them with the dress and said I could keep them.'

Marie wore a short red skirt of stoutly woven cloth, a white bodice and kirtle, a yellow silk turban wound low over her brown curls, and long coral pendants in her ears. Her ears had been pierced against a piece of cork by her great-aunt when she was seven years old. In those germless days she had worn bits of broomstraw, plucked from the common sweeping-broom, in the lobes until the holes were healed and ready for little gold rings.

When Emil came back from the village, he lingered outside on the terrace with the boys. Marie could hear him talking and strumming on his guitar while Raoul Marcel sang falsetto. She was vexed with him for staying out there. It made her very nervous to hear him and not to see him; for, certainly, she told herself, she was not going out to look for him. When the supper bell rang and the boys came trooping in to get seats at the first table, she forgot all about her annoyance and ran to greet the tallest of the crowd, in his conspicuous attire. She didn't mind showing her embarrassment at all. She blushed and laughed excitedly as she gave Emil her hand, and looked delightedly at the black velvet coat that brought out his fair skin and fine blond head. Marie was incapable of being lukewarm about anything that pleased her. She simply did not know how to give a half-hearted response. When she was delighted, she was as likely as not to stand on her tip-toes and clap her hands. If people laughed at her, she laughed with them.

'Do the men wear clothes like that every day, in the street?' She caught Emil by his sleeve and turned him about. 'Oh, I wish I lived where people wore things like that! Are the buttons real silver? Put on the hat, please. What a heavy thing! How do you ever wear it? Why don't you tell us about the bull-fights?'

She wanted to wring all his experiences from him at once, without waiting a moment. Emil smiled tolerantly and stood looking down at her with his old, brooding gaze, while the French girls fluttered about him in their white dresses and ribbons, and Alexandra watched the scene with pride. Several of the French girls, Marie knew, were hoping that Emil would take them to supper, and she was relieved when he took only his sister. Marie caught Frank's arm and dragged him to the same table, managing to get seats opposite the Bergsons, so that she could hear what they were talking about. Alexandra made Emil tell Mrs Xavier Chevalier, the mother of the twenty, about how he had seen a famous matador killed in the bull-ring. Marie listened to every word, only taking her eyes from Emil to watch Frank's plate and keep it filled. When Emil finished his account,—bloody enough to satisfy Mrs Xavier and to make her feel thankful that she was not a matador,—Marie broke out with a volley of questions. How did the women dress when they went to bull-fights? Did they wear mantillas? Did they never wear hats?

After supper the young people played charades for the amusement of their elders, who sat gossiping between their guesses. All the shops in Sainte-Agnes were closed at eight o'clock that night, so that the merchants and their clerks could attend the fair. The auction was the liveliest part of the entertainment, for the French boys always lost their heads when they began to bid, satisfied that their extravagance was in a good cause. After all the pincushions and sofa pillows and embroidered slippers were sold, Emil precipitated a panic by taking out one of his turquoise shirt studs, which every one had been admiring, and handing it to the auctioneer. All the French girls clamored for it, and their sweethearts bid against each other recklessly. Marie wanted it, too, and she kept making signals to Frank, which he took a sour pleasure in disregarding. He didn't see the use of making a fuss over a fellow just because he was dressed like a clown. When the turquoise went to Malvina Sauvage, the French banker's daughter, Marie shrugged her shoulders and betook herself to her little tent of shawls, where she began to shuffle her cards by the light of a tallow candle, calling out, 'Fortunes, fortunes!'

The young priest, Father Duchesne, went first to have his fortune read. Marie took his long white hand, looked at it, and then began to run off her cards. 'I see a long journey across water for you, Father. You will go to a town all cut up by water; built on islands, it seems to be, with rivers and green fields all about. And you will visit an old lady with a white cap and gold hoops in her ears, and you will be very happy there.'

'Mais, oui,' said the priest, with a melancholy smile. 'C'est L'Isle-Adam, chez ma mère. Vous êtes très savante, ma fille.' He patted her yellow turban, calling, 'Venez donc, mes garçons! Il y a ici une véritable clairvoyante!'

Marie was clever at fortune-telling, indulging in a light irony that amused the crowd. She told old Brunot, the miser, that he would lose all his money, marry a girl of sixteen, and live happily on a crust. Sholte, the fat Russian boy, who lived for his stomach, was to be disappointed in love, grow thin, and shoot himself from despondency. Amédée was to have twenty children, and nineteen of them were to be girls. Amédée slapped Frank on the back and asked him why he didn't see what the fortune-teller would promise him. But Frank shook off his friendly hand and grunted, 'She tell my fortune long ago; bad enough!' Then he withdrew to a corner and sat glowering at his wife.

Frank's case was all the more painful because he had no one in particular to fix his jealousy upon. Sometimes he could have thanked the man who would bring him evidence against his wife. He had discharged a good farmboy, Jan Smirka, because he thought Marie was fond of him; but she had not seemed to miss Jan when he was gone, and she had been just as kind to the next boy. The farm-hands would always do anything for Marie; Frank couldn't find one so surly that he would not make an effort to please her. At the bottom of his heart Frank knew well enough that if he could once give up his grudge, his wife would come back to him. But he could never in the world do that. The grudge was fundamental. Perhaps he could not have given it up if he had tried. Perhaps he got more satisfaction out of feeling himself abused than he would have got out of being loved. If he could once have made Marie thoroughly unhappy, he might have relented and raised her from the dust. But she had never humbled herself. In the first days of their love she had been his slave; she had admired him abandonedly. But the moment he began to bully her and to be unjust, she began to draw away; at first in tearful amazement, then in quiet, unspoken disgust. The distance between them had widened and hardened. It no longer contracted and brought them suddenly together. The spark of her life went somewhere else, and he was always watching to surprise it. He knew that somewhere she must get a feeling to live upon, for she was not a woman who could live without loving. He wanted to prove to himself the wrong he felt. What did she hide in her heart? Where did it go? Even Frank had his churlish delicacies; he never reminded her of how much she had once loved him. For that Marie was grateful to him.

While Marie was chattering to the French boys, Amédée called Emil to the back of the room and whispered to him that they were going to play a joke on the girls. At eleven o'clock, Amédée was to go up to the switchboard in the vestibule and turn off the electric lights, and every boy would have a chance to kiss his sweetheart before Father Duchesne could find his way up the stairs to turn the current on again. The only difficulty was the candle in Marie's tent; perhaps, as Emil had no sweetheart, he would oblige the boys by blowing out the candle. Emil said he would undertake to do that.

At five minutes to eleven he sauntered up to Marie's booth, and the French boys dispersed to find their girls. He leaned over the card-table and gave himself up to looking at her. 'Do you think you could tell my fortune?' he murmured. It was the first word he had had alone with her for almost a year. 'My luck hasn't changed any. It's just the same.'

Marie had often wondered whether there was anyone else who could look his thoughts to you as Emil could. Tonight, when she met his steady, powerful eyes, it was impossible not to feel the sweetness of the dream he was dreaming; it reached her before she could shut it out, and hid itself in her heart. She began to shuffle her cards furiously. 'I'm angry with you, Emil,' she broke out with petulance. 'Why did you give them that lovely blue stone to sell? You might have known Frank wouldn't buy it for me, and I wanted it awfully!'

Emil laughed shortly. 'People who want such little things surely ought to have them,' he said dryly. He thrust his hand into the pocket of his velvet trousers and brought out a handful of uncut turquoises, as big as marbles. Leaning over the table he dropped them into her lap. 'There, will those do? Be careful, don't let any one see them. Now, I suppose you want me to go away and let you play with them?'

Marie was gazing in rapture at the soft blue color of the stones. 'Oh, Emil! Is everything down there beautiful like these? How could you ever come away?'

At that instant Amédée laid hands on the switchboard. There was a shiver and a giggle, and every one looked toward the red blur that Marie's candle made in the dark. Immediately that, too, was gone. Little shrieks and currents of soft laughter ran up and down the dark hall. Marie started up,—directly into Emil's arms. In the same instant she felt his lips. The veil that had hung uncertainly between them for so long was dissolved. Before she knew what she was doing, she had committed herself to that kiss that was at once a boy's and a man's, as timid as it was tender; so like Emil and so unlike any one else in the world. Not until it was over did she realize what it meant. And Emil, who had so often imagined the shock of this first kiss, was surprised at its gentleness and naturalness. It was like a sigh which they had breathed together; almost sorrowful, as if each were afraid of wakening something in the other.

When the lights came on again, everybody was laughing and shouting, and all the French girls were rosy and shining with mirth. Only Marie, in her little tent of shawls, was pale and quiet. Under her yellow turban the red coral pendants swung against white cheeks. Frank was still staring at her, but he seemed to see nothing. Years ago, he himself had had the power to take the blood from her cheeks like that. Perhaps he did not remember—perhaps he had never noticed! Emil was already at the other end of the hall, walking about with the shoulder-motion he had acquired among the Mexicans, studying the floor with his intent, deep-set eyes. Marie began to take down and fold her shawls. She did not glance up again. The young people drifted to the other end of the hall where the guitar was sounding. In a moment she heard Emil and

Raoul singing:—

> 'Across the Rio Grand-e
> There lies a sunny land-e,
> My bright-eyed Mexico!'

Alexandra Bergson came up to the card booth. 'Let me help you, Marie. You look tired.'

She placed her hand on Marie's arm and felt her shiver. Marie stiffened under that kind, calm hand. Alexandra drew back, perplexed and hurt.

There was about Alexandra something of the impervious calm of the fatalist, always disconcerting to very young people, who cannot feel that the heart lives at all unless it is still at the mercy of storms; unless its strings can scream to the touch of pain.

CHAPTER 2

SIGNA'S wedding supper was over. The guests, and the tiresome little Norwegian preacher who had performed the marriage ceremony, were saying goodnight. Old Ivar was hitching the horses to the wagon to take the wedding presents and the bride and groom up to their new home, on Alexandra's north quarter. When Ivar drove up to the gate, Emil and Marie Shabata began to carry out the presents, and Alexandra went into her bedroom to bid Signa goodbye and to give her a few words of good counsel. She was surprised to find that the bride had changed her slippers for heavy shoes and was pinning up her skirts. At that moment Nelse appeared at the gate with the two milk cows that Alexandra had given Signa for a wedding present.

Alexandra began to laugh. 'Why, Signa, you and Nelse are to ride home. I'll send Ivar over with the cows in the morning.'

Signa hesitated and looked perplexed. When her husband called her, she pinned her hat on resolutely. 'I ta-ank I better do yust like he say,' she murmured in confusion.

Alexandra and Marie accompanied Signa to the gate and saw the party set off, old Ivar driving ahead in the wagon and the bride and groom following on foot, each leading a cow. Emil burst into a laugh before they were out of hearing.

'Those two will get on,' said Alexandra as they turned back to the house. 'They are not going to take any chances. They will feel safer with those cows in their own stable. Marie, I am going to send for an old woman next. As soon as I get the girls broken in, I marry them off.'

'I've no patience with Signa, marrying that grumpy fellow!' Marie declared. 'I wanted her to marry that nice Smirka boy who worked for us last winter. I think she liked him, too.'

'Yes, I think she did,' Alexandra assented, 'but I suppose she was too much afraid of Nelse to marry any one else. Now that I think of it, most of my girls have married men they were afraid of. I believe there is a good deal of the cow in most Swedish girls. You high-strung Bohemians can't understand us. We're a terribly practical people, and I guess we think a cross man makes a good manager.'

Marie shrugged her shoulders and turned to pin up a lock of hair that had fallen on her neck. Somehow Alexandra had irritated her of late. Everybody irritated her. She was tired of everybody. 'I'm going home alone, Emil, so you needn't get your hat,' she said as she wound her scarf quickly about her head. 'Goodnight, Alexandra,' she called back in a strained voice, running down the gravel walk.

Emil followed with long strides until he overtook her. Then she began to walk slowly. It was a night of warm wind and faint starlight, and the fireflies were glimmering over the wheat.

'Marie,' said Emil after they had walked for a while, 'I wonder if you know how unhappy I am?'

Marie did not answer him. Her head, in its white scarf, drooped forward a little.

Emil kicked a clod from the path and went on:—

'I wonder whether you are really shallow-hearted, like you seem? Sometimes I think one boy does just as well as another for you. It never seems to make much difference whether it is me or Raoul Marcel or Jan Smirka. Are you really like that?'

'Perhaps I am. What do you want me to do? Sit round and cry all day? When I've cried until I can't cry any more, then—then I must do something else.'

'Are you sorry for me?' he persisted.

'No, I'm not. If I were big and free like you, I wouldn't let anything make me unhappy. As old Napoleon Brunot said at the fair, I wouldn't go lovering after no woman. I'd take the first train and go off and have all the fun there is.'

'I tried that, but it didn't do any good. Everything reminded me. The nicer the place was, the more I wanted you.' They had come to the stile and Emile pointed to it persuasively. 'Sit down a moment, I want to ask you something.' Marie sat down on the top step and Emil drew nearer. 'Would you tell me something that's none of my business if you thought it would help me out? Well, then, tell me, *please* tell me, why you ran away with Frank Shabata!'

Marie drew back. 'Because I was in love with him,' she said firmly.

'Really?' he asked incredulously.

'Yes, indeed. Very much in love with him. I think I was the one who suggested our running away. From the first it was more my fault than his.'

Emil turned away his face.

'And now,' Marie went on, 'I've got to remember that. Frank is just the same now as he was then, only then I would see him as I wanted him to be. I would have my own way. And now I pay for it.'

'You don't do all the paying.'

'That's it. When one makes a mistake, there's no telling where it will stop. But you can go away; you can leave all this behind you.'

'Not everything. I can't leave you behind. Will you go away with me, Marie?'

Marie started up and stepped across the stile. 'Emil! How wickedly you talk! I am not that kind of a girl, and you know it. But what am I going to do if you keep tormenting me like this!' she added plaintively.

'Marie, I won't bother you any more if you will tell me just one thing. Stop a minute and look at me. No, nobody can see us. Everybody's asleep. That was only a firefly. Marie, *stop* and tell me!'

Emil overtook her and catching her by the shoulders shook her gently, as if he were trying to awaken a sleepwalker.

Marie hid her face on his arm. 'Don't ask me anything more. I don't know anything except how miserable I am. And I thought it would be all right when you came back. Oh, Emil,' she clutched his sleeve and began to cry, 'what am I to do if you don't go away? I can't go, and one of us must. Can't you see?'

Emil stood looking down at her, holding his shoulders stiff and stiffening the arm to which she clung. Her white dress looked gray in the darkness. She seemed like a troubled spirit, like some shadow out of the earth, clinging to him and entreating him to give her peace. Behind her the fireflies were weaving in and out over the wheat. He put his hand on her bent head. 'On my honor, Marie, if you will say you love me, I will go away.'

She lifted her face to his. 'How could I help it? Didn't you know?'

Emil was the one who trembled, through all his frame. After he left Marie at her gate, he wandered about the fields all night, till morning put out the fireflies and the stars.

CHAPTER 3

ONE evening, a week after Signa's wedding, Emil was kneeling before a box in the sitting-room, packing his books. From time to time he rose and wandered about the house, picking up stray volumes and bringing them listlessly back to his box. He was packing without enthusiasm. He was not very sanguine about his future. Alexandra sat sewing by the table. She had helped him pack his trunk in the afternoon. As Emil came and went by her chair with his books, he thought to himself that it had not been so hard to leave his sister since he first went away to school. He was going directly to Omaha, to read law in the office of a Swedish lawyer until October, when he would enter the law school at Ann Arbor. They had planned that Alexandra was to come to Michigan—a long journey for her—at Christmas time, and spend several weeks with him. Nevertheless, he felt that this leavetaking would be more final than his earlier ones had been; that it meant a definite break with his old home and the beginning of something new—he did not know what. His ideas about the future would not crystallize; the more he tried to think about it, the vaguer his conception of it became. But one thing was clear, he told himself; it was high time that he made good to Alexandra, and that ought to be incentive enough to begin with.

As he went about gathering up his books he felt as if he were uprooting things. At last he threw himself down on the old slat lounge where he had slept when he was little, and lay looking up at the familiar cracks in the ceiling.

'Tired, Emil?' his sister asked.

'Lazy,' he murmured, turning on his side and looking at her. He studied Alexandra's face for a long time in the lamplight. It had never occurred to him that his sister was a handsome woman until Marie Shabata had told him so. Indeed, he had never thought of her as being a woman at all, only a sister. As he studied her bent head, he looked up at the picture of John Bergson above the lamp. 'No,' he thought to himself, 'she didn't get it there. I suppose I am more like that.'

'Alexandra,' he said suddenly, 'that old walnut secretary you use for a desk was father's, wasn't it?'

Alexandra went on stitching. 'Yes. It was one of the first things he bought for the old log house. It was a great extravagance in those days. But he wrote a great many letters back to the old country. He had many friends there, and they wrote to him up to the time he died. No one ever blamed him for grandfather's disgrace. I can see him now, sitting there on Sundays, in his white shirt, writing pages and pages, so carefully. He wrote a fine, regular hand, almost like engraving. Yours is something like his, when you take pains.'

'Grandfather was really crooked, was he?'

'He married an unscrupulous woman, and then—then I'm afraid he was really crooked. When we first came here father used to have dreams about making a great fortune and going back to Sweden to pay back to the poor sailors the money grandfather had lost.'

Emil stirred on the lounge, 'I say, that would have been worth while, wouldn't it? Father wasn't a bit like Lou or Oscar, was he? I can't remember much about him before he got sick.'

'Oh, not at all!' Alexandra dropped her sewing on her knee. 'He had better opportunities; not to make money, but to make something of himself. He was a quiet man, but he was very intelligent. You would have been proud of him, Emil.'

Alexandra felt that he would like to know there had been a man of his kin whom he could admire. She knew that Emil was ashamed of Lou and Oscar, because they were bigoted and self-satisfied. He never said much about them, but she could feel his disgust. His brothers had shown their disapproval of him ever since he first went away to school. The only thing that would have satisfied them would have been his failure at the University. As it was, they resented every change in his speech, in his dress, in his point of view; though the latter they had to conjecture, for Emil avoided talking to them about any but family matters. All his interests they treated as affectations.

Alexandra took up her sewing again. 'I can remember father when he was quite a young man. He belonged to some kind of a musical society, a male chorus, in Stockholm. I can remember going with mother to hear them sing. There must have been a hundred of them, and they all wore long black coats and white neckties. I was used to seeing father in a blue coat, a sort of jacket, and when I recognized him on the platform, I was very proud. Do you remember that Swedish song he taught you, about the ship boy?'

'Yes. I used to sing it to the Mexicans. They like anything different.' Emil paused. 'Father had a hard fight here, didn't he?' he added thoughtfully.

'Yes, and he died in a dark time. Still, he had hope. He believed in the land.'

'And in you, I guess,' Emil said to himself. There was another period of silence; that warm, friendly silence, full of perfect understanding, in which Emil and Alexandra had spent many of their happiest half-hours.

At last Emil said abruptly, 'Lou and Oscar would be better off if they were poor, wouldn't they?'

Alexandra smiled. 'Maybe. But their children wouldn't. I have great hopes of Milly.'

Emil shivered. 'I don't know. Seems to me it gets worse as it goes on. The worst of the Swedes is that they're never willing to find out how much they don't know. It was like that at the University. Always so pleased with themselves! There's no getting behind that conceited

Swedish grin. The Bohemians and Germans were so different.'

'Come, Emil, don't go back on your own people. Father wasn't conceited, Uncle Otto wasn't. Even Lou and Oscar weren't when they were boys.'

Emil looked incredulous, but he did not dispute the point. He turned on his back and lay still for a long time, his hands locked under his head, looking up at the ceiling. Alexandra knew that he was thinking of many things. She felt no anxiety about Emil. She had always believed in him, as she had believed in the land. He had been more like himself since he got back from Mexico; seemed glad to be at home, and talked to her as he used to do. She had no doubt that his wandering fit was over, and that he would soon be settled in life.

'Alexandra,' said Emil suddenly, 'do you remember the wild duck we saw down on the river that time?'

His sister looked up. 'I often think of her. It always seems to me she's there still, just like we saw her.'

'I know. It's queer what things one remembers and what things one forgets.' Emil yawned and sat up. 'Well, it's time to turn in.' He rose, and going over to Alexandra stooped down and kissed her lightly on the cheek. 'Goodnight, sister. I think you did pretty well by us.'

Emil took up his lamp and went upstairs. Alexandra sat finishing his new nightshirt, that must go in the top tray of his trunk.

CHAPTER 4

THE next morning Angélique, Amédée's wife, was in the kitchen baking pies, assisted by old Mrs Chevalier. Between the mixing-board and the stove stood the old cradle that had been Amédée's, and in it was his black-eyed son. As Angélique, flushed and excited, with flour on her hands, stopped to smile at the baby, Emil Bergson rode up to the kitchen door on his mare and dismounted.

"Médée is out in the field, Emil,' Angélique called as she ran across the kitchen to the oven. 'He begins to cut his wheat today; the first wheat ready to cut anywhere about here. He bought a new header, you know, because all the wheat's so short this year. I hope he can rent it to the neighbors, it cost so much. He and his cousins bought a steam thresher on shares. You ought to go out and see that header work. I watched it an hour this morning, busy as I am with all the men to feed. He has a lot of hands, but he's the only one that knows how to drive the header or how to run the engine, so he has to be everywhere at once. He's sick, too, and ought to be in his bed.'

Emil bent over Hector Baptiste, trying to make him blink his round, bead-like black eyes. 'Sick? What's the matter with your daddy, kid? Been making him walk the floor with you?'

Angélique sniffed. 'Not much! We don't have that kind of babies. It was his father that kept Baptiste awake. All night I had to be getting up and making mustard plasters to put on his stomach. He had an awful colic. He said he felt better this morning, but I don't think he ought to be out in the field, overheating himself.'

Angélique did not speak with much anxiety, not because she was indifferent, but because she felt so secure in their good fortune. Only good things could happen to a rich, energetic, handsome young man like Amédée, with a new baby in the cradle and a new header in the field.

Emil stroked the black fuzz on Baptiste's head. 'I say, Angélique, one of 'Médée's grandmothers, 'way back, must have been a squaw. This kid looks exactly like the Indian babies.'

Angélique made a face at him, but old Mrs Chevalier had been touched on a sore point, and she let out such a stream of fiery *patois* that Emil fled from the kitchen and mounted his mare.

Opening the pasture gate from the saddle, Emil rode across the field to the clearing where the thresher stood, driven by a stationary engine and fed from the header boxes. As Amédée was not on the engine, Emil rode on to the wheatfield, where he recognized, on the header, the slight, wiry figure of his friend, coatless, his white shirt puffed out by the wind, his straw hat stuck jauntily on the side of his head. The six big work-horses that drew, or rather pushed, the header, went abreast at a rapid walk, and as they were still green at the work they required a good deal of management on Amédée's part; especially when they turned the corners, where they divided, three and three, and then swung round into line again with a movement that looked as complicated as a wheel of artillery. Emil felt a new thrill of admiration for his friend, and with it the old pang of envy at the way in which Amédée could do with his might what his hand found to do, and feel that, whatever it was, it was the most important thing in the world. 'I'll have to bring Alexandra up to see this thing work,' Emil thought; 'it's splendid!'

When he saw Emil, Amédée waved to him and called to one of his twenty cousins to take the reins. Stepping off the header without stopping it, he ran up to Emil who had dismounted. 'Come along,' he called. 'I have to go over to the engine for a minute. I gotta green man running it, and I gotta to keep an eye on him.'

Emil thought the lad was unnaturally flushed and more excited than even the cares of managing a big farm at a critical time warranted. As they passed behind a last year's stack, Amédée clutched at his right side and sank down for a moment on the straw.

'Ouch! I got an awful pain in me, Emil. Something's the matter with my insides, for sure.'

Emil felt his fiery cheek. 'You ought to go straight to bed, 'Médée, and telephone for the doctor; that's what you ought to do.'

Amédée staggered up with a gesture of despair. 'How can I? I got no time to be sick. Three thousand dollars' worth of new machinery to manage, and the wheat so ripe it will begin to shatter next week. My wheat's short, but it's gotta grand full berries. What's he slowing down for? We haven't got header boxes enough to feed the thresher, I guess.'

Amédée started hot-foot across the stubble, leaning a little to the right as he ran, and waved to the engineer not to stop the engine.

Emil saw that this was no time to talk about his own affairs. He mounted his mare and rode on to Sainte-Agnes, to bid his friends there goodbye. He went first to see Raoul Marcel, and found him innocently practising the 'Gloria' for the big confirmation service on Sunday while he polished the mirrors of his father's saloon.

As Emil rode homewards at three o'clock in the afternoon, he saw Amédée staggering out of the wheatfield, supported by two of his cousins. Emil stopped and helped them put the boy to bed.

CHAPTER 5

WHEN Frank Shabata came in from work at five o'clock that evening, old Moses Marcel, Raoul's father, telephoned him that Amédée had had a seizure in the wheatfield, and that Doctor Paradis was going to operate on him as soon as the Hanover doctor got there to help. Frank dropped a word of this at the table, bolted his supper, and rode off to Sainte-Agnes, where there would be sympathetic discussion of Amédée's case at Marcel's saloon.

As soon as Frank was gone, Marie telephoned Alexandra. It was a comfort to hear her friend's voice. Yes, Alexandra knew what there was to be known about Amédée. Emil had been there when they carried him out of the field, and had stayed with him until the doctors operated for appendicitis at five o'clock. They were afraid it was too late to do much good; it should have been done three days ago. Amédée was in a very bad way. Emil had just come home, worn out and sick himself. She had given him some brandy and put him to bed.

Marie hung up the receiver. Poor Amédée's illness had taken on a new meaning to her, now that she knew Emil had been with him. And it might so easily have been the other way—Emil who was ill and Amédée who was sad! Marie looked about the dusky sitting-room. She had seldom felt so utterly lonely. If Emil was asleep, there was not even a chance of his coming; and she could not go to Alexandra for sympathy. She meant to tell Alexandra everything, as soon as Emil went away. Then whatever was left between them would be honest.

But she could not stay in the house this evening. Where should she go? She walked slowly down through the orchard, where the evening air was heavy with the smell of wild cotton. The fresh, salty scent of the wild roses had given way before this more powerful perfume of midsummer. Wherever those ashes-of-rose balls hung on their milky stalks, the air about them was saturated with their breath. The sky was still red in the west and the evening star hung directly over the Bergsons' windmill. Marie crossed the fence at the wheatfield corner, and walked slowly along the path that led to Alexandra's. She could not help feeling hurt that Emil had not come to tell her about Amédée. It seemed to her most unnatural that he should not have come. If she were in trouble, certainly he was the one person in the world she would want to see. Perhaps he wished her to understand that for her he was as good as gone already.

Marie stole slowly, flutteringly, along the path, like a white night-moth out of the fields. The years seemed to stretch before her like the land; spring, summer, autumn, winter, spring; always the same patient fields, the patient little trees, the patient lives; always the same yearning, the same pulling at the chain—until the instinct to live had torn itself and bled and weakened for the last time, until the chain secured a dead woman, who might cautiously be released. Marie walked on, her face lifted toward the remote, inaccessible evening star.

When she reached the stile she sat down and waited. How

terrible it was to love people when you could not really share their lives!

Yes, in so far as she was concerned, Emil was already gone. They couldn't meet any more. There was nothing for them to say. They had spent the last penny of their small change; there was nothing left but gold. The day of love-tokens was past. They had now only their hearts to give each other. And Emil being gone, what was her life to be like? In some ways, it would be easier. She would not, at least, live in perpetual fear. If Emil were once away and settled at work, she would not have the feeling that she was spoiling his life. With the memory he left her, she could be as rash as she chose. Nobody could be the worse for it but herself; and that, surely, did not matter. Her own case was clear. When a girl had loved one man, and then loved another while that man was still alive, everybody knew what to think of her. What happened to her was of little consequence, so long as she did not drag other people down with her. Emil once away, she could let everything else go and live a new life of perfect love.

Marie left the stile reluctantly. She had, after all, thought he might come. And how glad she ought to be, she told herself, that he was asleep. She left the path and went across the pasture. The moon was almost full. An owl was hooting somewhere in the fields. She had scarcely thought about where she was going when the pond glittered before her, where Emil had shot the ducks. She stopped and looked at it. Yes, there would be a dirty way out of life, if one chose to take it. But she did not want to die. She wanted to live and dream—a hundred years, forever! As long as this sweetness welled up in her heart, as long as her breast could hold this treasure of pain! She felt as the pond must feel when it held the moon like that; when it encircled and swelled with that image of gold.

In the morning, when Emil came downstairs, Alexandra met him in the sitting-room and put her hands on his shoulders. 'Emil, I went to your room as soon as it was light, but you were sleeping so sound I hated to wake you. There was nothing you could do, so I let you sleep. They telephoned from Sainte-Agnes that Amédéed died at three o'clock this morning.'

CHAPTER 6

THE Church has always held that life is for the living. On Saturday, while half the village of Sainte-Agnes was mourning for Amédée and preparing the funeral black for his burial on Monday, the other half was busy with white dresses and white veils for the great confirmation service tomorrow, when the bishop was to confirm a class of one hundred boys and girls. Father Duchesne divided his time between the living and the dead. All day Saturday the church was a scene of bustling activity, a little hushed by the thought of Amédée. The choir were busy rehearsing a mass of Rossini, which they had studied and practised for this occasion. The women were trimming the altar, the boys and girls were bringing flowers.

On Sunday morning the bishop was to drive overland to Sainte-Agnes from Hanover, and Emil Bergson had been asked to take the place of one of Amédée's cousins in the cavalacade of forty French boys who were to ride across country to meet the bishop's carriage. At six o'clock on Sunday morning the boys met at the church. As they stood holding their horses by the bridle, they talked in low tones of their dead comrade. They kept repeating that Amédée had always been a good boy, glancing toward the red brick church which had played so large a part in Amédée's life, had been the scene of his most serious moments and of his happiest hours. He had played and wrestled and sung and courted under its shadow. Only three weeks ago he had proudly carried his baby there to be christened. They could not doubt that that invisible arm was still about Amédée; that through the church on earth he had passed to the church triumphant, the goal of the hopes and faith of so many hundred years.

When the word was given to mount, the young men rode at a walk out of the village; but once out among the wheatfields in the morning sun, their horses and their own youth got the better of them. A wave of zeal and fiery enthusiasm swept over them. They longed for a Jerusalem to deliver. The thud of their galloping hoofs interrupted many a country breakfast and brought many a woman and child to the door of the farmhouses as they passed. Five miles east of Sainte-Agnes they met the bishop in his open carriage, attended by two priests. Like one man the boys swung off their hats in a broad salute, and bowed their heads as the handsome old man lifted his two fingers in the episcopal blessing. The horsemen closed about the carriage like a guard, and whenever a restless horse broke from control and shot down the road ahead of the body, the bishop laughed and rubbed his plump hands together. 'What fine boys!' he said to his priests. 'The Church still has her cavalry.'

As the troop swept past the graveyard half a mile east of the town,—the first frame church of the parish had stood there,—old Pierre Séguin was already out with his pick and spade, digging Amédée's grave. He knelt and uncovered as the bishop passed. The boys with one accord looked away from old Pierre to the red church on the hill, with the gold cross flaming on its steeple.

Mass was at eleven. While the church was filling, Emil Bergson waited outside, watching the wagons and buggies drive up the hill. After the bell began to ring, he saw Frank Shabata ride up on horseback and tie his horse to the hitch-bar. Marie, then, was not coming. Emil turned and went into the church. Amédée's was the only empty pew, and he sat down in it. Some of Amédée's cousins were there, dressed in black and weeping. When all the pews were full, the old men and boys packed the open space at the back of the church, kneeling on the floor. There was scarcely a family in town that was not represented in the confirmation class, by a cousin, at least. The new communicants, with their clear, reverent faces, were beautiful to look upon as they entered in a body and took the front benches reserved for them. Even before the Mass began, the air was charged with feeling. The choir had never sung so well and Raoul Marcel, in the 'Gloria,' drew even the bishop's eyes to the organ loft. For the offertory he sang Gounod's 'Ave Maria,'—always spoken of in Sainte-Agnes as 'the Ave Maria.'

Emil began to torture himself with questions about Marie. Was she ill? Had she quarreled with her husband? Was she too unhappy to find comfort even here? Had she, perhaps, thought that he would come to her? Was she waiting for him? Overtaxed by excitement and sorrow as he was, the rapture of the service took hold upon his body and mind. As he listened to Raoul, he seemed to emerge from the conflicting emotions which had been whirling him about and sucking him under. He felt as if a clear light broke upon his mind, and with it a conviction that good was, after all, stronger than evil, and that good was possible to men. He seemed to discover that there was a kind of rapture in which he could love forever without faltering and without sin. He looked across the heads of the people at Frank Shabata with calmness. That rapture was for those who could feel it; for people who could not, it was non-existent. He coveted nothing that was Frank Shabata's. The spirit he had met in music was his own. Frank Shabata had never found it; would never find it if he lived beside it a thousand years; would have destroyed it if he had found it, as Herod slew the innocents, as Rome slew the martyrs.

San—cta Mari-i-i-a,

wailed Raoul from the organ loft;

O—ra pro no-o-bis!

And it did not occur to Emil that any one had ever reasoned thus before, that music had ever before given a man this equivocal revelation.

The confirmation service followed the Mass. When it was over, the congregation thronged about the newly confirmed. The girls, and even the boys, were kissed and embraced and wept over. All the aunts and grandmothers wept with joy. The housewives had much ado to tear themselves away from the general rejoicing and hurry back to their kitchens. The country parishioners were staying in town for dinner, and nearly every house in Sainte-Agnes entertained visitors that day. Father Duchesne, the bishop, and the visiting priests dined with Fabien Sauvage, the banker. Emil and Frank Shabata were both guests of old Moïse Marcel. After dinner Frank and old Moïse retired to the rear room of the saloon to play California Jack and drink their cognac, and Emil went over to the banker's with Raoul, who had been asked to sing for the bishop.

At three o'clock, Emil felt that he could stand it no longer. He slipped out under cover of 'The Holy City,' followed by Malvina's wistful eye, and went to the stable for his mare. He was at that height of excitement from which everything is foreshortened, from which life seems short and simple, death very near, and the soul seems to soar like an eagle. As he rode past the graveyard he looked at the brown hole in the earth where Amédée was to lie, and felt no horror. That, too, was beautiful, that simple doorway into forgetfulness. The heart, when it is too much alive, aches for that brown earth, and ecstasy has no fear of death. It is the old and the poor and the maimed who shrink from that brown hole; its wooers are found among the young, the passionate, the gallant-hearted. It was not until he had passed the graveyard that Emil realized where he was going. It was the hour for saying goodbye. It might be the last time that he would see her alone, and today he could leave her without rancor, without bitterness.

Everywhere the grain stood ripe and the hot afternoon was full of the smell of the ripe wheat, like the smell of bread baking in an oven. The breath of the wheat and the sweet clover passed him like pleasant things in a dream. He could feel nothing but the sense of diminishing distance. It seemed to him that his mare was flying, or running on wheels, like a railway train. The sunlight, flashing on the window-glass of the big red barns, drove him wild with joy. He was like an arrow shot from the bow. His life poured itself out along the road before him as he rode to the Shabata farm.

When Emil alighted at the Shabatas' gate, his horse was in a lather. He tied her in the stable and hurried to the house. It was empty. She might be at Mrs Hiller's or with Alexandra. But anything that reminded him of her would be enough, the orchard, the mulberry tree . . . When he reached the orchard the sun was hanging low over the wheatfield. Long fingers of light reached through the apple branches as through a net; the orchard was riddled and shot with gold; light was the reality, the trees were merely interferences that reflected and refracted light. Emil went softly down between the cherry trees toward the wheatfield. When he came to the corner, he stopped short and put his hand over his mouth. Marie was lying on her side under the white mulberry tree, her face half hidden in the grass, her eyes closed, her hands lying limply where they had happened to fall. She had lived a day of her new life of perfect love, and it had left her like this. Her breast rose and fell faintly, as if she were asleep. Emil threw himself down beside her and took her in his arms. The blood came back to her cheeks, her amber eyes opened slowly, and in them Emil saw his own face and the orchard and the sun. 'I was dreaming this,' she whispered, hiding her face against him, 'don't take my dream away!'

CHAPTER 7

WHEN Frank Shabata got home that night, he found Emil's mare in his stable. Such an impertinence amazed him. Like everybody else, Frank had had an exciting day. Since noon he had been drinking too much, and he was in a bad temper. He talked bitterly to himself while he put his own horse away, and as he went up the path and saw that the house was dark he felt an added sense of injury. He approached quietly and listened on the doorstep. Hearing nothing, he opened the kitchen door and went softly from one room to another. Then he went through the house again, upstairs and down, with no better result. He sat down on the bottom step of the box stairway and tried to get his wits togethers. In that unnatural quiet there was no sound but his own heavy breathing. Suddenly an owl began to hoot out in the fields. Frank lifted his head. An idea flashed into his mind, and his sense of injury and outrage grew. He went into his bedroom and took his murderous 405 Winchester from the closet.

When Frank took up his gun and walked out of the house, he had not the faintest purpose of doing anything with it. He did not believe that he had any real grievance. But it gratified him to feel like a desperate man. He had got into the habit of seeing himself always in desperate straits. His unhappy temperament was like a cage; he could never get out of it; and he felt that other people, his wife in particular, must have put him there. It had never more than dimly occurred to Frank that he made his own unhappiness. Though he took up his gun with dark projects in his mind, he would have been paralyzed with fright had he known that there was the slightest probability of his ever carrying any of them out.

Frank went slowly down to the orchard gate, stopped and stood for a moment lost in thought. He retraced his steps and looked through the barn and the hayloft. Then he went out to the road, where he took the footpath along the outside of the orchard hedge. The hedge was twice as tall as Frank himself, and so dense that one could see through it only by peering closely between the leaves. He could see the empty path a long way in the moonlight. His mind traveled ahead to the stile, which he always thought of as haunted by Emil Bergson. But why had he left his horse?

At the wheatfield corner, where the orchard hedge ended and the path led across the pasture to the Bergsons', Frank stopped. In the warm, breathless night air he heard a murmuring sound, perfectly inarticulate, as low as the sound of water coming from a spring, where there is no fall, and where there are no stones to fret it. Frank strained his ears. It ceased. He held his breath and began to tremble. Resting the butt of his gun on the ground, he parted the mulberry leaves softly with his fingers and peered through the hedge at the dark figures on the grass, in the shadow of the mulberry tree. It seemed to him that they must feel his eyes, that they must hear him breathing. But they did not. Frank, who had always wanted to see things blacker than they were, for once wanted to believe less than he saw. The woman lying in the shadow might so easily be one of the Bergsons' farm-girls . . . Again the murmur, like water welling out of the ground. This time he heard it more distinctly, and his blood was quicker than his brain. He began to act, just as a man who falls into the fire begins to act. The gun sprang to his shoulder, he sighted mechanically and fired three times without stopping, stopped without knowing why. Either he shut his eyes or he had vertigo. He did not see anything while he was firing. He thought he heard a cry simultaneous with the second report, but he was not sure. He peered again through the hedge, at the two dark figures under the tree. They had fallen a little apart from each other, and were perfectly still— No, not quite; in a white patch of light, where the moon shone through the branches a man's hand was plucking spasmodically at the grass.

Suddenly the woman stirred and uttered a cry, then another, and another. She was living! She was dragging herself toward the hedge! Frank dropped his gun and ran back along the path, shaking, stumbling, gasping. He had never imagined such horror. The cries followed him. They grew fainter and thicker, as if she were choking. He dropped on his knees beside the hedge and crouched like a rabbit, listening; fainter, fainter; a sound like a whine; again—a moan—another—silence. Frank scrambled to his feet and ran on, groaning and praying. From habit he went toward the house, where he was used to being soothed when he had worked himself into a frenzy, but at the sight of the black, open door, he started back. He knew that he had murdered somebody, that a woman was bleeding and moaning in the orchard, but he had not realized before that it was his wife. The gate stared him in the face. He threw his hands over his head. Which way to turn? He lifted his tormented face and looked at the sky. 'Holy Mother of God, not to suffer! She was a good girl—not to suffer!'

Frank had been wont to see himself in dramatic situations; but now, when he stood by the windmill, in the bright space between the barn and the house, facing his own black doorway, he did not see himself at all. He stood like the hare when the dogs are approaching from all sides. And he ran like a hare, back and forth about that moonlit space, before he could make up his mind to go into the dark stable for a horse. The thought of going into a doorway was terrible to him. He caught Emil's horse by the bit and led it out. He could not have buckled a bridle on his own. After two or three attempts, he lifted himself into the saddle and started for Hanover. If he could catch the one o'clock train, he had money enough to get as far as Omaha.

While he was thinking dully of this in some less sensitized part of his brain, his acuter faculties were going over and over the cries he had heard in the orchard. Terror was the only thing that kept him from going back to her, terror that she might still be she, that she might still be suffering. A woman, mutilated and bleeding in his orchard—it was because it was a woman that he was so afraid. It was inconceivable that he should have hurt a woman. He would rather be eaten by wild beasts than see her move on the ground as she had moved in the orchard. Why had she been so careless? She knew he was like a crazy man when he was angry. She had more than once taken that gun away from him and held it, when he was angry with other people. Once it had gone off while they were struggling over it. She was never afraid. But, when she knew him, why hadn't she been more careful? Didn't she have all summer before her to love Emil Bergson in, without taking such chances? Probably she had met the Smirka boy, too, down there in the orchard. He didn't care. She could have met all the men on the Divide there, and welcome, if only she hadn't brought this horror on him.

There was a wrench in Frank's mind. He did not honestly believe that of her. He knew that he was doing her wrong. He stopped his horse to admit this to himself the more directly, to think it out the more clearly. He knew that he was to blame. For three years he had been trying to break her spirit. She had a way of making the best of things that seemed to him a sentimental affectation. He wanted his wife to resent that he was wasting his best years among these stupid and unappreciative people; but she had seemed to find the people quite good enough. If he ever got rich he meant to buy her pretty clothes and take her to California in a Pullman car, and treat her like a lady; but in the mean time he wanted her to feel that life was as ugly and as unjust as he felt it. He had tried to make her life ugly. He had refused to share any of the little pleasures she was so plucky about making for herself. She could be gay about the least thing in the world; but she must be gay! When she first came to him, her faith in him, her adoration—Frank struck the mare with his fist. Why had Marie made him do this thing; why had she brought this upon him? He was overwhelmed by sickening misfortune. All at once he heard her cries again—he had forgotten for a moment. 'Maria,' he sobbed aloud, 'Maria!'

When Frank was halfway to Hanover, the motion of his horse brought on a violent attack of nausea. After it had passed, he rode on again, but he could think of nothing except his physical weakness and his desire to be comforted by his wife. He wanted to get into his own bed. Had his wife been at home, he would have turned and gone back to her meekly enough.

CHAPTER 8

WHEN old Ivar climbed down from his loft at four o'clock the next morning, he came upon Emil's mare, jaded and lather-stained, her bridle broken, chewing the scattered tufts of hay outside the stable door. The old man was thrown into a fright at once. He put the mare in her stall, threw her a measure of oats, and then set out as fast as his bow-legs could carry him on the path to the nearest neighbor.

'Something is wrong with that boy. Some misfortune has come upon us. He would never have used her so, in his right senses. It is not his way to abuse his mare,' the old man kept muttering, as he scuttled through the short, wet pasture grass on his bare feet.

While Ivar was hurrying across the fields, the first long rays of the sun were reaching down between the orchard boughs to those two dew-drenched figures. The story of what had happened was written plainly on the orchard grass, and on the white mulberries that had fallen in the night and were covered with dark stain. For Emil the chapter had been short. He was shot in the heart, and had rolled over on his back and died. His face was turned up to the sky and his brows were drawn in a frown, as if he had realized that something had befallen him. But for Marie Shabata it had not been so easy. One ball had torn through her right lung, another had shattered the carotid artery. She must have started up and gone toward the hedge, leaving a trail of blood. There she had fallen and bled. From that spot there was another trail, heavier than the first, where she must have dragged herself back to Emil's body. Once there, she seemed not to have struggled any more. She ·had lifted her head to her lover's breast, taken his hand in both her own, and bled quietly to death. She was lying on her right side in an easy and natural position, her cheek on Emil's shoulder. On her face there was a look of ineffable content. Her lips were parted a little; her eyes were lightly closed, as if in a day-dream or a light slumber. After she lay down there, she seemed not to have moved an eyelash. The hand she held was covered with dark stains, where she had kissed it.

But the stained, slippery grass, the darkened mulberries, told only half the story. Above Marie and Emil, two white butterflies from Frank's alfalfa field were fluttering in and out among the interlacing shadows; diving and soaring, now close together, now far apart; and in the long grass by the fence the last wild roses of the year opened their pink hearts to die.

When Ivar reached the path by the hedge, he saw Shabata's rifle lying in the way. He turned and peered through the branches, falling upon his knees as if his legs had been mowed from under him. 'Merciful God!' he groaned; 'merciful, merciful God!'

Alexandra, too, had risen early that morning, because of her anxiety about Emil. She was in Emil's room upstairs when, from the window, she saw Ivar coming along the path that led from the Shabatas'. He was running like a spent man, tottering and lurching from side to side. Ivar never drank, and Alexandra thought at once that one of his spells had come upon him, and that he must be in a very bad way indeed. She ran downstairs and hurried out to meet him, to hide his infirmity from the eyes of her household. The old man fell in the road at her feet and caught her hand, over which he bowed his shaggy head. 'Mistress, mistress,' he sobbed, 'it has fallen! Sin and death for the young ones! God have mercy upon us!'

PART V

ALEXANDRA

CHAPTER 1

IVAR was sitting at a cobbler's bench in the barn, mending harness by the light of a lantern and repeating to himself the 101st Psalm. It was only five o'clock of a mid-October day, but a storm had come up in the afternoon, bringing black clouds, a cold wind and torrents of rain. The old man wore his buffalo-skin coat, and occasionally stopped to warm his fingers at the lantern. Suddenly a woman burst into the shed, as if she had been blown in, accompanied by a shower of rain-drops. It was Signa, wrapped in a man's overcoat and wearing a pair of boots over her shoes. In time of trouble Signa had come back to stay with her mistress, for she was the only one of the maids from whom Alexandra would accept much personal service. It was three months now since the news of the terrible thing that had happened in Frank Shabata's orchard had first run like a fire over the Divide. Signa and Nelse were staying on with Alexandra until winter.

'Ivar,' Signa exclaimed as she wiped the rain from her face, 'do you know where she is?'

The old man put down his cobbler's knife. 'Who, the mistress?'

'Yes. She went away about three o'clock. I happened to look out of the window and saw her going across the fields in her thin dress and sun hat. And now this storm has come on. I thought she was going to Mrs Hiller's, and I telephoned as soon as the thunder stopped, but she had not been there. I'm afraid she is out somewhere and will get her death of cold.'

Ivar put on his cap and took up the lantern. '*Ja, ja*, we will see. I will hitch the boy's mare to the cart and go.'

Signa followed him across the wagon shed to the horses' stable. She was shivering with cold and excitement. 'Where do you suppose she can be, Ivar?'

The old man lifted a set of single harness carefully from its peg. 'How should I know?'

'But you think she is at the graveyard, don't you?' Signa persisted. 'So do I. Oh, I wish she would be more like herself! I can't believe it's Alexandra Bergson come to this, with no head about anything. I have to tell her when to eat and when to go to bed.'

'Patience, patience, sister,' muttered Ivar as he settled the bit in the horse's mouth. 'When the eyes of the flesh are shut, the eyes of the spirit are open. She will have a message from those who are gone, and that will bring her peace. Until then we must bear with her. You and I are the only ones who have weight with her. She trusts us.'

'How awful it's been these last three months.' Signa held the lantern so that he could see to buckle the straps. 'It don't seem right that we must all be so miserable. Why do we all have to be punished? Seems to me like good times would never come again.'

Ivar expressed himself in a deep sigh, but said nothing. He stooped and took a sandburr from his toe.

'Ivar,' Signa asked suddenly, 'will you tell me why you go barefoot? All the time I lived here in the house I wanted to ask you. Is it for a penance, or what?'

'No, sister. It is for the indulgence of the body. From my youth up I have had a strong, rebellious body, and have been subject to every kind of temptation. Even in age my temptations are prolonged. It was necessary to make some allowances; and the feet, as I understand it, are free members. There is no divine prohibition for them in the Ten Commandments. The hands, the tongue, the eyes, the heart, all the bodily desires we are commanded to subdue; but the feet are free members. I indulge them without harm to any one, even to trampling in filth when my desires are low. They are quickly cleaned again.'

Signa did not laugh. She looked thoughtful as she followed Ivar out to the wagon-shed and held the shafts up for him, while he backed in the mare and buckled the hold-backs. 'You have been a good friend to the mistress, Ivar,' she murmured.

'And you, God be with you,' replied Ivar as he clambered into the cart and put the lantern under the oilcloth lap-cover. 'Now for a ducking, my girl,' he said to the mare, gathering up the reins.

As they emerged from the shed, a stream of water, running off the thatch, struck the mare on the neck. She tossed her head indignantly, then struck out bravely on the soft ground, slipping back again and again as she climbed the hill to the main road. Between the rain and the darkness Ivar could see very little, so he let Emil's mare have the rein, keeping her head in the right direction. When the ground was level, he turned her out of the dirt road upon the sod, where she was able to trot without slipping.

Before Ivar reached the graveyard, three miles from the house, the storm had spent itself, and the downpour had died into a soft, dripping rain. The sky and the land were a dark smoke color, and seemed to be coming together, like two waves. When Ivar stopped at the gate and swung out his lantern, a white figure rose from beside John Bergson's white stone.

The old man sprang to the ground and shuffled toward the gate calling, 'Mistress, mistress!'

Alexandra hurried to meet him and put her hand on his shoulder. '*Tyst!* Ivar. There's nothing to be worried about. I'm sorry if I've scared you all. I didn't notice the storm till it was on me, and I couldn't walk against it. I'm glad you've come. I am so tired I didn't know how I'd ever get home.'

Ivar swung the lantern up so that it shone in her face. '*Gud!* You are enough to frighten us, mistress. You look like a drowned woman. How could you do such a thing!'

Groaning and mumbling he led her out of the gate and helped her into the cart, wrapping her in the dry blankets on which he had been sitting.

Alexandra smiled at his solicitude. 'Not much use in that, Ivar. You will only shut the wet in. I don't feel so cold now; but I'm heavy and numb. I'm glad you came.'

Ivar turned the mare and urged her into a sliding trot. Her feet sent back a continual spatter of mud.

Alexandra spoke to the old man as they jogged along through the sullen gray twilight of the storm. 'Ivar, I think it has done me good to get cold clear through like this, once. I don't believe I shall suffer so much any more. When you get so near the dead, they seem more real than the living. Worldly thoughts leave one. Ever since Emil died, I've suffered so when it rained. Now that I've been out in it with him, I shan't dread it. After you once get cold clear through, the feeling of the rain on you is sweet. It seems to bring back feelings you had when you were a baby. It carries you back into the dark, before you were born; you can't see things, but they come to you, somehow, and you know them and aren't afraid of them. Maybe it's like that with the dead. If they feel anything at all, it's the old things, before they were born, that comfort people like the feeling of their own bed does when they are little.'

'Mistress,' said Ivar reproachfully, 'those are bad thoughts. The dead are in Paradise.'

Then he hung his head, for he did not believe that Emil was in Paradise.

When they got home, Signa had a fire burning in the sitting-room stove. She undressed Alexandra and gave her a hot footbath, while Ivar made ginger tea in the kitchen. When Alexandra was in bed, wrapped in hot blankets, Ivar came in with his tea and saw that she drank it. Signa asked permission to sleep on the slat lounge outside her door. Alexandra endured their attentions patiently, but she was glad when they put out the lamp and left her. As she lay alone in the dark, it occurred to her for the first time that perhaps she was actually tired of life. All the physical operations of life seemed difficult and painful. She longed to be free from her own body, which ached and was so heavy. And longing itself was heavy: she yearned to be free of that.

As she lay with her eyes closed, she had again, more vividly than for many years, the old illusion of her girlhood, of being lifted and carried lightly by some one very strong. He was with her a long while this time, and carried her very far, and in his arms she felt free from pain. When he laid her down on her bed again, she opened her eyes, and, for the first time in her life, she saw him, saw him clearly, though the room was dark, and his face was covered. He was standing in the doorway of her room. His white cloak was thrown over his face, and his head was bent a little forward. His shoulders seemed as strong as the foundations of the world. His right arm, bared from the elbow, was dark and gleaming, like bronze, and she knew at once that it was the arm of the mightiest of all lovers. She knew at last for whom it was she had waited, and where he would carry her. That, she told herself, was very well. Then she went to sleep.

Alexandra wakened in the morning with nothing worse than a hard cold and a stiff shoulder. She kept her bed for several days, and it was during that time that she formed a resolution to go to Lincoln to see Frank Shabata. Ever since she last saw him in the courtroom, Frank's haggard face and wild eyes had haunted her. The trial had lasted only three days. Frank had given himself up to the police in Omaha and pleaded guilty of killing without malice and without premeditation. The gun was, of course, against him, and the judge had given him the full sentence,—ten years. He had now been in the State Penitentiary for a month.

Frank was the only one, Alexandra told herself, for whom

anything could be done. He had been less in the wrong than any of them, and he was paying the heaviest penalty. She often felt that she herself had been more to blame than poor Frank. From the time the Shabatas had first moved to the neighboring farm, she had omitted no opportunity of throwing Marie and Emil together. Because she knew Frank was surly about doing little things to help his wife, she was always sending Emil over to spade or plant or carpenter for Marie. She was glad to have Emil see as much as possible of an intelligent, city-bred girl like their neighbor; she noticed that it improved his manners. She knew that Emil was fond of Marie, but it had never occurred to her that Emil's feeling might be different from her own. She wondered at herself now, but she had never thought of danger in that direction. If Marie had been unmarried,—oh, yes! Then she would have kept her eyes open. But the mere fact that she was Shabata's wife, for Alexandra, settled everything. That she was beautiful, impulsive, barely two years older than Emil, these facts had had no weight with Alexandra. Emil was a good boy, and only bad boys ran after married women.

Now, Alexandra could in a measure realize that Marie was, after all, Marie; not merely a 'married woman.' Sometimes, when Alexandra thought of her, it was with an aching tenderness. The moment she had reached them in the orchard that morning, everything was clear to her. There was something about those two lying in the grass, something in the way Marie had settled her cheek on Emil's shoulder, that told her everything. She wondered then how they could have helped loving each other; how she could have helped knowing that they must. Emil's cold, frowning face, the girl's content—Alexandra had felt awe of them, even in the first shock of her grief.

The idleness of those days in bed, the relaxation of body which attended them, enabled Alexandra to think more calmly than she had done since Emil's death. She and Frank, she told herself, were left out of that group of friends who had been overwhelmed by disaster. She must certainly see Frank Shabata. Even in the courtroom her heart had grieved for him. He was in a strange country, he had no kinsmen or friends, and in a moment he had ruined his life. Being what he was, she felt, Frank could not have acted otherwise. She could understand his behavior more easily than she could understand Marie's. Yes, she must go to Lincoln to see Frank Shabata.

The day after Emil's funeral, Alexandra had written to Carl Linstrum; a single page of notepaper, a bare statement of what had happened. She was not a woman who could write much about such a thing, and about her own feelings she could never write very freely. She knew that Carl was away from post-offices, prospecting somewhere in the interior. Before he started he had written her where he expected to go, but her ideas about Alaska were vague. As the weeks went by and she heard nothing from him, it seemed to Alexandra that her heart grew hard against Carl. She began to wonder whether she would not do better to finish her life alone. What was left of life seemed unimportant.

CHAPTER 2

LATE in the afternoon of a brilliant October day, Alexandra Bergson, dressed in a black suit and traveling-hat, alighted at the Burlington depot in Lincoln. She drove to the Lindell Hotel, where she had stayed two years ago when she came up for Emil's Commencement. In spite of her usual air of sureness and self-possession, Alexandra felt ill at ease in hotels, and she was glad, when she went to the clerk's desk to register, that there were not many people in the lobby. She had her supper early, wearing her hat and black jacket down to the dining-room and carrying her handbag. After supper she went out for a walk.

It was growing dark when she reached the university campus. She did not go into the grounds, but walked slowly up and down the stone walk outside the long iron fence, looking through at the young men who were running from one building to another, at the lights shining from the armory and the library. A squad of cadets were going through their drill behind the armory, and the commands of their young officer rang out at regular intervals, so sharp and quick that Alexandra could not understand them. Two stalwart girls came down the library steps and out through one of the iron gates. As they passed her, Alexandra was pleased to hear them speaking Bohemian to each other. Every few moments a boy would come running down the flagged walk and dash out into the street as if he were rushing to announce some wonder to the world. Alexandra felt a great tenderness for them all. She wished one of them would stop and speak to her. She wished she could ask them whether they had known Emil.

As she lingered by the south gate she actually did encounter one of the boys. He had on his drill cap and was swinging his books at the end of a long strap. It was dark by this time; he did not see her and ran against her. He snatched off his cap and stood bareheaded and panting. 'I'm awfully sorry,' he said in a bright, clear voice, with a rising inflection, as if he expected her to say something.

'Oh, it was my fault!' said Alexandra eagerly. 'Are you an old student here, may I ask?'

'No, ma'am. I'm a Freshie, just off the farm. Cherry County. Were you hunting somebody?'

'No, thank you. That is—' Alexandra wanted to detain him. 'That is, I would like to find some of my brother's friends. He graduated two years ago.'

'Then you'd have to try the Seniors, wouldn't you? Let's see; I don't know any of them yet, but there'll be sure to be some of them around the library. That red building, right there,' he pointed.

'Thank you, I'll try there,' said Alexandra lingeringly.

'Oh that's all right! Goodnight.' The lad clapped his cap on his head and ran straight down Eleventh Street. Alexandra looked after him wistfully.

She walked back to her hotel unreasonably comforted. 'What a nice voice that boy had, and how polite he was. I know Emil was always like that to women.' And again, after she had undressed and was standing in her nightgown, brushing her long, heavy hair by the electric light, she remembered him and said to herself: 'I don't think I ever heard a nicer voice than that boy had. I hope he will get on well here. Cherry County; that's where the hay is so fine, and the coyotes can scratch down to water.'

At nine o'clock the next morning Alexandra presented herself at the warden's office in the State Penitentiary. The warden was a German, a ruddy, cheerful-looking man who had formerly been a harness-maker. Alexandra had a letter to him from the German banker in Hanover. As he glanced at the letter, Mr Schwartz put away his pipe.

'That big Bohemian, is it? Sure, he's gettin' along fine,' said Mr Schwartz cheerfully.

'I am glad to hear that. I was afraid he might be quarrelsome and get himself into more trouble. Mr Schwartz, if you have time, I would like to tell you a little about Frank Shabata, and why I am interested in him.'

The warden listened genially while she told him briefly something of Frank's history and character, but he did not seem to find anything unusual in her account.

'Sure, I'll keep an eye on him. We'll take care of him all right,' he said, rising. 'You can talk to him here, while I go to see to things in the kitchen. I'll have him sent in. He ought to be done washing out his cell by this time. We have to keep 'em clean, you know.'

The warden paused at the door, speaking back over his shoulder to a pale young man in convicts' clothes who was seated at a desk in the corner, writing in a big ledger.

'Bertie, when 1037 is brought in, you just step out and give this lady a chance to talk.'

The young man bowed his head and bent over his ledger again.

When Mr Schwartz disappeared, Alexandra thrust her black-edged handkerchief nervously into her handbag. Coming out on the streetcar she had not had the least dread of meeting Frank. But since she had been here the sounds and smells in the corridor, the look of the men in convicts' clothes who passed the glass door of the warden's office, affected her unpleasantly.

The warden's clock ticked, the young convict's pen scratched busily in the big book, and his sharp shoulders were shaken every few seconds by a loose cough which he tried to smother. It was easy to see that he was a sick man. Alexandra looked at him timidly, but he did not once raise his eyes. He wore a white shirt under his striped jacket, a high collar, and a necktie, very carefully tied. His hands were thin and white and well cared for, and he had a seal ring on his little finger. When he heard steps approaching in the corridor, he rose, blotted his book, put his pen in the rack, and left the room without raising his eyes. Through the door he opened a guard came in, bringing Frank Shabata.

'You the lady that wanted to talk to 1037? Here he is. Be on your good behavior, now. He can set down, lady,' seeing that Alexandra remained standing. 'Push that white button when you're through with him, and I'll come.'

The guard went out and Alexandra and Frank were left alone.

Alexandra tried not to see his hideous clothes. She tried to look straight into his face, which she could scarcely believe was his. It was already bleached to a chalky gray. His lips were colorless, his fine teeth looked yellowish. He glanced at Alexandra sullenly, blinked as if he had come from a dark place, and one eyebrow twitched continually. She felt at once that this interview was a terrible ordeal to him. His shaved head, showing the conformation of his skull, gave him a criminal look which he had not had during the trial.

Alexandra held out her hand. 'Frank,' she said, her eyes filling suddenly, 'I hope you'll let me be friendly with you. I understand how you did it. I don't feel hard toward you. They were more to blame than you.'

Frank jerked a dirty blue handkerchief from his trousers pocket. He had begun to cry. He turned away from Alexandra. 'I never did mean to do not'ing to dat woman,' he muttered. 'I never mean to do not'ing to dat boy. I ain't had not'ing ag'in'dat boy. I always like dat boy fine. An' then I find him—' He stopped. The feeling went out of his face and eyes. He dropped into a chair and sat looking stolidly at the floor, his hands hanging loosely between his knees, the handkerchief lying across his striped leg. He seemed to have stirred up in his mind a disgust that had paralyzed his faculties.

'I haven't come up here to blame you, Frank. I think they were more to blame than you.' Alexandra, too, felt benumbed.

Frank looked up suddenly and stared out of the office window. 'I guess dat place all go to hell what I work so hard on,' he said with a slow, bitter smile. 'I not care a damn.' He stopped and rubbed the palm of his hand over the light bristles on his head with annoyance. 'I no can t'ink without my hair,' he complained. 'I forget English. We not talk here, except swear.'

Alexandra was bewildered. Frank seemed to have undergone a change of personality. There was scarcely anything by which she could recognize her handsome Bohemian neighbor. He seemed, somehow, not altogether human. She did not know what to say to him.

'You do not feel hard to me, Frank?' she asked at last.

Frank clenched his fist and broke out in excitement. 'I not feel hard at no woman. I tell you I not that kind-a man. I never hit my wife. No, never I hurt her when she devil me something awful!' He struck his fist down on the warden's desk so hard that he afterward stroked it absently. A pale pink crept over his neck and face. 'Two, t'ree years I know dat woman don' care no more 'bout me, Alexandra Bergson. I know she after some other man. I know her, oo-oo! An' I ain't never hurt her. I never would-a done dat, if I ain't had dat gun along. I don' know what in hell make me take dat gun. She always say I ain't no man to carry gun. If she been in dat house, where she ought-a been—But das a foolish talk.'

Frank rubbed his head and stopped suddenly, as he had stopped before. Alexandra felt that there was something strange in the way he chilled off, as if something came up in him that extinguished his power of feeling or thinking.

'Yes, Frank,' she said kindly. 'I know you never meant to hurt Marie.'

Frank smiled at her queerly. His eyes filled slowly with tears. 'You know, I most forgit dat woman's name. She ain't got no name for me no more. I never hate my wife, but dat woman what make me do dat—Honest to God, but I hate her! I no man to fight. I don' want to kill no boy and no woman. I not care how many men she take under dat tree. I no care for not'ing but dat fine boy I kill, Alexandra Bergson. I guess I go crazy sure 'nough.'

Alexandra remembered the little yellow cane she had found in Frank's clothes-closet. She thought of how he had come to this country a gay young fellow, so attractive that the prettiest Bohemian girl in Omaha had run away with him. It seemed unreasonable that life should have landed him in such a place as this. She blamed Marie bitterly. And why, with her happy, affectionate nature, should she have brought destruction and sorrow to all who had loved her, even to poor old Joe Tovesky, the uncle who used to carry her about so proudly when she was a little girl? That was the strangest thing of all. Was there, then, something wrong in being warm-hearted and impulsive like that? Alexandra hated to think so. But there was Emil, in the Norwegian graveyard at home, and here was Frank Shabata. Alexandra rose and took him by the hand.

'Frank Shabata, I am never going to stop trying until I get you pardoned. I'll never give the Governor any peace. I know I can get you out of this place.'

Frank looked at her distrustfully, but he gathered confidence from her face. 'Alexandra,' he said earnestly, 'if I git out-a here, I not trouble dis country no more. I go back where I come from; see my mother.'

Alexandra tried to withdraw her hand, but Frank held on to it nervously. He put out his finger and absently touched a button on her black jacket. 'Alexandra,' he said in a low tone, looking steadily at the button, 'you ain' t'ink I use dat girl awful bad before—'

'No Frank. We won't talk about that,' Alexandra said, pressing his hand. 'I can't help Emil now, so I'm going to do what I can for you. You know I don't go away from home often, and I came up here on purpose to tell you this.'

The warden at the glass door looked in inquiringly. Alexandra nodded, and he came in and touched the white button on his desk. The guard appeared, and with a sinking heart Alexandra saw Frank led away down the corridor. After a few words with Mr Schwartz she left the prison and made her way to the streetcar. She had refused with horror the warden's cordial invitation to 'go through the institution.' As the car lurched over its uneven roadbed, back towards Lincoln, Alexandra thought of how she and Frank had been wrecked by the same storm and of how, although she could come out into the sunlight, she had not much more left in her life than he. She remembered some lines from a poem she had liked in her schooldays:—

> Henceforth the world will only be
> A wider prison-house to me,—

and sighed. A disgust of life weighed upon her heart; some such feeling as had twice frozen Frank Shabata's features while they talked together. She wished she were back on the Divide.

When Alexandra entered her hotel, the clerk held up one finger and beckoned to her. As she approached his desk, he handed her a telegram. Alexandra took the yellow envelope and looked at it in perplexity, then stepped into the elevator without opening it. As she walked down the corridor toward her room, she reflected that she was, in a manner, immune from evil tidings. On reaching her room she locked the door, and sitting down on a chair by the dresser, opened the telegram. It was from Hanover, and it read:—

Arrived Hanover last night. Shall wait here until you come. Please hurry.

CARL LINSTRUM.

Alexandra put her head down on the dresser and burst into tears.

CHAPTER 3

THE next afternoon Carl and Alexandra were walking across the fields from Mrs Hiller's. Alexandra had left Lincoln after midnight, and Carl had met her at the Hanover station early in the morning. After they reached home, Alexandra had gone over to Mrs Hiller's to leave a little present she had bought for her in the city. They stayed at the old lady's door but a moment, and then came out to spend the rest of the afternoon in the sunny fields.

Alexandra had taken off her black traveling-suit and put on a white dress; partly because she saw that her black clothes made Carl uncomfortable and partly because she felt oppressed by them herself. They seemed a little like the prison where she had worn them yesterday, and to be out of place in the open fields. Carl had changed very little. His cheeks were browner and fuller. He looked less like a tired scholar than when he went away a year ago, but no one, even now, would have taken him for a man of business. His soft, lustrous black eyes, his whimsical smile, would be less against him in the Klondike than on the Divide. There are always dreamers on the frontier.

Carl and Alexandra had been talking since morning. Her letter had never reached him. He had first learned of her misfortune from a San Francisco paper, four weeks old, which he had picked up in a saloon, and which contained a brief account of Frank Shabata's trial. When he put down the paper, he had already made up his mind that he could reach Alexandra as quickly as a letter could; and ever since he had been on the way; day and night, by the fastest boats and trains he could catch. His steamer had been held back two days by rough weather.

As they came out of Mrs Hiller's garden they took up their talk again where they had left it.

'But could you come away like that, Carl, without arranging things? Could you just walk off and leave your business?' Alexandra asked.

Carl laughed. 'Prudent Alexandra! You see, my dear, I happen to have an honest partner. I trust him with everything. In fact, it's been his enterprise from the beginning, you know. I'm in it only because he took me in. I'll have to go back in the spring. Perhaps you will want to go with me then. We haven't turned up millions yet, but we've got a start that's worth following. But this winter I'd like to spend with you. You won't feel that we ought to wait longer, on Emil's account, will you, Alexandra?'

Alexandra shook her head. 'No, Carl; I don't feel that way about it. And surely you needn't mind anything Lou and Oscar say now. They are much angrier with me about Emil, now, than about you. They say it was all my fault. That I ruined him by sending him to college.'

'No, I don't care a button for Lou or Oscar. The moment I knew you were in trouble, the moment I thought you might need me, it all looked different. You've always been a triumphant kind of person.' Carl hesitated, looking sidewise at her strong, full figure. 'But you do need me now, Alexandra?'

She put her hand on his arm. 'I needed you terribly when it happened, Carl. I cried for you at night. Then everything seemed to get hard inside of me, and I thought perhaps I should never care for you again. But when I got your telegram yesterday, then—then it was just as it used be. You are all I have in the world, you know.'

Carl pressed her hand in silence. They were passing the Shabatas' empty house now, but they avoided the orchard path and took one that led over by the pasture pond.

'Can you understand it, Carl?' Alexandra mumured. 'I have had nobody but Ivar and Signa to talk to. Do talk to me. Can you understand it? Could you have believed that of Marie Tovesky? I would have been cut to pieces, little by little, before I would have betrayed her trust in me!'

Carl looked at the shining spot of water before them. 'Maybe she was cut to pieces, too, Alexandra. I am sure she tried hard; they both did. That was why Emil went to Mexico, of course. And he was going away again, you tell me, though he had only been home three weeks. You remember that Sunday when I went with Emil up to the French Church fair? I thought that day there was some kind of feeling, something unusual, between them. I meant to talk to you about it. But on my way back I met Lou and Oscar and got so angry that I forgot everything else. You mustn't be hard on them, Alexandra. Sit down here by the pond a minute. I want to tell you something.'

They sat down on the grass-tufted bank and Carl told her how he had seen Emil and Marie out by the pond that morning, more than a year ago, and how young and charming and full of grace they had seemed to him. 'It happens like that in the world sometimes,

Alexandra,' he added earnestly. 'I've seen it before. There are women who spread ruin around them through no fault of theirs, just by being too beautiful, too full of life and love. They can't help it. People come to them as people go to a warm fire in winter. I used to feel that in her when she was a little girl. Do you remember how all the Bohemians crowded round her in the store that day, when she gave Emil her candy? You remember those yellow sparks in her eyes?'

Alexandra sighed. 'Yes. People couldn't help loving her. Poor Frank does, even now, I think; though he's got himself in such a tangle that for a long time his love has been bitterer than his hate. But if you saw there was anything wrong, you ought to have told me, Carl.'

Carl took her hand and smiled patiently. 'My dear, it was something one felt in the air, as you feel the spring coming, or a storm in summer. I didn't *see* anything. Simply, when I was with those two young things, I felt my blood go quicker, I felt—how shall I say it?— an acceleration of life. After I got away, it was all too delicate, too intangible, to write about.'

Alexandra looked at him mournfully. 'I try to be more liberal about such things than I used to be. I try to realize that we are not all made alike. Only, why couldn't it have been Raoul Marcel, or Jan Smirka? Why did it have to be my boy?'

'Because he was the best there was, I suppose. They were both the best you had here.'

The sun was dropping low in the west when the two friends rose and took the path again. The straw-stacks were throwing long shadows, the owls were flying home to the prairie-dog town. When they came to the corner where the pastures joined, Alexandra's twelve young colts were galloping in a drove over the brow of the hill.

'Carl,' said Alexandra, 'I should like to go up there with you in the spring. I haven't been on the water since we crossed the ocean, when

I was a little girl. After we first came out here I used to dream sometimes about the shipyard where father worked, and a little sort of inlet, full of masts.' Alexandra paused. After a moment's thought she said, 'But you would never ask me to go away for good, would you?'

'Of course not, my dearest. I think I know how you feel about this country as well as you do yourself.' Carl took her hand in both his own and pressed it tenderly.

'Yes, I still feel that way, though Emil is gone. When I was on the train this morning, and we got near Hanover, I felt something like I did when I drove back with Emil from the river that time, in the dry year. I was glad to come back to it. I've lived here a long time. There is great peace here, Carl, and freedom . . . I thought when I came out of that prison, where poor Frank is, that I should never feel free again. But I do, here.' Alexandra took a deep breath and looked off into the red west.

'You belong to the land,' Carl murmured, 'as you have always said. Now more than ever.'

'Yes, now more than ever. You remember what you once said about the graveyard, and the old story writing itself over? Only it is we who write it, with the best we have.'

They paused on the last ridge of the pasture, overlooking the house and the windmill and the stables that marked the site of John Bergson's homestead. On every side the brown waves of the earth rolled away to meet the sky.

'Lou and Oscar can't see those things,' said Alexandra suddenly. 'Suppose I do will my land to their children, what difference will that make? The land belongs to the future, Carl; that's the way it seems to me. How many of the names on the county clerk's plat will be there in fifty years? I might as well try to will the sunset over there to my brother's children. We come and go, but the land is always here. And the people who love it and understand it are the people who own it—

for a little while.'

Carl looked at her wonderingly. She was still gazing into the west, and in her face there was that exalted serenity that sometimes came to her at moments of deep feeling. The level rays of the sinking sun shone in her clear eyes.

'Why are you thinking of such things now, Alexandra?'

'I had a dream before I went to Lincoln—But I will tell you about that afterward, after we are married. It will never come true, now, in the way I thought it might.' She took Carl's arm and they walked toward the gate. 'How many times we have walked this path together, Carl. How many times we will walk it again! Does it seem to you like coming back to your own place? Do you feel at peace with the world here? I think we shall be very happy. I haven't any fears. I think when friends marry, they are safe. We don't suffer like—those young ones.' Alexandra ended with a sigh.

They had reached the gate. Before Carl opened it, he drew Alexandra to him and kissed her softly, on her lips and on her eyes.

She leaned heavily on his shoulder. 'I am tired,' she murmured. 'I have been very lonely, Carl.'

They went into the house together, leaving the Divide behind them, under the evening star. Fortunate country, that is one day to receive hearts like Alexandra's into its bosom, to give them out again in the yellow wheat, in the rustling corn, in the shining eyes of youth!

BEFORE THE GRINGO CAME

by Gertrude Atherton

THE EARS OF TWENTY AMERICANS

CHAPTER 1

'God of my soul! Do not speak of hope to me. Hope? For what are those three frigates, swarming with a horde of foreign bandits, creeping about our bay? For what have the persons of General Vallejo and Judge Leese been seized and imprisoned? Why does a strip of cotton, painted with a gaping bear, flaunt itself above Sonoma? Oh, abomination! Oh, execrable profanation! Mother of God, open thine ocean and suck them down! Smite them with pestilence if they put foot in our capital! Shrivel their fingers to the bone if they dethrone our Aztec Eagle and flourish their stars and stripes above our fort! O California! That thy sons and thy daughters should live to see thee plucked like a rose by the usurper! And why? Why? Not because these piratical Americans have the right to one league of our land; but because, Holy Evangelists! they want it! Our lands are rich, our harbors are fine, gold veins our valleys, therefore we must be plucked. The United States of America are mightier than Mexico, therefore they sweep down upon us with mouths wide open. Holy God! That I could choke but one with my own strong fingers. Oh!' Doña Eustaquia paused abruptly and smote her hands together,—'O that I were a man! That the women of California were men!'

On this pregnant morning of July seventh, eighteen hundred and forty-six, all aristocratic Monterey was gathered in the sala of Doña Modeste Castro. The hostess smiled sadly. 'That is the wish of my husband,' she said, 'for the men of our country want the Americans.'

'And why?' asked one of the young men, flicking a particle of dust from his silken riding jacket. 'We shall then have freedom from the constant war of opposing factions. If General Castro and Governor Pico are not calling Juntas in which to denounce each other, a Carillo is pitting his ambition against an Alvarado. The Gringos will rule us lightly and bring us peace. They will not disturb our grants, and will give us rich prices for our lands—'

'Oh, fool!' interrupted Doña Eustaquia. 'Thrice fool! A hundred years from now, Fernando Altimira, and our names will be forgotten in California. Fifty years from now and our walls will tumble upon us whilst we cook our beans in the rags that charity—American charity—has flung us! I tell you that the hour the American flag waves above the fort of Monterey is the hour of the Californians' doom. We have lived in Arcadia—ingrates that you are to complain—they will run over us like ants and sting us to death!'

'That is the prediction of my husband;' said Doña Modeste. 'Liberty, Independence, Decency, Honour, how long will they be his watch words?'

'Not a day longer!' cried Doña Eustaquia, 'for the men of California are cowards.'

'Cowards! We? No man should say that to us!' The caballeros were on their feet, their eyes flashing, as if they faced in uniform the navy of the United States, rather than confronted, in lace ruffles and silken small-clothes, an angry scornful woman.

'Cowards!' continued Fernando Altimira. 'Are not men flocking about General Castro at San Juan Bautista, willing to die in a cause already lost? If our towns were sacked or our women outraged would not the weakest of us fight until we died in our blood? But what is coming is for the best, Doña Eustaquia, despite your prophecy; and as we cannot help it—we, a few thousand men against a great nation—we resign ourselves because we are governed by reason instead of by passion. No one reverences our General more than Fernando Altimira. No grander man ever wore a uniform! But he is fighting in a hopeless cause, and the fewer who uphold him the less blood will flow, the sooner the struggle will finish.'

Doña Modeste covered her beautiful face and wept. Many of the women sobbed in sympathy. Bright eyes, from beneath gay rebosas or delicate mantillas, glanced approvingly at the speaker. Brown old men and women stared gloomily at the floor. But the greater number followed every motion of their master-spirit, Doña Eustaquia Ortega.

She walked rapidly up and down the long room, too excited to sit down, flinging the mantilla back as it brushed her hot cheek. She was a woman not yet forty, and very handsome, although the peachness of youth had left her face. Her features were small but sharply cut; the square chin and firm mouth had the lines of courage and violent emotions, her piercing intelligent eyes interpreted a terrible power of love and hate. But if her face was so strong as to be almost unfeminine, it was frank and kind.

Doña Eustaquia might watch with joy her bay open and engulf the hated Americans, but she would nurse back to life the undrowned bodies flung upon the shore. If she had been born a queen she would have slain in anger, but she would not have tortured. General Castro had flung his hat at her feet many times, and told her that she was born to command. Even the nervous irregularity of her step today could not affect the extreme elegance of her carriage, and she carried her small head with the imperious pride of a sovereign. She did not speak again for a moment, but as she passed the group of young men at the end of the room her eyes flashed from one languid face to another. She hated their rich breeches and embroidered jackets buttoned with silver and gold, the lace handkerchiefs knotted about their shapely throats. No man was a man who did not wear a uniform.

Don Fernando regarded her with a mischievous smile as she approached him a second time.

'I predict, also,' he said, 'I predict that our charming Doña Eustaquia will yet wed an American—'

'What!' she turned upon him with the fury of a lioness. 'Hold thy prating tongue! I marry an American? God! I would give every league of my ranchos for a necklace made from the ears of twenty Americans. I would throw my jewels to the pigs, if I could feel here upon my neck the proof that twenty American heads looked ready to be fired from the cannon on the hill!'

Everybody in the room laughed, and the atmosphere felt lighter. Muslin gowns began to flutter, and the seal of disquiet sat less heavily upon careworn or beautiful faces. But before the respite was a moment old a young man entered hastily from the street, and throwing his hat on the floor burst into tears.

'What is it?' The words came mechanically from every one in the room.

The herald put his hands to his throat to control the swelling muscles. 'Two hours ago,' he said, 'Commander Sloat sent one Captain William Mervine on shore to demand of our Commandante the surrender of the town. Don Mariano walked the floor, wringing his hands, until a quarter of an hour ago, when he sent word to the insolent servant of a pirate-republic that he had no authority to deliver up the capital, and bade him go to San Juan Bautista and confer with General Castro. Whereupon the American thief ordered two hundred and fifty of his men to embark in boats—do not you hear?'

A mighty cheer shook the air amidst the thunder of cannon; then another, and another.

Every lip in the room was white.

'What is that?' asked Doña Eustaquia. Her voice was hardly audible.

'They have raised the American flag upon the Custom-house,' said the herald.

For a moment no one moved; then as by one impulse, and without a word, Doña Modeste Castro and her guests rose and ran through the streets to the Custom-house on the edge of the town.

In the bay were three frigates of twenty guns each. On the rocks, in the street by the Custom-house and on its corridors, was a small army of men in the naval uniform of the United States, respectful but determined. About them and the little man who read aloud from a long roll of paper, the aristocrats joined the rabble of the town. Men with sunken eyes who had gambled all night, leaving even serape and sombrero on the gaming table; girls with painted faces staring above cheap and gaudy satins, who had danced at fandangos in the booths until dawn, then wandered about the beach, too curious over the movements of the American squadron to go to bed; shopkeepers, black and rusty of face, smoking big pipes with the air of philosophers; Indians clad in a single garment of calico, falling in a straight line from the neck; eagle-beaked old crones with black shawls over their heads; children wearing only a smock twisted about their little waists and tied in a knot behind; a few American residents, glancing triumphantly at each other; caballeros, gay in the silken attire of summer, sitting in angry disdain upon their plunging, superbly trapped horses; last of all, the elegant women in their lace mantillas and flowered rebosas, weeping and clinging to each other. Few gave ear to the reading of Sloat's proclamation.

Benicia, the daughter of Doña Eustaquia, raised her clasped hands, the tears streaming from her eyes. 'Oh, these Americans! How I hate them!' she cried, a reflection of her mother's violent spirit on her sweet face.

Doña Eustaquia caught the girl's hands and flung herself upon her neck. 'Ay! California! California!' she cried wildly. 'My country is flung to its knees in the dirt.'

A rose from the upper corridor of the Custom-house struck her daughter full in the face.

CHAPTER 2

THE same afternoon Benicia ran into the sala where her mother was lying on a sofa, and exclaimed excitedly: 'My mother! My mother! It is not so bad. The Americans are not so wicked as we have thought. The proclamation of the Commodore Sloat has been pasted on all the walls of the town and promises that our grants shall be secured to us under the new government, that we shall elect our own alcaldes, that we shall continue to worship God in our own religion, that our priests shall be protected, that we shall have all the rights and advantages of the American citizen—'

'Stop!' cried Doña Eustaquia, springing to her feet. Her face still burned with the bitter experience of the morning. 'Tell me of no more lying promises! They will keep their word! Ay, I do not doubt but they will take advantage of our ignorance, with their Yankee sharpness! I know them! Do not speak of them to me again. If it must be, it must; and at least I have thee.' She caught the girl in her arms, and covered the flower-like face with passionate kisses. 'My little one! My darling! Thou lovest thy mother—better than all the world? Tell me!'

The girl pressed her soft, red lips to the dark face which could express such fierceness of love and hate.

'My mother! Of course I love thee. It is because I have thee that I do not take the fate of my country to deeper heart. So long as they do not put their ugly bayonets between us, what difference whether the eagle or the stars wave above the fort?'

'Ah, my child, thou hast not that love of country which is part of my soul! But perhaps it is as well, for thou lovest thy mother the more. Is it not so, my little one?'

'Surely, my mother; I love no one in the world but you.'

Doña Eustaquia leaned back and tapped the girl's fair cheek with her finger.

'Not even Don Fernando Altimira?'

'No, my mother.'

'Nor Flujencio Hernandez? Nor Juan Perez? Nor any of the caballeros who serenade beneath thy window?'

'I love their music, but it comes as sweetly from one throat as from another.'

Her mother gave a long sigh of relief. 'And yet I would have thee marry some day, my little one. I was happy with thy father—thanks to God he did not live to see this day—I was as happy, for two little years, as this poor nature of ours can be, and I would have thee be the same. But do not hasten to leave me alone. Thou art so young! Thine eyes have yet the roguishness of youth; I would not see love flash it aside. Thy mouth is like a child's; I shall shed the saddest tears of my life the day it trembles with passion. Dear little one! Thou hast been more than a daughter to me; thou hast been my only companion. I have striven to impart to thee the ambition of thy mother and the intellect of thy father. And I am proud of thee, very, very proud of thee.'

Benicia pinched her mother's chin, her mischievous eyes softening. 'Ay, my mother, I have done my little best, but I never shall be you. I am afraid I love to dance through the night and flirt my breath away better than I love the intellectual conversation of the few people you think worthy to sit about you in the evenings. I am like a little butterfly sitting on the mane of a mountain lion—'

'Tush! Tush! Thou knowest more than any girl in Monterey, and I am satisfied with thee. Think of the books thou hast read, the languages thou hast learned from the Señor Hartnell. Ay, my little one, nobody but thou wouldst dare to say thou cared for nothing but dancing and flirting, although I will admit that even Ysabel Herrera could scarce rival thee at either.'

'Ay, my poor Ysabel! My heart breaks every night when I say a prayer for her.' She tightened the clasp of her arms and pressed her face close to her mother's. 'Mamacita, darling,' she said coaxingly, 'I have a big favour to beg. Ay, an enormous one! How dare I ask it?'

'Aha! What is it? I should like to know. I thought thy tenderness was a little anxious.'

'Ay, mamacita! Do not refuse me or it will break my heart. On Wednesday night Don Thomas Larkin gives a ball at his house to the officers of the American squadron. Oh, mamacita! mamacita! *darling!* do, do let me go!'

'Benicia! Thou wouldst meet those men? Válgame Dios! And thou art a child of mine!'

She flung the girl from her, and walked rapidly up and down the room, Benicia following with her little white hands outstretched. 'Dearest one, I know just how you feel about it! But think a moment. They have come to stay. They will never go. We shall meet them everywhere—every night—every day. And my new gown, mamacita! The beautiful silver spangles! There is not such a gown in Monterery! Ay, I must go. And they say the Americans hop like puppies when they dance. How I shall laugh at them! And it is not once in the year that I have a chance to speak English, and none of the other girls can. And all the girls, all the girls, all the girls, will go to this ball. Oh, mamacita!'

Her mother was obliged to laugh. 'Well, well, I cannot refuse you anything; you know that! Go to the ball! Ay, yi, do not smother me! As you have said—that little head can think—we must meet these insolent braggarts sooner or later. So I would not—' her cheeks blanched suddenly, she caught her daughter's face between her hands, and bent her piercing eyes above the girl's soft depths. 'Mother of God! That could not be. My child! Thou couldst never love an American! A Gringo! A Protestant! Holy Mary!'

Benicia threw back her head and gave a long laugh—the light rippling laugh of a girl who has scarcely dreamed of lovers. 'I love an

American? Oh, my mother! A great, big, yellow-haired bear! When I want only to laugh at their dancing! No, mamacita, when I love an American thou shalt have his ears for thy necklace.'

CHAPTER 3

THOMAS O. LARKIN, United States Consul to California until the occupation left him without duties, had invited Monterey to meet the officers of the *Savannah, Cyane,* and *Levant,* and only Doña Modeste Castro had declined. At ten o'clock the sala of his large house on the rise of the hill was thronged with robed girls in every shade and device of white, sitting demurely behind the wide shoulders of coffee-colored dowagers, also in white, and blazing with jewels. The young matrons were there, too, although they left the sala at intervals to visit the room set apart for the nurses and children; no Montereña ever left her little ones at home. The old men and the caballeros wore the black coats and white trousers which Monterey fashion dictated for evening wear; the hair of the younger men was braided with gay ribbons, and diamonds flashed in the lace of their ruffles.

The sala was on the second floor; the musicians sat on the corridor beyond the open windows and scraped their fiddles and twanged their guitars, awaiting the coming of the American officers. Before long the regular tramp of many feet turning from Alvarado Street up the little Primera del Este, facing Mr Larkin's house, made dark eyes flash, lace and silken gowns flutter. Benicia and a group of girls were standing by Doña Eustaquia. They opened their large black fans as if to wave back the pink that had sprung to their cheeks. Only Benicia held her head saucily high, and her large brown eyes were full of defiant sparkles.

'Why art thou so excited, Blandina?' she asked of a girl who had grasped her arm. 'I feel as if the war between the United States and

Mexico began tonight.'

'Ay, Benicia, thou hast so gay a spirit that nothing ever frightens thee! But, Mary! How many they are! They tramp as if they would go through the stair. Ay, the poor flag! No wonder—'

'Now, do not cry over the flag any more. Ah! there is not one to compare with General Castro!'

The character of the Californian sala had changed for ever; the blue and gold of the United States had invaded it.

The officers, young and old, looked with much interest at the faces, soft, piquant, tropical, which made the effect of pansies looking inquisitively over a snowdrift. The girls returned their glances with approval, for they were as fine and manly a set of men as ever had faced death or woman. Ten minutes later California and the United States were flirting outrageously.

Mr Larkin presented a tall officer to Benicia. That the young man was very well-looking even Benicia admitted. True, his hair was golden, but it was cut short, and bore no resemblance to the coat of a bear; his mustache and brows were brown; his gray eyes were as laughing as her own.

'I suppose you do not speak any English, señorita,' he said, helplessly.

'No? I spik Eenglish like the Spanish. The Spanish people no have difficult at all to learn the other langues. But Señor Hartnell he say it no is easy at all for the Eenglish to spik the French and the Spanish, so I suppose you no spik one word our langue, no?'

He gallantly repressed a smile. 'Thankfully I may say that I do not, else would I not have the pleasure of hearing you speak English. Never have I heard it so charmingly spoken before.'

Benica took her skirt between the tips of her fingers and swayed her graceful body forward, as a tule bends in the wind.

'You like dip the flag of the conqueror in honey, señor. Ay! We need have one compliment for every tear that fall since your eagle stab his beak in the neck de ours.'

'Ah, the loyal women of Monterey! I have no words to express my admiration for them, señorita. A thousand compliments are not worth one tear.'

Benicia turned swiftly to her mother, her eyes glittering with pleasure. 'Mother, you hear! You hear!' she cried in Spanish. 'These Americans are not so bad, after all.'

Doña Eustaquia gave the young man one of her rare smiles; it flashed over her strong dark face, until the light of youth was there once more.

'Very pretty speech,' she said, with slow precision. 'I thank you, Señor Russell, in the name of the women of Monterey.'

'By Jove! Madam—señora—I assure you I never felt so cut up in my life as when I saw all those beautiful women crying down there by the Custom-house. I am a good American, but I would rather have thrown the flag under your feet than have seen you cry like that. And I assure you, dear señora, every man among us felt the same. As you have been good enough to thank me in the name of the women of Monterey, I, in behalf of the officers of the United States squadron, beg that you will forgive us.'

Doña Eustaquia's cheek paled again, and she set her lips for a moment; then she held out her hand.

'Señor,' she said, 'we are conquered, but we are Californians; and although we do not bend the head, neither do we turn the back. We have invite you to our houses, and we cannot treat you like enemies. I will say with—how you say it—truth?—we did hate the thought that you come and take the country that was ours. But all is over and cannot be changed. So, it is better we are good friends than poor ones; and—and—my house is open to you, señor.'

Russell was a young man of acute perceptions; moreover, he had heard of Doña Eustaquia; he divined in part the mighty effort by which good breeding and philosophy had conquered bitter resentment. He raised the little white hand to his lips.

'I would that I were twenty men, señora. Each would be your devoted servant.'

'And then she have her necklace!' cried Benicia, delightedly.

'What is that?' asked Russell; but Doña Eustaquia shook her fan threateningly and turned away.

'I no tell you everything,' said Benicia, 'so no be too curiosa. You no dance the contradanza, no?'

'I regret to say that I do not. But this is a plain waltz; will you not give it to me?'

Benicia, disregarding the angry glances of approaching caballeros, laid her hand on the officer's shoulder, and he spun her down the room.

'Why, you no dance so bad!' she said with surprise. 'I think always the Americanos dance so terreeblay.'

'Who could not dance with a fairy in his arms?'

'What funny things you say. I never been called fairy before.'

'You have never been interpreted.' And then, in the whirl-waltz of that day, both lost their breath.

When the dance was over and they stood near Doña Eustaquia, he took the fan from Benicia's hand and waved it slowly before her. She laughed outright.

'You think I am so tired I no can fan myself?' she demanded. 'How queer are these Americanos! Why, I have dance for three days and three nights and never estop.'

'Señorita!'

'Si, señor. Oh, we estop sometimes, but no for long. It was at Sonoma two months ago. At the house de General Vallejo.'

'You certainly are able to fan yourself; but it is no reflection upon your muscle. It is only a custom we have.'

'Then I think much better you no have the custom. You no look like a man at all when you fan like a girl.'

He handed her back the fan with some choler.

'Really, señorita, you are very frank. I suppose you would have a man lie in a hammock all day and roll cigaritos.'

'Much better do that than take what no is yours.'

'Which no American ever did!'

'Excep' when he pulled California out the pocket de Mexico.'

'And what did Mexico do first? Did she not threaten the United States with hostilities for a year, and attack a small detachment of our troops with a force of seven thousand men—'

'No make any difference what she do. Si she do wrong, that no is excuse for you do wrong.'

Two angry young people faced each other.

'You steal our country and insult our men. But they can fight, Madre de Dios! I like see General Castro take your little Commodore Sloat by the neck. He look like a little gray rat.'

'Commodore Sloat is a brave and able man, Miss Ortega, and no officer in the United States navy will hear him insulted.'

'Then much better you lock up the ears.'

'My dear Captain Russell! Benicia! what is the matter?'

Mr Larkin stood before them, an amused smile on his thin intellectual face. 'Come, come, have we not met tonight to dance the waltz of peace? Benicia, your most humble admirer has a favor to crave of you. I would have my countrymen learn at once the utmost grace of the Californian. Dance El Jarabe, please, and with Don Fernando Altimira.'

Benicia lifted her dainty white shoulders. She was not unwilling to avenge herself upon the American by dazzling him with her grace and beauty. Her eye's swift invitation brought Don Fernando, scowling, to her side. He led her to the middle of the room, and the musicians played the stately jig.

Benica swept one glance of defiant coquetry at Russell from beneath her curling lashes, then fixed her eyes upon the floor, nor raised them again. She held her reed-like body very erect and took either side of her spangled skirt in the tips of her fingers, lifting it just enough to show the arched little feet in their embroidered stockings and satin slippers. Don Fernando crossed his hands behind him, and together they rattled their feet on the floor with dexterity and precision, whilst the girls sang the words of the dance. The officers gave genuine applause, delighted with this picturesque fragment of life on the edge of the Pacific. Don Fernando listened to their demonstrations with sombre contempt on his dark handsome face; Benicia indicated her pleasure by sundry archings of her narrow brows, or coquettish curves of her red lips. Suddenly she made a deep courtesy and ran to her mother, with a long sweeping movement, like the bending and lifting of grain in the wind. As she approached Russell he took a rose from his coat and threw it at her. She caught it, thrust it carelessly in one of her thick braids, and the next moment he was at her side again.

CHAPTER 4

DOÑA EUSTAQUIA slipped from the crowd and out of the house. Drawing a reboso about her head she walked swiftly down the street and across the plaza. Sounds of ribaldry came from the lower end of the town, but the aristocratic quarter was very quiet, and she walked unmolested to the house of General Castro. The door was open, and she went down the long hall to the sleeping room of Doña Modeste. There was no response to her knock, and she pushed open the door and entered. The room was dimly lit by the candles on the altar. Doña Modeste was not in the big mahogany bed, for the heavy satin coverlet was still over it. Doña Eustaquia crossed the room to the altar and lifted in her arms the small figure kneeling there.

'Pray no more, my friend,' she said. 'Our prayers have been unheard, and thou art better in bed or with thy friends.'

Doña Modeste threw herself wearily into a chair, but took Doña Eustaquia's hand in a tight clasp. Her white skin shone in the dim light, and with her black hair and green tragic eyes made her look like a little witch queen, for neither suffering nor humiliation could bend that stately head.

'Religion is my solace,' she said, 'my only one; for I have not a brain of iron nor a soul of fire like thine. And, Eustaquia, I have more cause to pray tonight.'

'It is true, then, that José is in retreat? Ay, Mary!'

'My husband, deserted by all but one hundred men, is flying southward from San Juan Bautista. I have it from the wash-tub mail. That never is wrong.'

'Ingrates! Traitors! But it is true, Modeste—surely, no?—that our general will not surrender? That he will stand against the Americans?'

'He will not yield. He would have marched upon Monterey and forced them to give him battle here but for this base desertion. Now he wil go to Los Angeles and command the men of the South to rally about him.'

'I knew that he would not kiss the boots of the Americans like the rest of our men! Oh, the cowards! I could almost say tonight that I like better the Americans than the men of my own race. *They* are Castros! I shall hate their flag so long as life is in me; but I cannot hate the brave men who fight for it. But my pain is light to thine. Thy heart is wrung, and I am sorry for thee.'

'My day is over. Misfortune is upon us. Even if my husband's life is spared—ay! shall I ever see him again?—his position will be taken from him, for the Americans will conquer in the end. He will be Commandante-General of the army of the Californias no longer, but—holy God!—a ranchero, a caballero! He at whose back all California has galloped! Thou knowest his restless aspiring soul, Eustaquia, his ambition, his passionate love of California. Can there be happiness for such a man humbled to the dust—no future! no hope? Ay!'—she sprang to her feet with arms uplifted, her small slender form looking twice its height as it palpitated against the shadows, 'I feel the bitterness of that spirit! I know how that great heart is torn. And he is alone!' She flung herself across Doña Eustaquia's knees and burst into violent sobbing.

Doña Eustaquia laid her strong arm about her friend, but her eyes were more angry than soft. 'Weep no more, Modeste,' she said. 'Rather, arise and curse those who have flung a great man into the dust. But comfort thyself. Who can know? Thy husband, weary with fighting, disgusted with men, may cling the closer to thee, and with thee and thy children forget the world in thy redwood forests or between the golden hills of thy ranchos.'

Doña Modeste shook her head. 'Thou speakest the words of kindness, but thou knowest José. Thou knowest that he would not be content to be as other men. And, ay! Eustaquia, to think that it was opposite our own dear home, our favourite home, that the American flag should first have been raised! Opposite the home of José Castro!'

'To perdition with Frémont! Why did he, of all places, select San Juan Bautista in which to hang up his American rag?'

'We never can live there again. The Gabilan Mountains would shut out the very face of the sun from my husband.'

'Do not weep, my Modeste; remember thy other beautiful ranchos. Dios de mi alma!' she added with a flash of humor, 'I revere San Juan Bautista for your husband's sake, but I weep not that I shall visit you there no more. Every day I think to hear that the shaking earth of that beautiful valley has opened its jaws and swallowed every hill and adobe. God grant that Frémont's hair stood up more than once. But go to bed, my friend. Look, I will put you there.' As if Doña Modeste were an infant, she undressed and laid her between the linen sheets with their elaborate drawn work, then made her drink a glass of angelica, folded and laid away the satin coverlet, and left the house.

She walked up the plaza slowly, holding her head high. Monterey at that time was infested by dogs, some of them very strange. Doña Eustaquia's strong soul had little acquaintance with fear, and on her way to General Castro's house she had paid no attention to the snarling muzzles thrust against her gown. But suddenly a cadaverous creature sprang upon her with a savage yelp and would have caught her by the throat had not a heavy stick cracked its skull. A tall officer in the uniform of the United States navy raised his cap from iron-gray hair and looked at her with blue eyes as piercing as her own.

'You will pardon me, madam,' he said, 'if I insist upon attending you to your door. It is not safe for a woman to walk alone in the streets of Monterey at night.'

Doña Eustaquia bent her head somewhat haughtily. 'I thank you much, señor, for your kind rescue. I would not like, at all, to be eaten by the dogs. But I not like to trouble you to walk with me. I go only to the house of the Señor Larkin. It is there, at the end of the little street beyond the plaza.'

'My dear madam, you must not deprive the United States of the pleasure of protecting California. Pray grant my humble request to walk behind you and keep off the dogs.'

Her lips pressed each other, but pride put down the bitter retort.

'Walk by me, if you wish,' she said graciously. 'Why are you not at the house of Don Thomas Larkin?'

'I am on my way there now. Circumstances prevented my going earlier.' His companion did not seem disposed to pilot the conversation, and he continued lamely, 'Have you noticed, madam, that the English frigate *Collingwood* is anchored in the bay?'

'I saw it in the morning.' She turned to him with sudden hope. 'Have they—the English—come to help California?'

'I am afraid, dear madam, that they came to capture California at the first whisper of war between Mexico and the United States; you know that England has always cast a covetous eye upon your fair

185

land. It is said that the English admiral stormed about the deck in a mighty rage today when he saw the American flag flying on the fort.'

'All are alike!' she exclaimed bitterly, then controlled herself. 'You—do you admeer our country, señor? Have you in America something more beautiful than Monterey?'

The officer looked about him enthusiastically, glad of a change of topic, for he suspected to whom he was talking. 'Madam, I have never seen anything more perfect than this beautiful town of Monterey. What a situation! What exquisite proportions! That wide curve of snow-white sand about the dark blue bay is as exact a crescent as if cut with a knife. And that semicircle of hills behind the town, with its pine and brush forest tapering down to the crescent's points! Nor could anything be more picturesque than this scattered little town with its bright red tiles above the white walls of the houses and the gray walls of the yards; its quaint church surrounded by the ruins of the old presidio; its beautiful, strangely dressed women and men who make this corner of the earth resemble the pages of some romantic old picture-book—'

'Ay!' she interrupted him. 'Much better you feel proud that you conquer us; for surely, señor, California shall shine like a diamond in the very centre of America's crown.' Then she held out her hand impulsively. 'Mucho gracias, señor—pardon—thank you very much. If you love my country, señor, you must be my friend and the friend of my daughter. I am the Señora Doña Eustaquia Carillo de Ortega, and my house is there on the hill—you can see the light, no? Always we shall be glad to see you.'

He doffed his cap again and bent over her hand.

'And I, John Brotherton, a humble captain in the United States navy, do sincerely thank the most famous woman of Monterey for her gracious hospitality. And if I abuse it, lay it to the enthusiasm of the American who is not the conqueror but the conquered.'

'That was very pretty—speech. When you abuse me I put you out the door. This is the house of Don Thomas Larkin, where is the ball. You come in, no? You like I take your arm? Very well.'

And so the articles of peace were signed.

CHAPTER 5

'YES, yes, indeed, Blandina,' exclaimed Benicia, 'they had no chance at all last night, for we danced until dawn, and perhaps they were afraid of Don Thomas Larkin. But we shall talk and have music tonight, and those fine new tables that come on the last ship from Boston must not be destroyed.'

'Well, if you really think—' said Blandina, who always thought exactly as Benicia did. She opened a door and called:—

'Flujencio.'

'Well, my sister?'

A dreamy-looking young man in short jacket and trousers of red silk entered the room, sombrero in one hand, a cigarito in the other.

'Flujencio, you know it is said that these 'Yankees' always 'whittle' everything. We are afraid they will spoil the furniture tonight; so tell one of the servants to cut a hundred pine slugs, and you go down to the store and buy a box of penknives. Then they will have plenty to amuse themselves with and will not cut the furniture.'

'True! True! What a good idea! Was it Benicia's?' He gave her a glance of languid adoration. 'I will buy those knives at once, before I forget it,' and he tossed the sombrero on his curls and strode out of the house.

'How dost thou like the Señor Lieutenant Russell, Benicia?'

Benicia lifted her chin, but her cheeks became very pink.

'Well enough. But he is like all the Americans, very proud, and thinks too well of his hateful country. But I shall teach him how to flirt. He thinks he can, but he cannot.'

'Thou canst do it, Benicia—look! look!'

Lieutenant Russell and a brother officer were sauntering slowly by and looking straight through the grated window at the beautiful girls in their gayly flowered gowns. They saluted, and the girls bent their slender necks, but dared not speak, for Doña Francesca Hernandez was in the next room and the door was open. Immediately following the American officers came Don Fernando Altimira on horseback. He scowled as he saw the erect swinging figures of the conquerors, but Benicia kissed the tips of her fingers as he flung his sombrero to the ground, and he galloped, smiling, on his way.

That night the officers of the United States squadron met the society of Monterey at the house of Don Jorje Hernandez. After the contradanza, to which they could be admiring spectators only, much to the delight of the caballeros, Benicia took the guitar presented by Flujencio, and letting her head droop a little to one side like a lily bent on its stalk by the breeze, sang the most coquettish song she knew. Her mahogany brown hair hung unconfined over her white shoulders and gown of embroidered silk with its pointed waist and full skirt. Her large brown eyes were alternately mischievous and tender, now and again lighted by a sudden flash. Her cheeks were pink; her round babylike arms curved with all the grace of the Spanish woman. As she finished the song she dropped her eyelids for a moment, then raised them slowly and looked straight at Russell.

'By Jove, Ned, you are a lucky dog!' said a brother officer. 'She's the prettiest girl in the room! Why don't you fling your hat at her feet, as these ardent Californians do?'

'My cap is in the next room, but I will go over and fling myself there instead.'

Russell crossed the room and sat down beside Benicia.

'I should like to hear you sing under those cypresses out on the ocean about six or eight miles from here,' he said to her. 'I rode down the coast yesterday. Jove! what a coast it is!'

'We will have a merienda there on some evening,' said Doña

Eustaquia, who sat beside her daughter. 'It is very beautiful on the big rocks to watch the ocean, under the moonlight.'

'A merienda?'

'A peek-neck.'

'Good! You will not forget that?'

She smiled at his boyishness. 'It will be at the next moon. I promise.'

Benicia sang another song, and a half-dozen caballeros stood about her, regarding her with glances languid, passionate, sentimental, reproachful, determined, hopeless. Russell, leaning back in his chair, listened to the innocent thrilling voice of the girl, and watched her adorers, amused and stimulated. The Californian beauty was like no other woman he had known, and the victory would be as signal as the capture of Monterey. 'More blood, perhaps,' he thought, 'but a victory is a poor affair unless painted in red. It will do these seething caballeros good to learn that American blood is quite as swift as Californian.'

As the song finished, the musicians began a waltz; Russell took the guitar from Benicia's hand and laid it on the floor.

'This waltz is mine, señorita,' he said.

'I no know—'

'Señorita!' said Don Fernando Altimira, passionately, 'the first waltz is always mine. Thou wilt not give it to the American?'

'And the next is mine!'

'And the next contradanza!'

The girl's faithful retinue protested for their rights. Russell could not understand, but he translated their glances, and bent his lips to Benicia's ear. That ear was pink and her eyes were bright with roguish triumph.

'I want this dance, dear señorita. I may go away any day. Orders may come tomorrow which will send me where I never can see you again. You can dance with these men every night of the year—'

'I give to you,' said Benicia, rising hurriedly. 'We must be hospitable to the stranger who comes today and leaves tomorrow,' she said in Spanish to the other men. 'I have plenty more dances for you.'

After the dance, salads and cakes, claret and water, were brought to the women by Indian girls, who glided about the room with borrowed grace, their heads erect, the silver trays held well out. They wore bright red skirts and white smocks of fine embroidered linen, open at the throat, the sleeves very short. Their coarse hair hung in heavy braids; their bright little eyes twinkled in square faces scrubbed until they shone like copper.

'Captain,' said Russell to Brotherton, as the men followed the host into the supper room, 'let us buy a ranch, marry two of these stunning girls, and lie round in hammocks whilst these Western houris bring us aguardiente and soda. What an improvement on Byron and Tom Moore! It is all so unhackneyed and unexpected. In spite of Dana and Robinson I expected mud huts and whooping savages. This is Arcadia, and the women are the most elegant in America.'

'Look here, Ned,' said his captain, 'you had better do less flirting and more thinking while you are in this odd country. Your talents will get rusty, but you can rub them up when you get home. Neither Californian men nor women are to be trifled with. This is the land of passion, not of drawing-room sentiment.'

'Perhaps I am more serious than you think. What is the matter?' He spoke to a brother officer who had joined them and was laughing immoderately.

'Do you see those Californians grinning over there?' The speaker beckoned to a group of officers, who joined him at once. 'What job do you suppose they have put up on us? What do you suppose that mysterious table in the sala means, with its penknives and wooden sticks? I thought it was a charity bazaar. Well, it is nothing more nor less than a trick to keep us from whittling up the furniture. We are all Yankess to them, you know. Preserve my Spanish!'

The officers shouted with delight. They marched solemnly back into the sala, and seating themselves in a deep circle about the table, whittled the slugs all over the floor, much to the satisfaction of the Californians.

CHAPTER 6

AFTER the entertainment was over, Russell strolled about the town. The new moon was on the sky, the stars thick and bright; but dark corners were everywhere, and he kept his hand on his pistol. He found himself before the long low house of Doña Eustaquia Ortega. Not a light glimmered; the shutters were of solid wood. He walked up and down, trying to guess which was Benicia's room.

'I am growing as romantic as a Californian,' he thought; 'but this wonderful country pours its color all through one's nature. If I could find her window, I believe I should serenade her in true Spanish fashion. By Jove, I remember now, she said something about looking through her window at the pines on the hill. It must be at the back of the house, and how am I going to get over that great adobe wall? That gate is probably fastened with an iron bar—ah!'

He had walked to the corner of the wall surrounding the large yard behind and at both sides of Doña Eustaquia's house, and he saw, ascending a ladder, a tall figure, draped in a serape, its face concealed by the shadow of a sombrero. He drew his pistol, then laughed at himself, although not without annoyance. 'A rival; and he has got ahead of me. He is going to serenade her.'

The caballero seated himself uncomfortably on the tiles that roofed the wall, removed his sombrero, and Russell recognized Fernando Altimira. A moment later the sweet thin chords of the guitar quivered in the quiet air, and a tenor, so fine that even Russell

191

stood entranced, sang to Benicia one of the old songs of Monterey:—

El SUSPIRO

Una mirada un suspiro,
Una lagrima querida,
Es balsamo à la herida
Que abriste en mi corazón.

Por esa lagrima cara
Objeto de mi termina,
Yo te amé bella criatura
Desde que te ví llorar.

Te acuerdas de aquella noche
En que triste y abatida
Una lagrima querida
Vi de tus ojos brotar.

Although Russell was at the base of the high wall he saw that a light flashed. The light was followed by the clapping of little hands. 'Jove!' he thought, 'am I really jealous? But damn that Californian!'

Altimira sang two more songs and was rewarded by the same demonstrations. As he descended the ladder and reached the open street he met Russell face to face. The two men regarded each other for a moment. The Californian's handsome face was distorted by a passionate scowl; Russell was calmer, but his brows were lowered.

Altimira flung the ladder to the ground, but fireblooded as he was, the politeness of his race did not desert him, and his struggle with English flung oil upon his passion.

'Señor,' he said, 'I no know what you do it by the house of the Señorita Benicia so late in the night. I suppose you have the right to walk in the town si it please yourself.'

'Have I not the same right as you—to serenade the Señorita Benicia? If I had known her room, I should have been on the wall before you.'

Altimira's face flushed with triumph. 'I think the Señorita Benicia no care for the English song, señor. She love the sweet words of her country; she no care for words of ice.'

Russell smiled. 'Our language may not be as elastic as yours, Don Fernando, but it is a good deal more sincere. And it can express as much and perhaps—'

'You love Benicia?' interrupted Altimira, fiercely.

'I admire the Señorita Ortega tremendously. But I have seen her twice only, and although we may love longer, we take more time to get there, perhaps, than you do.'

'Ay! Dios de mi vida! You have the heart of rock! You chip it off in little pieces, one today, another tomorrow, and give to the woman. I, señor, I love Benicia, and I marry her. You understand? Si you take her, I cut the heart from your body. You understand?'

'I understand. We understand each other.' Russell lifted his cap. The Californian took his sombrero from his head and made a long sweeping bow; and the two men parted.

CHAPTER 7

ON the twenty-third of July, Commodore Sloat transferred his authority to Commodore Stockton, and the new commander of the Pacific squadron organized the California Battalion of Mounted Riflemen, appointing Frémont major and Gillespie captain. He ordered them South at once to intercept Castro. On the twenty-eighth, Stockton issued a proclamation in which he asserted that Mexico was the instigator of the present difficulties, and justified the United States in seizing the Californias. He denounced Castro in violent terms as an usurper, a boasting and abusive chief, and accused him of having violated every principle of national hospitality and good faith toward Captain Frémont and his surveying party. Stockton sailed for the South the same day in the *Congress*, leaving a number of officers to Monterey and the indignation of the people.

'By Jove, I don't dare to go near Doña Eustaquia,' said Russell to Brotherton. 'And I'm afraid we won't have our picnic. It seems to me the Commodore need not have used such strong language about California's idol. The very people in the streets are ready to unlimb us; and as for the peppery Doña—'

'Speak more respectfully of Doña Eustaquia, young man,' said the older officer, severely. 'She is a very remarkable woman and not to be spoken slightingly of by young men who are in love with her daughter.'

'God forbid that I should slight her, dear Captain. Never have I so respected a woman. She frightens the life out of me every time she flashes those eyes of hers. But let us go and face the enemy at once, like the brave Americans we are.'

'Very well.' And together they walked along Alvarado Street from the harbor, then up the hill to the house of Doña Eustaquia.

That formidable lady and her daughter were sitting on the corridor dressed in full white gowns, slowly wielding large black fans, for the night was hot. Bernicia cast up her eyes expressively as she rose and courtesied to the officers, but her mother merely bent her head; nor did she extend her hand. Her face was very dark.

Brotherton went directly to the point.

'Dear Doña Eustaquia, we deeply regret that our Commodore has used such harsh language in regard to General Castro. But remember that he has been here a few days only and has had no chance to learn the many noble and valiant qualities of your General. He doubtless has been prejudiced against him by some enemy, and he adores Frémont:—there is the trouble. He resents Castro's treating Frémont as an enemy before the United States had declared its intentions. But had he been correctly informed, he undoubtedly would have conceived the same admiration and respect for your brave General that is felt by every other man among us.'

Doña Eustaquia looked somewhat mollified, but shook her head sternly. 'Much better he took the trouble to hear true. He insult all Californians by those shemful words. All the enemies of our dear General be glad. And the poor wife! Poor my Modeste! She fold the arms and raise the head, but the heart is broken.'

'Jove! I almost wish they had driven us out! Dear señora—' Russell and Benicia were walking up and down the corridor—'we have become friends, true friends, as sometimes happens—not often—between man and woman. Cease to think of me as an officer of the United States navy, only as a man devoted to your service. I have already spent many peasant hours with you. Let me hope that while I remain here neither Commodore Stockton nor party feeling will exclude me from many more.'

She raised her graceful hand to her chin with a gesture peculiar to her, and looked upward with a glance half sad, half bitter.

'I much appreciate your friendship, Capitan Brotherton. You give me much advice that is good for me, and tell me many things. It is like the ocean wind when you have live long in the hot valley. Yes, dear friend, I forget you are in the navy of the conqueror.'

'Mamacita,' broke in Benicia's light voice, 'tell us now when we can have the peek-neek.'

'Tomorrow night.'

'Surely?'

'Surely, niñita.'

'Castro,' said Russell, lifting his cap, 'peace be with thee.'

CHAPTER 8

THE great masses of rock on the ocean's coast shone white in the moonlight. Through the gaunt outlying rocks, lashed apart by furious storms, boiled the ponderous breakers, tossing aloft the sparkling clouds of spray, breaking in the pools like a million silver fishes. High above the waves, growing out of the crevices of the massive rocks of the shore, were weird old cypresses, their bodies bent from the ocean as if petrified in flight before the mightier foe. On their gaunt outstretched arms and gray bodies, seamed with time, knobs like human muscles jutted; between the broken bark the red blood showed. From their angry hands, clutching at the air or doubled in imprecation, long strands of gray-green moss hung, waving and coiling, in the night wind. Only one old man was on his hands and knees as if to crawl from the field; but a comrade spurned him with his foot and wound his bony hand about the coward's neck. Another had turned his head to the enemy, pointing his index finger in scorn, although he stood alone on high.

All along the cliffs ran the ghostly army, sometimes with straining arms fighting the air, sometimes thrust blankly outward, all with life quivering in their arrested bodies, silent and scornful in their defeat. Who shall say what winter winds first beat them, what great waves first fought their deathless trunks, what young stars first shone over them? They have outstood centuries of raging storm and rending earthquake. Tradition says that until convulsion wrenched the Golden Gate apart the San Franciscan waters rolled through the long valleys and emptied into the Bay of Monterey. But the old cypresses were on the ocean just beyond; the incoming and the outgoing of the inland ocean could not trouble them; and perhaps they will stand there until the end of time.

Down the long road by the ocean rode a gay cavalcade. The caballeros had haughtily refused to join the party, and the men wore the blue and gold of the United States. But the women wore fluttering mantillas, and their prancing high-stepping horses were trapped with embossed leather and silver. In a lumbering 'wagon of the country,' drawn by oxen, running on solid wheels cut from the trunks of trees, but padded with silk, rode some of the older people of the town, disapproving, but overridden by the impatient enthusiasm of Doña Eustaquia. Through the pine woods with their softly moving shadows and splendid aisles, out between the cypresses and rocky beach, wound the stately cavalcade, their voices rising above the sociable converse of the seals and the screeching of the sea-gulls spiking the rocks where the waves fought and foamed. The gold on the shoulders of the men flashed in the moonlight; the jewels of the woman sparkled and winked. Two by two they came like a conquering army to the rescue of the cypresses. Brotherton, who rode ahead with Doña Eustaquia, half expected to see the old trees rise upright with a deep shout of welcome.

When they reached a point where the sloping rocks rose high above surf and spray, they dismounted, leaving the Indian servants to tether the horses. They climbed down the big smooth rocks and sat about in groups, although never beyond the range of older eyes, the cypresses lowering above them, the ocean tearing through the outer rocks to swirl and grumble in the pools. The moon was so bright, its light so broad and silver, they almost could imagine they saw the gorgeous mass of color in the pools below.

'You no have seaweed like that in Boston,' said Benicia, who had a comprehensive way of symbolizing the world by the city from which she got many of her clothes and all of her books.

'Indeed, no!' said Russell. 'The other day I sat for hours watching those great bunches and strands that look like richly colored chenille. And there were stones that looked like big opals studded with vivid jewels. God of my soul, as you say, it was magnificent! I never saw such brilliant color, such delicate tints! And those great rugged defiant rocks out there, lashed by the waves! Look at that one; misty with spray one minute, bare and black the next! They look like an old castle which has been battered down with cannon. Captain, do you not feel romantic?'

'I feel that I never want to go into an art gallery again. No wonder the women of California are original.'

'Benicia,' said Russell, 'I have tried in vain to learn a Spanish song. But teach me a Spanish phrase of endearment. All our 'darlings' and 'dearests' are too flat for California.'

'Bueno; I teach you. Say after me: Mi muy querida prima. That is very sweet. Say.'

'Mi muy—'

'Querida prima.'

'Que—What is it in English?'

'My—very—darling—first. It no sound so pretty, in English.'

'It does very well. My—very—darling—first—if all these people were not about us, I should kiss you. You look exactly like a flower.'

'Si you did, Señor Impertinencio, you get that for thanks.'

Russell jumped to his feet with a shout, and shook from his neck a little crab with a back like green velvet and legs like carven garnet.

'Did you put that crab on my neck, señorita?'

'Si, señor.'

A sulky silence of ten minutes ensued, during which Benicia sent little stones skipping down into the silvered pools, and Russell, again recumbent, stared at the horizon.

'Si you no can talk,' she said finally, 'I wish you go way and let Don Henry Tallant come talk to me. He look like he want.'

'No doubt he does; but he can stay where he is. Let me kiss your hand, Benicia, and I will forgive you.'

Benicia hit his mouth lightly with the back of her hand, but he captured it and kissed it several times.

'Your mustache feels like the cat's,' said she.

He flung the hand from him, but laughed in a moment. 'How sentimental you are! Making love to you is like dragging a cannon uphill! Will you not at least sing me a love song? And please do not make faces in the tender parts.'

Benicia tossed her spirited head, but took her guitar from its case and called to the other girls to accompany her. They withdrew from their various flirtations with audible sighs, but it was Benicia's merienda, and in a moment a dozen white hands were sweeping the long notes from the strings.

Russell moved to a lower rock, and lying at Benicia's feet looked upward. The scene was all above him—the great mass of white rocks, whiter in the moonlight; the rigid cypresses aloft; the beautiful faces, dreamy, passionate, stolid, restless, looking from the lace mantillas; the graceful arms holding the guitars; the sweet rich voices threading through the roar of the ocean like the melody in a grand recitativo; the old men and women crouching like buzzards on the stones, their sharp eyes never closing; enfolding all with an almost palpable touch, the warm voluptuous air. Now and again a bird sang a few notes, a strange sound in the night, or the soft wind murmured like the ocean's echo through the pines.

The song finished. 'Benicia, I love you,' whispered Russell.

'We will now eat,' said Benicia. 'Mamma,'—she raised her voice,—'shall I tell Raphael to bring down the supper?'

'Yes, niña.'

The girl sprang lightly up on the rocks, followed by Russell. The Indian servants were some distance off, and as the young people ran through a pine grove the bold officer of the United States squadron captured the Californian and kissed her on the mouth. She boxed his ears and escaped to the light.

Benica gave her orders, Raphael and the other Indians followed her with the baskets, and spread the supper of tomales and salads, dulces and wine, on a large table-like rock, just above the threatening spray; the girls sang each in turn, whilst the others nibbled the dainties Doña Eustaquia had provided, and the Americans wondered if it were not a vision that would disappear into the fog bearing down upon them.

A great white bank, writhing and lifting, rolling and bending, came across the ocean slowly, with majestic stealth, hiding the swinging waves on which it rode so lightly, shrouding the rocks, enfolding the men and women, wreathing the cypresses, rushing onward to the pines.

'We must go,' said Doña Eustaquia, rising. 'There is danger to stay. The lungs, the throat, my children. Look at the poor old cypresses.'

The fog was puffing through the gaunt arms, festooning the rigid hands. It hung over the green heads, it coiled about the gray trunks. The stern defeated trees looked like the phantoms of themselves, a long silent battalion of petrified ghosts. Even Benicia's gay spirit was oppressed, and during the long ride homeward through the pine woods she had little to say to her equally silent companion.

CHAPTER 9

DOÑA EUSTAQUIA seldom gave balls, but once a week she opened her salas to the more intellectual people of the town. A few Americans were ever attendant; General Vallejo often came from Sonoma to hear the latest American and Mexican news in her house; Castro rarely had been absent; Alvarado, in the days of his supremacy, could always be found there, and she was the first woman upon whom Pio Pico called when he deigned to visit Monterey. A few young people came to sit in a corner with Benicia, but they had little to say.

The night after the picnic some fifteen or twenty people were gathered about Doña Eustaquia in the large sala on the right of the hall; a few others were glancing over the Mexican papers in the little sala on the left. The room was ablaze with many candles standing, above the heads of the guests, in twisted silver candelabra, the white walls reflecting their light. The floor was bare, the furniture of stiff mahogany and horse-hair, but no visitor to that quaint ugly room every thought of looking beyond the brilliant face of Doña Eustaquia, the lovely eyes of her daughter, the intelligence and animation of the people she gathered about her. As a rule Doña Modeste Castro's proud head and strange beauty had been one of the living pictures of that historical sala, but she was not there tonight.

As Captain Brotherton and Lieutenant Russell entered, Doña Eustaquia was waging war against Mr Larkin.

'And what hast thou to say to that proclamation of thy little American hero, thy Commodore'—she gave the word a satirical roll, impossible to transcribe—'who is heir to a conquest without blood, who struts into history as the Commander of the United States Squadron of the Pacific, holding a few hundred helpless Californians in subjection? O warlike name of Sloat! O heroic name of Stockton! O immortal Frémont, prince of strategists and tacticians, your country must be proud of you! Your newspapers will glorify you! Sometimes, perhaps, you will have a little history bound in red morocco all to yourselves; whilst Castro—' she sprang to her feet and brought her open palm down violently upon the table, 'Castro, the real hero of his country, the great man ready to die a thousand deaths for the liberty of the Californians, a man who was made for great deeds and born for fame, he will be left to rust and rot because we have no newspapers to glorify him, and the Gringos send what they wish to their country! Oh, profanation! That a great man should be covered from sight by an army of red ants!'

'By Jove!' said Russell, 'I wish I could understand her! Doesn't she look magnificent?'

Captain Brotherton made no reply. He was watching her closely, gathering the sense of her words, full of passionate admiration for the woman. Her tall majestic figure was quivering under the lash of her fiery temper, quick to spring and strike. The red satin of her gown and the diamonds on her finely moulded neck and in the dense coils of her hair grew dim before the angry brilliancy of her eyes.

The thin sensitive lips of Mr Larkin curled with their accustomed humor, but he replied sincerely, 'Yes, Castro is a hero, a great man on a small canvas—'

'And they are little men on a big canvas!' interrupted Doña Eustaquia.

Mr Larkin laughed, but his reply was non-committal. 'Remember, they have done all that they have been called upon to do, and they have done it well. Who can say that they would not be as heroic, if opportunity offered, as they have been prudent?'

Doña Eustaquia shrugged her shoulders disdainfully, but resumed her seat. 'You will not say, but you know what chance they would have with Castro in a fair fight. But what chance has even a great man, when at the head of a few renegades, against the navy of a big nation? But Frémont! Is he to cast up his eyes and draw down his mouth to the world, whilst the man who acted for the safety of his country alone, who showed foresight and wisdom, is denounced as a violator of international courtesy?'

'No,' said one of the American residents who stood near, 'history will right all that. Some day the world will know who was the great and who the little man.'

'Some day! When we are under our stones! This swaggering Commodore Stockton adores Frémont and hates Castro. His lying proclamation will be read in his own country—'

The door opened suddenly and Don Fernando Altimira entered the room. 'Have you heard?' he cried. 'All the South is in arms! The Departmental Assembly has called the whole country to war, and men are flocking to the standard! Castro has sworn that he will never give up the country under his charge. Now, Mother of God! let our men drive the usurper from the country.'

Even Mr Larkin sprang to his feet in excitement. He rapidly translated the news to Brotherton and Russell.

'Ah! There will be a little blood, then,' said the younger officer. 'It was too easy a victory to count.'

Every one in the room was talking at once. Doña Eustaquia smote her hands together, then clasped and raised them aloft.

'Thanks to God!' she cried. 'California has come to her senses at last!'

Altimira bent his lips to her ear. 'I go to fight the Americans,' he whispered.

She caught his hand between both her own and pressed it convulsively to her breast. 'Go,' she said, 'and may God and Mary protect thee. Go, my son, and when thou returnest I will give thee Benicia. Thou art a son after my heart, a brave man and a good Catholic.'

Benicia, standing near, heard the words. For the first time Russell saw the expression of careless audacity leave her face, her pink color fade.

'What is that man saying to your mother?' he demanded.

'She promise me to him when he come back; he go to join General Castro.'

'Benicia!' He glanced about. Altimira had left the house. Every one was too excited to notice them. He drew her across the hall and into the little sala, deserted since the startling news had come. 'Benicia,' he said hurriedly, 'there is no time to be lost. You are such a butterfly I hardly know whether you love me or not.'

'I no am such butterfly as you think,' said the girl, pathetically. 'I often am very gay, for that is my spirit, señor; but I cry sometimes in the night.'

'Well, you are not to cry any more, my very darling first!' He took her in his arms and kissed her, and she did not box his ears. 'I may be ordered off at any moment, and what may they not do with you while I am gone? So I have a plan! Marry me tomorrow!'

'Ay! Señor!'

'Tomorrow. At your friend Blandina's house. The Hernandez like the Americans; in fact, as we all know, Tallant is in love with Blandina and the old people do not frown. They will let us marry there.'

'Ay! Cielo santo! What my mother say? She kill me!'

'She will forgive you, no matter how angry she may be at first. She loves you—almost as much as I do.'

The girl withdrew from his arms and walked up and down the room. Her face was very pale, and she looked older. On one side of the room hung a large black cross, heavily mounted with gold. She leaned her face against it and burst into tears. 'Ay, my home! My mother!' she cried under her breath. 'How I can leave you? Ay, triste de mi!' She turned suddenly to Russell, whose face was as white as her own, and put to him the question which we have not yet answered. 'What is this love?' she said rapidly. 'I no can understand. I never feel before. Always I laugh when men say they love me; but I never laugh again. In my heart is something that shake me like a lion shake what it go to kill, and make me no care for my mother or my God—and you are a Protestant! I have love my mother like I have love that cross; and now a man come—a stranger! a conqueror! a Protestant! an American! And he twist my heart out with his hands! But I no can help. I love you and I go.'

CHAPTER 10

THE next morning, Doña Eustaquia looked up from her desk as Benicia entered the room. 'I am writing to Alvarado,' she said. 'I hope to be the first to tell him the glorious news. Ay! my child, go to thy altar and pray that the bandoleros may be driven wriggling from the land like snakes out of a burning field!'

'But, mother, I thought you had learned to like the Gringos.'

'I like the Gringos well enough, but I hate their flag! Ay! I will pull it down with my own hands if Castro and Pico roll Stockton and Frémont in the dust!'

'I am sorry for that, my mother, for I am going to marry an

American today.'

Her mother laughed and glanced over the closely written page.

'I am going to marry the Lieutenant Russell at Blandina's house this morning.'

'Ay, run, run. I must finish my letter.'

Benicia left the sala and crossing her mother's room entered her own. From the stout mahogany chest she took white silk stockings and satin slippers, and sitting down on the floor put them on. Then she opened the doors of her wardrobe and looked for some moments at the many pretty frocks hanging there. She selected one of fine white lawn, half covered with deshalados, and arrayed herself. She took from the drawer of the wardrobe a mantilla of white Spanish lace, and draped it about her head and shoulders, fastening it back above one ear with a pink rose. Around her throat she clasped a string of pearls, then stood quietly in the middle of the room and looked about her. In one corner was a little brass bedstead covered with a heavy quilt of satin and lace. The pillowcases were almost as fine and elaborate as her gown. In the opposite corner was an altar with little gold candlesticks and an ivory crucifix. The walls and floor were bare but spotless. The ugly wardrobe built into the thick wall never had been empty: Doña Eustaquia's generosity to the daughter she worshipped was unbounded.

Benicia drew a long hysterical breath and went over to the window. It looked upon a large yard enclosed by the high adobe wall upon which her lovers so often had sat and sung to her. No flowers were in the garden, not even a tree. It was as smooth and clean as the floor of a ballroom. About the well in the middle were three or four Indian servants quarrelling good-naturedly. The house stood on the rise of one of the crescent's horns. Benicia looked up at the dark pine woods on the hill. What days she had spent there with her mother! She whirled about suddenly and taking a large fan from the table returned to the sala.

Doña Eustaquia laughed. 'Thou silly child, to dress thyself like a bride. What nonsense is this?'

'I will be a bride in an hour, my mother.'

'Go! Go, with thy nonsense! I have spoiled thee! What other girl in Monterey would dare to dress herself like this at eleven in the morning? Go! And do not ruin that mantilla, for thou wilt not get another. Thou art going to Blandina's, no? Be sure thou goest no farther! I would not let thee go there alone were it not so near. And be sure thou speakest to no man in the street.'

'No, mamacita, I will speak to no man in the street, but one awaits me in the house. Hasta luego.' And she flitted out of the door and up the street.

CHAPTER 11

A few hours later Doña Eustaquia sat in the large and cooler sala with Captain Brotherton. He read Shakespeare to her whilst she fanned herself, her face aglow with intelligent pleasure. She had not broached to him the uprising in the South lest it should lead to bitter words. Although an American and a Protestant, few friends had ever stood so close to her.

He laid down the book as Russell and Benicia entered the room. Doña Eustaquia's heavy brows met.

'Thou knowest that I do not allow thee to walk with men on the street,' she said in Spanish.

'But, mamacita, he is my husband. We were married this morning at Blandina's.' Excitement had tuned Benicia's spirit to its accustomed pitch, and her eyes danced with mischief. Moreover, although she expected violent reproaches, she knew the tenacious strength of her mother's affection, and had faith in speedy forgiveness.

Brotherton opened his eyes, but Doña Eustaquia moved back her head impatiently. 'That silly joke!' Then she smiled at her own impatience. What was Benicia but a spoiled child, and spoiled children would disobey at times. 'Welcome, my son,' she said to Russell, extending her hand. 'We celebrate your marriage at the supper tonight, and the Captain helps us, no? my friend.'

'Let us have chicken with red pepper and tomato sauce,' cried Russell. 'And rice with saffron; and that delightful dish with which I remonstrate all night—olives and cheese and hard-boiled eggs and red peppers all rolled up in corn-meal cakes.'

'Enchiladas? You have them! Now, both you go over to the corner and talk not loud, for I wish to hear my friend read.'

Russell, lifting his shoulders, did as he was bidden. Benicia, with a gay laugh, kissed her mother and flitted like a butterfly about the room, singing gay little snatches of song.

'Oh, mamacita, mamacita,' she chanted. 'Thou wilt not believe thous hast lost thy little daughter. Thou wilt not believe thou hast a son. Thou wilt not believe I shall sleep no more in the little brass bed—'

'Benicia, hold thy saucy tongue! Sit down!' And this Benicia finally consented to do, although smothered laughter came now and again from the corner.

Doña Eustaquia sat easily against the straight back of her chair, looking very handsome and placid as Brotherton read and expounded *As You Like It* to her. Her gown of thin black silk threw out the fine gray tones of her skin; about her neck and chest was a heavy chain of Californian gold; her dense lustreless hair was held high with a shell comb banded with gold; superb jewels weighted her little white hands; in her small ears were large hoops of gold studded with black pearls. She was perfectly contented in that hour. Her woman's vanity was at peace and her eager mind expanding.

The party about the supper table in the evening was very gay. The long room was bare, but heavy silver was beyond the glass doors of the cupboard; a servant stood behind each chair; the wines were as fine as any in America, and the favourite dishes of the Americans had been prepared. Even Brotherton, although more nervous than was usual with him, caught the contagion of the hour and touched his glass more than once to that of the woman whose overwhelming personality had more than half captured a most indifferent heart.

After supper they sat on the corridor, and Benicia sang her mocking love-songs and danced El Son to the tinkling of her own guitar.

'Is she not a light-hearted child?' asked her mother. 'But she has her serious moments, my friend. We have been like the sisters. Every path of the pine woods we walk together, arm in arm. We ride miles on the beach and sit down on the rocks for hours and try to think what the seals say one to the other. Before you come I have friends, but no other companion; but it is good for me you come, for she think only of flirting since the Americans take Monterey. Mira! Look at her flash the eyes at Señor Russell. It is well he has the light heart like herself.'

Brotherton made no reply.

'Give to me the guitar,' she continued.

Benicia handed her the instrument and Doña Eustaquia swept the chords absently for a moment then sang the song of the troubador. Her rich voice was like the rush of the wind through the pines after the light trilling of a bird, and even Russell sat enraptured. As she sang the color came into her face, alight with the fire of youth. Her low notes were voluptuous, her high notes rang with piercing sadness. As she finished, a storm of applause came from Alvarado Street, which pulsed with life but a few yards below them.

'No American woman ever sang like that,' said Brotherton. He rose and walked to the end of the corridor. 'But it is a part of Monterey.'

'Most enchanting of mothers-in-law,' said Russell, 'you have made it doubly hard for us to leave you; but it grows late and my wife and I must go. Good night,' and he raised her hands to his lips.

'Good night, my son.'

'Mamacita, good night,' and Benicia, who had fluttered into the house and found a reboso, kissed her mother, waved her hand to Brotherton, and stepped from the corridor to the street.

'Come here, señorita!' cried her mother. 'No walk tonight, for I have not the wish to walk myself.'

'But I go with my husband, mamma.'

'Oh, no more of that joke without sense! Señor Russell, go home, that she have reason for one moment.'

'But, dear Doña Eustaquia, won't you understand that we are really married?'

Doña Eustaquia's patience was at an end. She turned to Brotherton and addressed a remark to him. Russell and Benicia conferred a moment, then the young man walked rapidly down the street.

'Has he gone?' asked Doña Eustaquia. 'Then let us go in the house, for the fog comes from the bay.'

They went into the little sala and sat about the table. Doña Eustaquia picked up a silver dagger she used as a paper cutter and tapped a book with it.

'Ay, this will not last long,' she said to Brotherton. 'I much am afraid your Commodore send you to the South to fight with our men.'

'I shall return,' said Brotherton, absently. His eyes were fixed on the door.

'But it will not be long that you will be there, my friend. Many people are not killed in our wars. Once there was a great battle at Point Rincon, near Santa Barbara, between Castro and Carillo. Carillo have been appointed governor by Mejico, and Alvarado refuse to resign. They fight for three days, and Castro manage so well he lose only one man, and the others run away and not lose any.'

Brotherton laughed. 'I hope all our battles may be as bloodless,' he said, and then drew a short breath.

Russell, accompanied by Don Jorje and Doña Francesca Hernandez and the priest of Monterey, entered the room.

Doña Eustaquia rose and greeted her guests with grace and hospitality.

'But I am glad to see you, my father, my friends. And you always are welcome, Señor Russell; but no more joke. Where is our Blandina? Sit down—Why, what is it?'

The priest spoke.

'I have that to tell you, Doña Eustaquia, which I fear will give you great displeasure. I hoped not to be the one to tell it. I was weak to consent, but these young people importuned me until I was weary. Doña Eustaquia, I married Benicia to the Señor Russell today.'

Doña Eustaquia's head had moved forward mechanically, her eyes staring incredulously from the priest to the other members of the apprehensive group. Suddenly her apathy left her, her arm curved upward like the neck of a snake; but as she sprang upon Benicia her ferocity was that of a tiger.

'What!' she shrieked, shaking the girl violently by the shoulder. 'What! ingrate! traitor! Thou hast married an American, a Protestant!'

Benicia burst into terrified sobs. Russell swung the girl from her mother's grasp and placed his arm around her.

'She is mine now,' he said. 'You must not touch her again.'

'Yours! Yours!' screamed Doña Eustaquia, beside herself. 'Oh, Mother of God!' She snatched the dagger from the table and, springing backward, plunged it into the cross.

'By that sign I curse thee,' she cried. 'Accursed be the man who has stolen my child! Accursed be the woman who has betrayed her mother and her country! God! God!—I implore thee, let her die in her happiest hour.'

CHAPTER 12

ON August twelfth Commodore Hull arrived on the frigate *Warren*, from Mazatlan, and brought the first positive intelligence of the declaration of war between Mexico and the United States. Before the middle of the month news came that Castro and Pico, after gallant defence, but overwhelmed by numbers, had fled, the one to Sonora, the other to Baja California. A few days after, Stockton issued a proclamation to the effect that the flag of the United States was flying over every town in the territory of California; and Alcalde Colton announced that the rancheros were more than satisfied with the change of government.

A month later a mounted courier dashed into Monterey with a note from the Alcalde of Los Angeles, wrapped about a cigarito and hidden in his hair. The note contained the information that all the South was in arms again, and that Los Angeles was in the hands of the Californians. Russell was ordered to go with Captain Mervine, on the *Savannah*, to join Gillespie at San Pedro; Brotherton was left at Monterey with Lieutenant Maddox and a number of men to quell a threatened uprising. Later came the news of Mervine's defeat and the flight of Talbot from Santa Barbara; and by November California was in a state of general warfare, each army receiving new recruits every day.

Doña Eustaquia, hard and stern, praying for the triumph of her people, lived alone in the old house. Benicia, praying for the return of her husband and the relenting of her mother, lived alone in her little house on the hill. Friends had interceded, but Doña Eustaquia had closed her ears. Brotherton went to her one day with the news that

Lieutenant Russell was wounded.

'I must tell Benicia,' he said, 'but it is you who should do that.'

'She betray me, my friend.'

'Oh, Eustaquia, make allowance for the lightness of youth. She barely realized what she did. But she loves him now, and suffers bitterly. She should be with you.'

'Ay! She suffer for another! She love a strange man—an American—better than her mother! And it is I who would die for her! Ay, you cold Americans! Never you know how a mother can love her child.'

'The Americans know how to love, señora. And Benicia was thoroughly spoiled by her devoted mother. She was carried away by her wild spirits, nothing more.'

'Then much better she live on them now.'

Doña Eustaquia sat with her profile against the light. It looked severe and a little older, but she was very handsome in her rich black gown and the gold chain about her strong throat. Her head, as usual, was held a little back. Brotherton sat down beside her and took her hand.

'Eustaquia,' he said, 'no friendship between man and woman was ever deeper and stronger than ours. In spite of the anxiety and excitement of these last months we have found time to know each other very intimately. So you will forgive me if I tell you that the more a friend loves you the more he must be saddened by the terrible iron in your nature. Only the great strength of your passions has saved you from hardening into an ugly and repellent woman. You are a mother; forgive your child; remember that she, too, is about to be a mother—'

She caught his hand between both of hers with a passionate gesture. 'Oh, my friend,' she said, 'do not too much reproach me! You never have a child, you cannot know! And remember we all are not make alike. If you are me, you act like myself. If I am you, I can forgive more easy. But I am Eustaquia Ortega, and as I am make, so I do feel now. No judge too hard, my friend, and—*infelez de mi!* do not forsake me.'

'I will never forsake you, Eustaquia.' He rose suddenly. 'I, too, am a lonely man, if not a hard one, and I recognize that cry of the soul's isolation.'

He left her and went up the hill to Benicia's little house, half hidden by the cypress trees that grew before it.

She was sitting in her sala working an elaborate deshalados on a baby's gown. Her face was pale, and the sparkle had gone out of it; but she held herself with all her mother's pride, and her soft eyes were deeper. She rose as Captain Brotherton entered, and took his hand in both of hers. 'You are so good to come to me, and I love you for your friendship for my mother. Tell me how she is.'

'She is well, Benicia.' Then he exclaimed suddenly: 'Poor little girl! What a child you are—not yet seventeen.'

'In a few months, señor. Sit down. No? And I no am so young now. When we suffer we grow more than by the years; and now I go to have the baby, that make me feel very old.'

'But it is very sad to see you alone like this, without your husband or your mother. She will relent some day, Benicia, but I wish she would do it now, when you most need her.'

'Yes, I wish I am with her in the old house,' said the girl, pathetically, although she winked back the tears. 'Never I can be happy without her, even si *he* is here, and you know how I love him. But I have love her so long; she is—how you say it?—like she is part of me, and when she no spik to me, how I can be happy with all myself when part is gone. You understand, señor?'

'Yes, Benicia, I understand.' He looked through the bending cypresses, down the hill, upon the fair town. He had no relish for the task which had brought him to her. She looked up and caught the expression of his face.

'Señor!' she cried sharply. 'What you go to tell me?'

'There is a report that Ned is slightly wounded; but it is not serious. It was Altimira who did it, I believe.'

She shook from head to foot, but was calmer than he had expected. She laid the gown on a chair and stood up. 'Take me to him. Si he is wound, I go to nurse him.'

'My child! You would die before you got there. I have sent a special courier to find out the truth. If Ned is wounded, I have arranged to have him sent home immediately.'

'I wait for the courier come back, for it no is right I hurt the baby si I can help. But si he is wound so bad he no can come, then I go to him. It no is use for you to talk at all, señor, I go.'

Brotherton looked at her in wonderment. Whence had the butterfly gone? Its wings had been struck from it and a soul had flown in.

'Let me send Blandina to you,' he said. 'You must not be alone.'

'I am alone till he or my mother come. I no want other. I love Blandina before, but now she make me feel tired. She talk so much and no say anything. I like better be alone.'

'Poor child!' said Brotherton, bitterly, 'truly do love and suffering age and isolate.' He motioned with his hand to the altar in her bedroom, seen through the open door. 'I have not your faith, I am afraid I have not much of any; but if I cannot pray for you, I can wish with all the strength of a man's heart that happiness will come to you yet, Benicia.'

She shook her head. 'I no know; I no believe much happiness come in this life. Before, I am like a fairy; but it is only because I no am *un*happy. But when the heart have wake up, señor, and the knife have gone in hard, then, after that, always, I think, we are a little sad.'

CHAPTER 13

GENERAL KEARNEY and Lieutenant Beale walked rapidly up and down before the tents of the wretched remnant of United States troops with which the former had arrived overland in California. It was bitterly cold in spite of the fine drizzling rain. Lonely buttes studded the desert, whose palms and cacti seemed to spring from the rocks; high on one of them was the American camp. On the other side of a river flowing at the foot of the butte, the white tents of the Californians were scattered among the dark huts of the little pueblo of San Pasqual.

'Let me implore you, General,' said Beale, 'not to think of meeting Andres Pico. Why, your men are half starved; your few horses are broken-winded; your mules are no match for the fresh trained mustangs of the enemy. I am afraid you do not appreciate the Californians. They are numerous, brave, and desperate. If you avoid them now, as Commodore Stockton wishes, and join him at San Diego, we stand a fair chance of defeating them. But now Pico's cavalry and foot are fresh and enthusiastic—in painful contrast to yours. And, moreover, they know every inch of the ground.'

Kearney impatiently knocked the ashes out of his pipe. He had little regard for Stockton, and no intention of being dictated to by a truculent young lieutenant who spoke his mind upon all occasions.

'I shall attack them at daybreak,' he said curtly. 'I have one hundred and thirty good men; and has not Captain Gillespie joined me with his battalion? Never shall it be said that I turned aside to avoid a handful of boasting Californians. Now go and get an hour's sleep before we start.'

The young officer shrugged his shoulders, saluted, and walked down the line of tents. A man emerged from one of them, and he recognized Russell.

'Hello, Ned,' he said. 'How's the arm?'

''Twas only a scratch. Is Altimira down there with Pico, do you know? He is a brave fellow! I respect that man; but we have an account to settle, and I hope it will be done on the battlefield.'

'He is with Pico, and he has done some good fighting. Most of the Californians have. They know how to fight and they are perfectly fearless. Kearney will find it out tomorrow. He is mad to attack them. Why, his men are actually cadaverous. Bueno! as they say here; Stockton sent me to guide him to San Diego. If he prefers to go through the enemy's lines, there is nothing for me to do but take him.'

'Yes, but we may surprise them. I wish to God this imitation war were over!'

'It will be real enough before you get through. Don't worry. Well, good night. Luck to your skin.'

At daybreak the little army marched down the butte, shivering with cold, wet to the skin. Those on horseback naturally proceeded more rapidly than those mounted upon the clumsy stubborn mules; and Captain Johnson, who led the advance guard of twelve dragoons, found himself, when he came in sight of the enemy's camp, some distance ahead of the main body of Kearney's small army. To his surprise he saw that the Californians were not only awake, but horsed and apparently awaiting him. Whether he was fired by valor or desperation at the sight is a disputed point; but he made a sudden dash down the hill and across the river, almost flinging himself upon the lances of the Californians.

Captain Moore, who was ambling down the hill on an old white horse at the head of fifty dragoons mounted on mules, spurred his beast as he witnessed the foolish charge of the advance, and arrived upon the field in time to see Johnson fall dead and to take his place. Pico, seeing that reinforcements were coming, began to retreat, followed hotly by Moore and the horsed dragoons. Suddenly,

216

however, Fernando Altimira raised himself in his stirrups, looked back, laughed and galloped across the field to General Pico.

'Look!' he said. 'Only a few men on horses are after us. The mules are stumbling half a mile behind.'

Pico wheeled about, gave the word of command, and bore down upon the Americans. Then followed a hand-to-hand conflict, the Californians lancing and using their pistols with great dexterity, the Americans doing the best they could with their rusty sabres and clubbed guns.

They were soon reinforced by Moore's dragoons and Gillespie's battalion, despite the unwilling mules; but the brutes kicked and bucked at every pistol shot and fresh cloud of smoke. The poor old horses wheezed and panted, but stood their ground when not flung out of position by the frantic mules. The officers and soldiers of the United States army were a sorry sight, and in pointed contrast to the graceful Californians on their groomed steeds, handsomely trapped, curvetting and rearing and prancing as lightly as if on the floor of a circus. Kearney cursed his own stupidity, and Pico laughed in his face. Beale felt satisfaction and compunction in saturating the silk and silver of one fine saddle with the blood of its owner. The point of the dying man's lance pierced his face, but he noted the bleaching of Kearney's, as one dragoon after another was flung upon the sharp rocks over which his bewildered brute stumbled, or was caught and held aloft in the torturing arms of the cacti.

On the edge of the battle two men had forgotten the Aztec Eagle and the Stars and Stripes; they fought for love of a woman. Neither had had time to draw his pistol; they fought with lance and sabre, thrusting and parrying. Both were skilful swordsmen, but Altimira's horse was far superior to Russell's, and he had the advantage of weapons.

'One or the other die on the rocks,' said the Californian, 'and si I kill you, I marry Benicia.'

Russell made no reply. He struck aside the man's lance and wounded his wrist. But Altimira was too excited to feel pain. His face was quivering with passion.

It is not easy to parry a lance with a sabre, and still more difficult to get close enough to wound the man who wields it. Russell rose suddenly in his stirrups, described a rapid half-circle with his weapon, brought it down midway upon the longer blade, and snapped the latter in two. Altimira gave a cry of rage, and spurring his horse sought to ride his opponent down; but Russell wheeled, and the two men simultaneously snatched their pistols from the holsters. Altimira fired first, but his hand was unsteady and his ball went through a cactus. Russell raised his pistol with firm wrist, and discharged it full in the face of the Californian.

Then he looked over the field. Moore, fatally lanced, lay under a palm, and many of his men were about him. Gillespie was wounded, Kearney had received an ugly thrust. The Californians, upon the arrival of the main body of the enemy's troops, had retreated unpursued; the mules attached to one of the American howitzers were scampering over to the opposite ranks, much to the consternation of Kearney. The sun, looking over the mountain, dissipated the gray smoke, and cast a theatrical light on the faces of the dead. Russell bent over Altimira. His head was shattered, but his death was avenged. Never had an American troop suffered a more humiliating defeat. Only six Californians lay on the field; and when the American surgeon, after attending to his own wounded, offered his services to Pico's, that indomitable general haughtily replied that he had none.

'By Jove!' said Russell to Beale that night, 'you know your Californians! I am prouder than ever of having married one! That army is of the stuff of which my mother-in-law is made!'

CHAPTER 14

THAT was a gay Christmas at Monterey, despite the barricades in the street. News had come of the defeat of Kearney at San Pasqual, and the Montereños, inflated with hope and pride, gave little thought to the fact that his forces were now joined with Stockton's at San Diego.

On Christmas eve light streamed from every window, bonfires flared on the hills; the streets were illuminated, and every one was abroad. The clear warm night was ablaze with fireworks; men and women were in their gala gowns; rockets shot upward amidst shrieks of delight which mingled oddly with the rolling of drums at muster; even the children caught the enthusiasm, religious and patriotic.

'I suppose you would be glad to see even your friends driven out,' said Brotherton to Doña Eustaquia, as they walked through the brilliant town toward the church: bells called them to witness the dramatic play of 'The Shepherds.'

'I be glad to see the impertinent flag come down,' said she, frankly; 'but you can make resignation from the army, and have a little store on Alvarado Street. You can have beautiful silks and crêpes from America. I buy of you.'

'Thanks,' he said grimly. 'You would put a dunce cap on poor America, and stand her in a corner. If I resign, Doña Eustaquia. it will be to become a ranchero, not a shopkeeper. To tell the truth, I have little desire to leave California again.'

'But you were make for the fight,' she said, looking up with some pride at the tall military figure, the erect head and strong features. 'You not were make to lie in the hammock and horseback all day.'

'But I should do a good deal else, señora. I should raise cattle with some method; and I should have a library—and a wife.'

'Ah! you go to marry?'

'Some day, I hope. It would be lonely to be a ranchero without a wife.'

'Truly.'

'What is the matter with those women?'

A group of old women stood by the roadside. Their forms were bent, their brown faces gnarled like apples. Some were a shapeless mass of fat, other were parchment and bone; about the head and shoulders of each was a thick black shawl. Near them stood a number of young girls clad in muslin petticoats, flowered with purple and scarlet. Bright satin shoes were on their feet, cotton rebosas covered their pretty, pert little heads. All were looking in one direction, whispering and crossing themselves.

Doña Eustaquia glanced over her shoulder, then leaned heavily on Brotherton's arm.

'It is Benicia,' she said. 'It is because she was cursed and is with child that they cross themselves.'

Brotherton held her arm closely and laid his hand on hers, but he spoke sternly.

'The curse is not likely to do her any harm. You prayed that she should die when happiest, and you have done your best to make her wretched.'

She did not reply, and they walked slowly onward. Benicia followed, leaning on the arm of an Indian servant. Her friends avoided her, for they bitterly resented Altimira's death. But she gave them little regret. Since her husband could not be with her on this Christmas eve, she wished only for reconciliation with her mother. In spite of the crowd she followed close behind Doña Eustaquia and Brotherton, holding her head proudly, but ready to fall at the feet of the woman she worshipped.

'My friend,' said Doña Eustaquia, after a moment, 'perhaps it is best that I do not forgive her. Were she happy, then might the curse come true.'

'She has enough else to make her unhappy. Besides, who ever heard of a curse coming true? It has worked its will already for the matter of that. You kept your child from happiness with her husband during the brief time she had him. The bitterness of death is a small matter beside the bitterness of life. You should be satisfied.'

'You are hard, my friend.'

'I see your other faults only to respect and love them.'

'Does she look ill, Captain?'

'She cannot be expected to look like the old Benicia. Of course she looks ill, and needs care.'

'Look over the shoulder. Does she walk heavily?'

'Very. But as haughtily as do you.'

'Talk of other things for a little while, my friend.'

'Truly there is much to claim the interest tonight. This may be an old scene to you, but it is novel and fascinating to me. How lovely are those stately girls, half hidden by their rebosas, telling their beads as they hurry along. It is the very coquetry of religion. And those—But here we are.'

The church was handsomer without than within, for the clever old padres that built it had more taste than their successors. About the whitewashed walls of the interior were poor copies of celebrated paintings—the Passion of Christ, and an extraordinary group of nude women and grinning men representing the temptation of St Anthony. In a glass case a beautiful figure of the Saviour reclined on a stiff couch clumsily covered with costly stuffs. The Virgin was dressed much like the aristocratic ladies of Monterey, and the altar was a rainbow of tawdry colors.

But the ceremonies were interesting, and Brotherton forgot Benicia for the hour. After the mass the priest held out a small waxen image of the infant Jesus, and all approached and kissed it. Then from without came the sound of a guitar; the worshippers arose and ranged themselves against the wall; six girls dressed as shepherdesses; a man

221

representing Lucifer; two others, a hermit and the lazy vagabond Bartola; a boy, the archangel Gabriel, entered the church. They bore banners and marched to the centre of the building, then acted their drama with religious fervor.

The play began with the announcement by Gabriel of the birth of the Saviour, and exhortations to repair to the manger. On the road came the temptation of Lucifer; the archangel appeared once more; a violent altercation ensued in which all took part, and finally the prince of darkness was routed. Songs and fanciful by-play, brief sermons, music, gay and solemn, diversified the strange performance. When all was over, the players were followed by an admiring crowd to the entertainment awaiting them.

'Is it not beautiful—our Los Pastores?' demanded Doña Eustaquia, looking up at Brotherton, her fine face aglow with enthusiasm. 'Do not you feel the desire to be a Catholic, my friend?'

'Rather would I see two good Catholics united, dear señora,' and he turned suddenly to Benicia, who also had remained in the church, almost at her mother's side.

'Mamacita!' cried Benicia.

Doña Eustaquia opened her arms and caught the girl passionately to her heart; and Brotherton left the church.

CHAPTER 15

The April flowers were on the hills. Beds of gold-red poppies and silver-blue baby eyes were set like tiles amidst the dense green undergrowth beneath the pines, and on the natural lawns about the white houses. Although hope of driving forth the intruder had gone forever in January, Monterey had resumed in part her old gayety; despair had bred philosophy. But Monterey was Monterey no longer. An American alcalde with a power vested in no judge of the United States ruled over her; to add injury to insult, he had started a newspaper. The town was full of Americans; the United States was constructing a fort on the hill; above all, worse than all, the Californians were learning the value of money. Their sun was sloping to the west.

A thick India shawl hung over the window of Benicia's old room in her mother's house, shutting out the perfume of the hills. A carpet had been thrown on the floor, candles burned in the pretty gold candlesticks that had stood on the altar since Benicia's childhood. On the little brass bedstead lay Benicia, very pale and very pretty, her transparent skin faintly reflecting the pink of the satin coverlet. By the bed sat an old woman of the people. Her ragged white locks were bound about by a fillet of black silk; her face, dark as burnt umber, was seamed and lined like a withered prune; even her long broad nose was wrinkled; her dull eyes looked like mud-puddles; her big underlip was pursed up as if she had been speaking mincing words, and her chin was covered with a short white stubble. Over her coarse smock and gown she wore a black cotton reboso. In her arms she held an infant, muffled in a white lace mantilla.

Doña Eustaquia came in and bent over the baby, her strong face alight with joy.

'Dist thou ever nurse so beautiful a baby?' she demanded.

The old woman grunted; she had heard that question before.

'See how pink and smooth it is—not red and wrinkled like other babies! How becoming is that mantilla! No, she shall not be wrapped in blankets, cap, and shawls.'

'She catch cold, most likely,' grunted the nurse.

'In this weather? No; it is soft as midsummer. I cannot get cool. Ay, she looks like a rosebud lying in a fog-bank!' She touched the baby's cheek with her finger, then sat on the bed, beside her daughter. 'And how dost thou feel, my little one? Thou wert a baby thyself but yesterday, and thou art not much more today.'

'I feel perfectly well, my mother, and—ay, Dios, so happy! Where is Edourdo?'

'Of course! Always the husband! They are all alike! Hast thou not thy mother and thy baby?'

'I adore you both, mamacita, but I want Edourdo. Where is he?'

Her mother grimaced. 'I suppose it is no use to protest. Well, my little one, I think he is at this moment on the hill with Lieutenant Ord.'

'Why did he not come to see me before he went out?'

'He did, my daughter, but thou wert asleep. He kissed thee and stole away.'

'Where?'

'Right there on your cheek, one inch below your eyelashes.'

'When will he return?'

'Holy Mary! For dinner, surely, and that will be in an hour.'

'When can I get up?'

'In another week. Thou art so well! I would not have thee draw too heavily on thy little strength. Another month and thou wilt not remember that thou hast been ill. Then we will go to the rancho, where thou and thy little one will have sun all day and no fog.'

'Have I not a good husband, mamacita?'

'Yes; I love him like my own son. Had he been unkind to thee, I should have killed him with my own hands; but as he has his lips to thy little slipper, I forgive him for being an American.'

'And you no longer wish for a necklace of American ears! Oh, mamma!'

Doña Eustaquia frowned, then sighed. 'I do not know the American head for which I have not more like than hate, and they are welcome to their ears; but *the spirit* of that wish is in my heart yet, my child. Our country has been taken from us; we are aliens in our own land; it is the American's. They—holy God!—permit us to live here!'

'But they like us better than their own women.'

'Perhaps; they are men and like what they have not had too long.'

'Mamacita, I am thirsty.'

'What wilt thou have? A glass of water?'

'Water has no taste.'

'I know!'

Doña Eustaquia left the room and returned with an orange. 'This will be cool and pleasant on so warm a day. It is just a little sour,' she said; but the nurse raised her bony hand.

'Do not give her that,' she said in her harsh voice. 'It is too soon.'

'Nonsense! The baby is two weeks old. Why, I ate fruit a week after childing. Look how dry her mouth is! It will do her good.'

She pared the orange and gave it to Benicia, who ate it gratefully.

'It is very good, mamita. You will spoil me always, but that is because you are so good. And one day I hope you will be as happy as your little daughter; for there are other good Americans in the world. No? mamma. I think—Mamacita!'

She sprang upward with a loud cry, the body curving rigidly; her soft brown eyes stared horribly; froth gathered about her mouth; she gasped once or twice, her body writhing from the agonized arms that strove to hold it, then fell limply down, her features relaxing.

'She is dead,' said the nurse.

'Benicia!' whispered Doña Eustaquia. 'Benicia!'

'You have killed her,' said the old woman, as she drew the mantilla about the baby's face.

Doña Eustaquia dropped the body and moved backward from the bed. She put out her hands and went gropingly from the room to her own, and from thence to the sala. Brotherton came forward to meet her. 'Eustaquia!' he cried. 'My friend! *My dear!* What has happened? What—'

She raised her hand and pointed to the cross. The mark of the dagger was still there.

'Benicia!' she uttered. 'The curse!' and then she fell at his feet.

SELECTED STORIES
by Bret Harte

THE OUTCASTS OF POKER FLAT

As Mr John Oakhurst, gambler, stepped into the main street of Poker Flat on the morning of the twenty-third of November, 1850, he was conscious of a change in its moral atmosphere since the preceding night. Two or three men, conversing earnestly together, ceased as he approached, and exchanged significant glances. There was a Sabbath lull in the air, which, in a settlement unused to Sabbath influences, looked ominous.

Mr Oakhurst's calm, handsome face betrayed small concern in these indications. Whether he was conscious of any predisposing cause, was another question. 'I reckon they're after somebody,' he reflected; 'likely it's me.' He returned to his pocket the handkerchief with which he had been whipping away the red dust of Poker Flat from his neat boots, and quietly discharged his mind of any further conjecture.

In point of fact, Poker Flat was 'after somebody.' It had lately suffered the loss of several thousand dollars, two valuable horses, and a prominent citizen. It was experiencing a spasm of virtuous reaction, quite as lawless and ungovernable as any of the acts that had provoked it. A secret committee had determined to rid the town of all improper persons. This was done permanently in regard of two men who were then hanging from the boughs of a sycamore in the gulch, and temporarily in the banishment of certain other objectionable characters. I regret to say that some of these were ladies. It is but due to the sex, however, to state that their impropriety was professional, and it was only in such easily established standards of evil that Poker Flat ventured to sit in judgment.

Mr Oakhurst was right in supposing that he was included in this category. A few of the committee had urged hanging him as a possible example, and a sure method of reimbursing themselves from his pockets of the sums he had won from them. 'It's agin justice,' said Jim Wheeler, 'to let this yer young man from Roaring Camp—an entire stranger—carry away our money.' But a crude sentiment of equity residing in the breasts of those who had been fortunate enough to win from Mr Oakhurst overruled this narrower local prejudice.

Mr Oakhurst received his sentence with philosophic calmness, none the less coolly that he was aware of the hesitation of his judges. He was too much of a gambler not to accept Fate. With him life was at best an uncertain game, and he recognized the usual percentage in favour of the dealer.

A party of armed men accompanied the deported wickedness of Poker Flat to the outskirts of the settlement. Besides Mr Oakhurst, who was known to be a coolly desperate man, and for whose intimidation the armed escort was intended, the expatriated party consisted of a young woman familiarly known as 'The Duchess;' another, who had born the title of 'Mother Shipton;' and 'Uncle Billy,' a suspected sluice-robber and confirmed drunkard. The cavalcade provoked no comments from the spectators, nor was any word uttered by the escort. Only when the gulch which marked the uttermost limit of Poker Flat was reached, the leader spoke briefly and to the point. The exiles were forbidden to return at the peril of their lives.

As the escort disappeared, their pent-up feelings found vent in a few hysterical tears from the Duchess, some bad language from Mother Shipton, and a Parthian volley of expletives from Uncle Billy. The philosophic Oakhurst alone remained silent. He listened calmly to Mother Shipton's desire to cut somebody's heart out, to the repeated statements of the Duchess that she would die in the road, and to the alarming oaths that seemed to be bumped out of Uncle Billy as he rode forward. With the easy good-humour characteristic of his class, he insisted upon exchanging his own riding-horse, 'Five Spot,' for the sorry mule which the Duchess rode. But even this act did not draw the party into any closer sympathy. The young woman readjusted her somewhat draggled plumes with a feeble, faded coquetry; Mother Shipton eyed the possessor of 'Five Spot' with malevolence; and Uncle Billy included the whole party in one sweeping anathema.

The road to Sandy Bar—a camp that, not having as yet experienced the regenerating influences of Poker Flat, consequently seemed to offer some invitation to the emigrants—lay over a steep mountain range. It was distant a day's severe travel. In that advanced season, the party soon passed out of the moist, temperate regions of the foothills into the dry, cold, bracing air of the Sierras. The trail was narrow and difficult. At noon the Duchess, rolling out of her saddle upon the ground, declared her intention of going no farther, and the party halted.

The spot was singularly wild and impressive. A wooded amphitheater, surrounded on three sides by precipitous cliffs of naked granite, sloped gently towards the crest of another precipice that overlooked the valley. It was, undoubtedly, the most suitable spot for a camp, had camping been advisable. But Mr Oakhurst knew that scarcely half the journey to Sandy Bar was accomplished, and the party were not equipped or provisioned for delay. This fact he pointed out to his companions curtly, with a philosophic commentary on the folly of 'throwing up their hand before the game was played out.' But they were furnished with liquor, which in this emergency stood them in place of food, fuel, rest, and prescience. In spite of his remonstrances, it was not long before they were more or less under its influence. Uncle Billy passed rapidly from a bellicose state into one of stupor, the Duchess became maudlin, and Mother Shipton snored. Mr Oakhurst alone remained erect, leaning against a rock, calmly surveying them.

Mr Oakhurst did not drink. It interfered with a profession which required coolness, impassiveness, and presence of mind, and, in his own language, he 'couldn't afford it.' As he gazed at his recumbent fellow-exiles, the loneliness begotten of his pariah-trade, his habits of life, his very vices, for the first time seriously oppressed him. He bestirred himself in dusting his black clothes, washing his hands and face, and other acts characteristic of his studiously neat habits, and for a moment forgot his annoyance. The thought of deserting his weaker and more pitiable companions never perhaps occurred to him. Yet he could not help feeling the want of that excitement which, singularly enough, was most conducive to that calm equanimity for which he was notorious. He looked at the gloomy walls that rose a thousand feet sheer above the circling pines around him; at the sky, ominously clouded; at the valley below, already deepening into shadow. And, doing so, suddenly he heard his own name called.

A horseman slowly ascended the trail. In the fresh, open face of the newcomer, Mr Oakhurst recognized Tom Simson, otherwise known as 'The Innocent' of Sandy Bar. He had met him some months before over a 'little game,' and had, with perfect equanimity, won the entire fortune—amounting to some forty dollars—of that guileless youth. After the game was finished, Mr Oakhurst drew the youthful speculator behind the door, and thus addressed him: 'Tommy, you're a good little man, but you can't gamble worth a cent. Don't try it over again.' He then handed him his money back, pushed him gently from the room, and so made a devoted slave of Tom Simson.

There was a remembrance of this in his boyish and enthusiastic greeting of Mr Oakhurst. He had started, he said, to go to Poker Flat to seek his fortune. 'Alone?' No, not exactly alone; in fact (a giggle), he had run away with Piney Woods. Didn't Mr Oakhurst remember Piney. She that used to wait on the table at the Temperance House. They had been engaged a long time, but old Jake Woods had objected, and so they had run away, and were going to Poker Flat to be married; and here they were. And they were tired out, and how lucky it was they had found a place to camp and company. All this the Innocent delivered rapidly, while Piney, a stout, comely damsel of fifteen, emerged from behind the pine tree, where she had been blushing unseen, and rode to the side of her lover.

Mr Oakhurst seldom troubled himself with sentiment, still less with propriety; but he had a vague idea that the situation was not fortunate. He retained, however, his presence of mind sufficiently to kick Uncle Billy, who was about to say something, and Uncle Billy was sober enough to recognize in Mr Oakhurst's kick a superior power that would not bear trifling. He then endeavoured to dissuade Tom Simson from delaying further, but in vain. He even pointed out the fact that there was no provision, nor means of making a camp. But, unluckily, the Innocent met this objection by assuring the party that he was provided with an extra mule loaded with provisions, and by the discovery of a rude attempt at a log house near the trail. 'Piney can stay with Mrs Oakhurst,' said the Innocent, pointing to the Duchess, 'and I can shift for myself.'

Nothing but Mr Oakhurst's admonishing foot saved Uncle Billy from bursting into a roar of laughter. As it was, he felt compelled to retire up the cañon until he could recover his gravity. There he confided the joke to the tall pine trees, with many slaps of his leg, contortions of his face, and the usual profanity. But when he returned to the party, he found them seated by a fire—for the air had grown strangely chill, and the sky overcast—in apparently amicable conversation. Piney was actually talking in an impulsive, girlish fashion to the Duchess, who was listening with an interest and animation she had not shown for many days. The Innocent was holding forth, apparently with equal effect, to Mr Oakhurst and Mother Shipton, who was actually relaxing into amiability. 'Is this yer a d—d pic-nic?' said Uncle Billy, with inward scorn, as he surveyed the sylvan group, the glancing firelight, and the tethered animals in the foreground. Suddenly an idea mingled with the alcoholic fumes that disturbed his brain. It was apparently of a jocular nature, for he felt impelled to slap his leg again and cram his fist into his mouth.

As the shadows crept slowly up the mountain, a slight breeze rocked the tops of the pine trees, and moaned through their long and gloomy aisles. The ruined cabin, patched and covered with pine boughs, was set apart for the ladies. As the lovers parted, they unaffectedly exchanged a kiss, so honest and sincere that it might have been heard above the swaying pines. The frail Duchess and the malevolent Mother Shipton were probably too stunned to remark upon this last evidence of simplicity, and so turned without a word to the hut. The fire was replenished, the men lay down before the door, and in a few minutes were asleep.

Mr Oakhurst was a light sleeper. Toward morning he awoke benumbed and cold. As he stirred the dying fire, the wind, which was now blowing strongly, brought to his cheek that which caused the blood to leave it,—snow!

He started to his feet with the intention of awakening the sleepers, for there was no time to lose. But turning to where Uncle Billy had been lying, he found him gone. A suspicion leaped to his brain and a curse to his lips. He ran to the spot where the mules had been tethered; they were no longer there. The tracks were already rapidly disappearing in the snow.

The momentary excitement brought Mr Oakhurst back to the fire with his usual calm. He did not waken the sleepers. The Innocent slumbered peacefully, with a smile on his good-humored, freckled face; the virgin Piney slept beside her frailer sisters as sweetly as though attended by celestial guardians, and Mr Oakhurst, drawing his blanket over his shoulders, stroked his mustaches and waited for the dawn. It came slowly in a whirling mist of snowflakes, that dazzled and confused the eye. What could be seen of the landscape appeared magically changed. He looked over the valley, and summed up the present and future in two words—'snowed in!'

A careful inventory of the provisions, which, fortunately for the party, had been stored within the hut, and so escaped the felonious fingers of Uncle Billy, disclosed the fact that with care and prudence they might last ten days longer. 'That is,' said Mr Oakhurst, *sotto voce* to the Innocent, 'if you're willing to board us. If you ain't—and perhaps you'd better not—you can wait till Uncle Billy gets back with provisions.' For some occult reason Mr Oakhurst could not bring himself to disclose Uncle Billy's rascality, and so offered the hypothesis that he had wondered from the camp and had accidentally stampeded the animals. He dropped a warning to the Duchess and Mother Shipton, who of course knew the facts of their associate's defection. 'They'll find out the truth about us *all* when they find out anything,' he added, significantly, 'and there's no good frightening them now.'

Tom Simson not only put all his worldly store at the disposal of Mr Oakhurst, but seemed to enjoy the prospect of their enforced seclusion. 'We'll have a good camp for a week, and then the snow'll melt, and we'll all go back together.' The cheerful gayety of the young man, and Mr Oakhurst's calm infected the others. The Innocent, with the aid of pine-boughs, extemporized a thatch for the roofless cabin, and the Duchess directed Piney in the rearrangement of the interior with a taste and tact that opened the blue eyes of that provincial maiden to their fullest extent. 'I reckon now you're used to fine things at Poker Flat,' said Piney. The Duchess turned away sharply to conceal something that reddened her cheeks through its professional tint, and Mother Shipton requested Piney not to 'chatter.' But when Mr Oakhurst returned from a weary search for the trail, he heard the sound of happy laughter echoed from the rocks. He stopped in some alarm, and his thoughts first naturally reverted to the whiskey, which he had prudently *cachéd*. 'And yet it don't somehow sound like whiskey,' said the gambler. It was not until he caught sight of the blazing fire through the still blinding storm and the group around it, that he settled to the conviction that it was 'square fun.'

Whether Mr Oakhurst had *cachéd* his cards with the whiskey as something debarred the free access of the community, I cannot say. It was certain that, in Mother Shipton's words, he 'didn't say cards once' during that evening. Haply the time was beguiled by an accordion, produced somewhat ostentatiously by Tom Simson from his pack. Notwithstanding some difficulties attending the manipulation of this instrument, Piney Woods managed to pluck several reluctant melodies from its keys, to an accompaniment by the Innocent on a pair of bone castinets. But the crowning festivity of the evening was reached in a rude camp-meeting hymn, which the lovers, joining hands, sang with great earnestness and vociferation. I fear that a certain defiant tone and Covenanter's swing to its chorus, rather than any devotional quality, caused it speedily to infect the others, who at last joined in the refrain:—

'I'm proud to live in the service of the Lord,
And I'm bound to die in His army.'

The pines rocked, the storm eddied and whirled above the miserable group, and the flames of their altar leaped heavenward, as if in token of the vow.

At midnight the storm abated, the rolling clouds parted, and the stars glittered keenly above the sleeping camp. Mr Oakhurst, whose professional habits had enabled him to live on the smallest possible amount of sleep, in dividing the watch with Tom Simson, somehow managed to take upon himself the greater part of that duty. He excused himself to the Innocent by saying that he had 'often been a week without sleep.' 'Doing what?' asked Tom. 'Poker!' replied Oakhurst, sententiously; 'when a man gets a streak of luck—nigger-luck—he don't get tired. The luck gives in first. Luck,' continued the gambler, reflectively, 'is a mighty queer thing. All you know about it for certain is that it's bound to change. And it's finding out when it's going to change that makes you. We've had a streak of bad luck since we left Poker Flat—you come along, and slap you get into it, too. If you can hold your cards right along you're all right. For,' added the gambler, with cheerful irelevance—

> '"I'm proud to live in the service of the Lord,
> And I'm bound to die in His army."'

The third day came, and the sun, looking through the white-curtained valley, saw the outcasts divide their slowly decreasing store of provisions for the morning meal. It was one of the peculiarities of that mountain climate that its rays diffused a kindly warmth over the wintry landscape, as if in regretful commiseration of the past. But it revealed drift on drift of snow piled high around the hut—a hopeless, unchartered, trackless sea of white lying below the rocky shores to which the castaways still clung. Through the marvellously clear air the smoke of the pastoral village of Poker Flat rose miles away. Mother Shipton saw it, and from a remote pinnacle of her rocky fastness, hurled in that direction a final malediction. It was her last vituperative attempt, and perhaps for that reason was invested with a certain degree of sublimity. It did her good, she privately informed the Duchess. 'Just you go out there and cuss, and see.' She then set herself to the task of amusing 'the child,' as she and the Duchess were pleased to call Piney. Piney was no chicken, but it was a soothing and original theory of the pair thus to account for the fact that she didn't swear and wasn't improper.

When night crept up again through the gorges, the reedy notes of the accordion rose and fell in fitful spasms and long-drawn gasps by the flickering camp-fire. But music failed to fill entirely the aching void left by insufficient food, and a new diversion was proposed by

Piney—story-telling. Neither Mr Oakhurst nor his female companions caring to relate their personal experiences, this plan would have failed, too, but for the Innocent. Some months before he had chanced upon a stray copy of Mr Pope's ingenious translation of the Iliad. He now proposed to narrate the principal incidents of that poem—having thoroughly mastered the argument and fairly forgotten the words—in the current vernacular of Sandy Bar. And so for the rest of that night the Homeric demigods again walked the earth. Trojan bully and wily Greek wrestled in the winds, and the great pines in the cañon seemed to bow to the wrath of the son of Peleus. Mr Oakhurst listened with quiet satisfaction. Most especially was he interested in the fate of 'Ash-heels,' as the Innocent persisted in denominating the 'swift-footed Achilles.'

So with small food and much of Homer and the accordion, a week passed over the heads of the outcasts. The sun again forsook them, and again from leaden skies the snowflakes were sifted over the land. Day by day closer around them drew the snowy circle, until at last they looked from their prison over drifted walls of drizzling white, that towered twenty feet above their heads. It became more and more difficult to replenish their fires, even from the fallen trees beside them, now half hidden in the drifts. And yet no one complained. The lovers turned from the dreary prospect, and looked into each other's eyes, and were happy. Mr Oakhurst settled himself coolly to the losing game before him. The Duchess, more cheerful than she had been, assumed the care of Piney. Only Mother Shipton—once the strongest of the party—seemed to sicken and fade. At midnight on the tenth day she called Oakhurst to her side. 'I'm going,' she said, in a voice of querulous weakness, 'but don't say anything about it. Don't waken the kids. Take the bundle from under my head and open it.' Mr Oakhurst did so. It contained Mother Shipton's rations for the last week, untouched. 'Give 'em to the child,' she said, pointing to the sleeping Piney. 'You've starved yourself,' said the gambler. 'That's what they call it,' said the woman, querulously, as she lay down again, and, turning her face to the wall, passed quietly away.

The accordion and the bones were put aside that day, and Homer was forgotten. When the body of Mother Shipton had been committed to the snow, Mr Oakhurst took the Innocent aside, and showed him a pair of snow-shoes, which he had fashioned from the old pack-saddle. 'There's one chance in a hundred to save her yet,' he said, pointing to Piney; 'but it's there,' he added, pointing toward Poker Flat. 'If you reach there in two days she's safe.' 'And you?' asked Tom Simson. 'I'll stay here,' was the curt reply.

The lovers parted with a long embrace. 'You are not going, too?' said the Duchess, as she saw Mr Oakhurst apparently waiting to accompany him. 'As far as the cañon,' he replied. He turned suddenly, and kissed the Duchess, leaving her pallid face aflame, and her trembling limbs rigid with amazement.

Night came, but not Mr Oakhurst. It brought the storm again and the whirling snow. Then the Duchess, feeding the fire, found that some one had quietly piled beside the hut enough fuel to last a few days longer. The tears rose to her eyes, but she hid them from Piney.

The women slept but little. In the morning, looking into each other's faces, they read their fate. Neither spoke; but Piney, accepting the position of the stronger, drew near and placed her arm around the Duchess's waist. They kept this attitude for the rest of the day. That night the storm reached its greatest fury, and, rending asunder the protecting pines, invaded the very hut.

Toward morning they found themselves unable to feed the fire, which gradually died away. As the embers slowly blackened, the Duchess crept closer to Piney, and broke the silence of many hours: 'Piney, can you pray?' 'No, dear,' said Piney, simply. The Duchess, without knowing exactly why, felt relieved, and, putting her head upon Piney's shoulder, spoke no more. And so reclining, the younger and purer pillowing the head of her soiled sister upon her virgin breast, they fell asleep.

The wind lulled as if it feared to waken them. Feathery drifts of snow, shaken from the long pine boughs, flew like white-winged birds, and settled about them as they slept. The moon through the rifted clouds looked down upon what had been the camp. But all human stain, all trace of earthly travail, was hidden beneath the spotless mantle mercifully flung from above.

They slept all that day and the next, nor did they waken when voices and footsteps broke the silence of the camp. And when pitying fingers brushed the snow from their wan faces, you could scarcely have told, from the equal peace that dwelt upon them, which was she that had sinned. Even the law of Poker Flat recognized this, and turned away, leaving them still locked in each other's arms.

But at the head of the gulch, on one of the largest pine-trees, they found the deuce of clubs pinned to the bark with a bowie-knife. It bore the following, written in pencil, in a firm hand:—

†

BENEATH THIS TREE
LIES THE BODY
OF
JOHN OAKHURST,
WHO STRUCK A STREAK OF BAD LUCK
ON THE 23RD OF NOVEMBER, 1850,
AND
HANDED IN HIS CHECKS
ON THE 7TH DECEMBER, 1850.

†

And pulseless and cold, with a Derringer by his side and a bullet in his heart, though still calm as in life, beneath the snow lay he who was at once the strongest and yet the weakest of the outcasts of Poker Flat.

THE MAN OF NO ACCOUNT

His name was Fagg—David Fagg. He came to California in '52 with us, in the 'Skyscraper.' I don't think he did it in an adventurous way. He probably had no other place to go to. When a knot of us young fellows would recite what splendid opportunities we resigned to go, and how sorry our friends were to have us leave, and show daguerreotypes and locks of hair, and talk of Mary and Susan, the man of no account used to sit by and listen with a pained, mortified expression on his plain face, and say nothing. I think he had nothing to say. He had no associates, except when we patronized him; and, in point of fact, he was a good deal of sport to us. He was always seasick whenever we had a capful of wind. He never got his sea-legs on either. And I never shall forget how we all laughed when Rattler took him the piece of pork on a string, and—But you know that time-honored joke. And then we had such a splendid lark with him. Miss Fanny Twinkler couldn't bear the sight of him, and we used to make Fagg think that she had taken a fancy to him, and send him little delicacies and books from the cabin. You ought to have witnessed the rich scene that took place when he came up, stammering and very sick, to thank her! Didn't she flash up grandly and beautifully and scornfully? So like 'Medora,' Rattler said,—Rattler knew Byron by heart,—and wasn't old Fagg awfully cut up? But he got over it, and when Rattler felt sick at Valparaiso, old Fagg used to nurse him. You see he was a good sort of fellow, but he lacked manliness and spirit.

He had absolutely no idea of poetry. I've seen him sit stolidly by, mending his old clothes, when Rattler delivered that stirring apostrophe of Byron's to the ocean. He asked Rattler once, quite seriously, if he thought Byron was ever seasick. I don't remember Rattler's reply, but I know we all laughed very much, and I have no doubt it was something good, for Rattler was smart.

When the 'Skyscraper' arrived at San Francisco, we had a grand 'feed.' We agreed to meet every year and perpetuate the occasion. Of course we didn't invite Fagg. Fagg was a steerage passenger, and it was necessary, you see, now we were ashore, to exercise a little discretion. But Old Fagg, as we called him,—he was only about twenty-five years old, by the way,—was the source of immense amusement to us that day. It appeared that he had conceived the idea that he could walk to Sacramento, and actually started off afoot. We had a good time, and shook hands with one another all around, and so parted. Ah me! only eight years ago, and yet some of those hands then clasped in amity have been clenched at each other, or have dipped furtively in one another's pockets. I know that we didn't dine together the next year, because young Barker swore he wouldn't put his feet under the same mahogany with such a very contemptible scoundrel as that Mixer; and Nibbles, who borrowed money at Valparaiso of young Stubbs, who was then a waiter in a restaurant, didn't like to meet such people.

When I bought a number of shares in the Coyote Tunnel at Mugginsville, in '54, I thought I'd take a run up there and see it. I stopped at the Empire Hotel, and after dinner I got a horse and rode round the town and out to the claim. One of those individuals whom newspaper correspondents call 'our intelligent informant,' and to whom in all small communities the right of answering questions is tacitly yielded, was quietly pointed out to me. Habit had enabled him to work and talk at the same time, and he never pretermitted either. He gave me a history of the claim, and added: 'You see, stranger' (he addressed the bank before him), 'gold is sure to come out 'er that theer claim (he put in a comma with his pick), but the old pro-pri-e-tor (he wriggled out the word and the point of his pick) warn't of much account (a long stroke of the pick for a period). He was green, and let the boys about here jump him,'—and the rest of his sentence was confided to his hat, which he had removed to wipe his manly brow with his red bandanna.

I asked him who was the original proprietor.

'His name was Fagg.'

I went to see him. He looked a little older and plainer. He had worked hard, he said, and was getting on 'so, so.' I took quite a liking to him, and patronized him to some extent. Whether I did so because I was beginning to have a distrust for such fellows as Rattler and Mixer is not necessary for me to state.

You remember how the Coyote Tunnel went in, and how awfully we shareholders were done! Well, the next thing I heard was that Rattler, who was one of the heaviest shareholders, was up at Mugginsville keeping bar for the proprietor of the Mugginsville Hotel, and that old Fagg had struck it rich, and didn't know what to do with his money. All this was told me by Mixer, who had been there, settling up matters, and likewise that Fagg was sweet upon the daughter of the proprietor of the aforesaid hotel. And so by hearsay and letter I eventually gathered that old Robins, the hotel man, was trying to get up a match between Nellie Robins and Fagg. Nellie was a pretty, plump, and foolish little thing, and would do just as her father wished. I thought it would be a good thing for Fagg if he should marry and settle down; that as a married man he might be of some account. So I ran up to Mugginsville one day to look after things.

It did me an immense deal of good to make Rattler mix my drinks for me,—Rattler? the gay, brilliant, and unconquerable Rattler, who had tried to snub me two years ago. I talked to him about old Fagg and Nellie, particularly as I thought the subject was distasteful. He never liked Fagg, and he was sure, he said, that Nellie didn't. Did Nellie like anybody else? He turned around to the mirror behind the bar and brushed up his hair; I understood the conceited wretch. I thought I'd put Fagg on his guard and get him to hurry up matters. I had a long talk with him. You could see by the way the poor fellow acted that he was badly struck. He sighed, and promised to pluck up courage to hurry matters to a crisis. Nellie was a good girl, and I think had a sort of quiet respect for old Fagg's unobtrusiveness. But her fancy was already taken captive by Rattler's superficial qualities, which were obvious and pleasing. I don't think Nellie was any worse than you or I. We are more apt to take acquaintances at their apparent value than their intrinsic worth. It's less trouble, and, except when we want to trust them, quite as convenient. The difficulty with women is that their feelings are apt to get interested sooner than ours, and then, you know, reasoning is out of the question. This is what old Fagg would have known had he been of any account. But he wasn't. So much the worse for him.

It was a few months afterward, and I was sitting in my office, when in walked old Fagg. I was surprised to see him down, but we talked over the current topics in that mechanical manner of people who know that they have something else to say, but are obliged to get at it in that formal way. After an interval Fagg in his natural manner said,—

'I'm going home!'

'Going home?'

'Yes,—that is, I think I'll take a trip to the Atlantic States. I came to see you, as you know I have some little property, and I have executed a power of attorney for you to manage my affairs. I have some papers I'd like to leave with you. Will you take charge of them?'

'Yes,' I said. 'But what of Nellie?'

His face fell. He tried to smile, and the combination resulted in one of the most startling and grotesque effects I ever beheld. At length he said,—

'I shall not marry Nellie,—that is,'—he seemed to apologize internally for the positive form of expression,—'I think that I had better not.'

'David Fagg,' I said with sudden severity, 'you're of no account!'

To my astonishment his face brightened. 'Yes,' said he, that's it!—I'm of no account! But I always knew it. You see I thought Rattler loved that girl as well as I did, and I knew she liked him better than she did me, and would be happier I dare say with him. But then I knew that old Robins would have preferred me to him, as I was better off,—and the girl would do as he said,—and, you see, I thought I was kinder in the way,—and so I left. But,' he continued, as I was about to interrupt him, 'for fear the old man might object to Rattler, I've lent him enough to set him up in business for himself in Dogtown. A pushing, active, brilliant fellow, you know, like Rattler, can get along, and will soon be in his old position again,—and you needn't be hard on him, you know, if he doesn't. Goodbye.'

I was too much disgusted with his treatment of that Rattler to be at all amiable, but as his business was profitable, I promised to attend to it, and he left. A few weeks passed. The return steamer arrived, and a terrible incident occupied the papers for days afterward. People in all parts of the State conned eagerly the details of an awful shipwreck, and those who had friends aboard went away by themselves, and read the long list of the lost under their breath. I read of the gifted, the gallant, the noble, and loved ones who had perished, and among them I think I was the first to read the name of David Fagg. For the 'man of no account' had 'gone home!'

THE TRAPPERS
OF ARKANSAS
(AN EXTRACT)
by Gustave Aimard

THE PRAIRIE

To the westward of the United States extended some years ago, many hundred miles beyond the Mississippi, an immense territory, composed of uncultivated lands, on which stood neither the log-house of the white man nor the hut of the Indian.

This vast desert, intersected by dark forests, with mysterious paths traced by the steps of wild beasts, and by verdant prairies with high and tufted herbage that undulates with the slightest breeze, is watered by powerful streams.

Over these plains, endowed with so rich a vegetation, wandered innumerable troops of wild horses, buffaloes, elks, big horns, and those thousands of animals which the civilisation of the other parts of America is every day driving back, and which regain their primitive liberty in these regions.

On this account, the most powerful Indian tribes have established their hunting grounds in this country.

Towards the end of the year 1837, in the latter days of the month of September, by the Indians called the moon of the falling leaves—a man, still young, and who, from his complexion, notwithstanding his costume was entirely like that of the Indians, it was easy to perceive was a white man, was seated, about an hour before sunset, near a fire, the want of which began to be felt at this period of the year, at one of the most unfrequented spots of the prairie we have just described.

This man was at most thirty-five to thirty-six years old, though a few deeply-marked wrinkles on his broad white forehead seemed to indicate a more advanced age.

His features were handsome and noble, and impressed with that pride and energy which a wild life imparts. His black, prominent eyes, crowned with thick eyebrows, had a mild and melancholy expression, that tempered their brilliancy and vivacity; the lower part of his face was hidden by a long, thick beard, the dark tint of which contrasted with the peculiar paleness of his countenance.

He was tall, slender, and well-proportioned; his nervous limbs, which displayed muscles of extreme rigidity, proved that he was endowed with more than common strength.

His remarkably simple attire was composed of a mitasse, or kind of close drawers falling down to his ankles, and fastened to his hips by a leather belt, and of a cotton hunting-shirt, embroidered with ornaments in wool of different colors, which descended to his mid-leg. This blouse, open in front, left exposed his embrowned chest, upon which hung a scapulary of black velvet, from a slight steel chain. Boots of untanned deer skin protected him from the bites of reptiles, and rose to his knees. A cap of beaver skin, whose tail hung down behind, covered his head, while long and luxuriant curls of black hair, which were beginning to be threaded with white, fell over his broad shoulders. This man was a hunter.

A magnificent rifle within reach of his hand, the game bag which was hung to his shoulder belt, and the two buffalo horns, suspended at his girdle, and filled with powder and balls, left no doubt in this respect. Two long double pistols were carelessly thrown near his rifle.

The hunter, armed with that long knife called a machete, or a short-bladed straight sabre, which the inhabitants of the prairies never lay aside, was occupied in conscientiously skinning a beaver, whilst carefully watching the haunch of a deer which was roasting at the fire, suspended by a string.

The spot where this man was seated was admirably chosen for a halt of a few hours.

It was a clearing at the summit of a moderately elevated hill, which, from its position, commanded the prairie for a great distance, and prevented a surprise. A spring bubbled up at a few paces from the place where the hunter had established his bivouac, and descended to the plain. The high and abundant grass afforded an excellent pasto for two superb horses, with wild and sparkling eyes, which, safely tethered, were enjoying their food. The fire, lighted with dry wood, and sheltered on three sides by the rock, only allowed a thin column of smoke to escape, scarcely perceptible at ten paces' distance, and a screen of tall trees concealed the encampment from the indiscreet looks of any who were in ambuscade in the neighborhood.

The red fires of the setting sun tinged with beautiful flickering rays the tops of the great trees, and the sun itself was on the point of disappearing behind the mountains which bounded the horizon, when the horses raised their heads and pricked their ears—signs of restlessness which did not escape the hunter.

Although he heard no suspicious sound, and all appeared calm, he hastened to place the skin of the beaver before the fire stretched upon two crossed sticks, and, without rising, put out his hand towards his rifle.

The cry of the jay was heard, and repeated thrice at regular intervals.

The hunter laid his rifle by his side again with a smile, and resumed his attention to the supper. Almost immediately the grass was violently shaken, and two magnificent bloodhounds bounded up and lay down by the hunter, who patted them for an instant, and not without difficulty quieted their caresses.

The dogs only preceded by a few minutes a second hunter.

This new personage, much younger than the first,—for he did not appear to be more than twenty-two years old,—was a tall, thin, agile and powerfully-built man, with a slightly-rounded head, lighted by two grey eyes, sparkling with intelligence, and endowed with an open and loyal physiognomy, to which long light hair gave a somewhat childish appearance.

He was clothed in the same costume as his companion, and on

arriving, threw down by the fire a string of birds which he was carrying at his shoulder.

The two hunters then, without exchanging a word, set about preparing a supper, that exercise always renders excellent.

The night had completely set in and the howlings of wild beasts already resounded in the prairie.

The hunters, after supping with a good appetite, lit their pipes, and placing their backs to the fire, in order that the flame should not prevent them from perceiving the approach of any suspicious visitor whom darkness might bring them, smoked with the enjoyment of people who, after a long and painful journey, taste an instant of repose which they may not meet with again for some time.

'Well!' the first hunter said laconically.

'You were right,' the other replied; 'we have kept too much to the right, it was that which made us lose the scent.'

'I was sure of it,' the first speaker replied; 'you see, Belhumeur, you trust too much to your Canadian habits: the Indians with whom we have to do here in no way resemble the Iroquois of your country.'

Belhumeur nodded his head in sign of acquiescence.

'After all,' the other continued, 'this is of very little importance at this moment; what is urgent is to know who are our thieves.'

'I know.'

'Good!' the other said; 'and who are the Indians who have dared to steal the traps marked with my cipher!'

'The Comanches.'

'I suspected as much. By heavens, ten of our best traps stolen during the night! I swear, Belhumeur, that they shall pay for them dearly! And where are the Comanches at this moment?'

'Within about three leagues of us. It is a party of plunderers composed of a dozen men; according to the direction they are following, they are returning to their mountains.'

'They shall not all reach home,' said the hunter.

'Parbleu!' said Belhumeur with a laugh, 'they will only get what they deserve. I leave it to you, Loyal Heart, to punish them for their insult; but you will be still more determined to avenge yourself when you know they are commanded by *Nehu Nutah*.'

'Eagle Head!' cried Loyal Heart, almost bounding from his seat. 'Oh, oh! yes, I know him, and God grant that this time I may settle the old account there is between us. His mocassins have long enough trodden the same path with me and barred my passage.'

After pronouncing these words with an accent of hatred that made Belhumeur shudder, the hunter resumed his pipe and continued to smoke with a feigned carelessness that did not deceive his companion.

The conversation ceased, and the two hunters appeared to be absorbed in profound reflections, smoking silently beside each other.

'Shall I watch?' asked Belhumeur suddenly.

'No,' Loyal Heart replied, in a low voice; 'sleep, I will be sentinel for both.'

Belhumeur, without making the least objection, laid himself down by the fire, and in a few minutes slept profoundly.

When the owl hooted its matin song, Loyal Heart, who during the night had remained motionless as a marble statue, awakened his companion.

'It is time,' said he.

'Very good!' Belhumeur replied.

The hunters saddled their horses, descended the hill with precaution, and galloped off upon the track of the Comanches.

THE HUNTERS

LOYAL HEART—the only name by which the hunter was known throughout the prairies of the West—enjoyed an immense reputation for skill, loyalty, and courage among the Indian tribes, with whom his adventurous existence had brought him in contact. All respected him. The white hunters and trappers, whether Spaniards, North-Americans, or half-breeds, had a high opinion of his experience, and often had recourse to his counsels.

The pirates of the prairies themselves, thorough food for the gallows, the refuse of civilization, who lived by rapine and plunder, did not dare attack him, and avoided as much as possible throwing themselves in his way.

This man had succeeded by the sheer force of intelligence and will, in creating for himself, and almost unknown to himself, a power accepted and recognized by the ferocious inhabitants of these vast deserts,—a power which he only employed for good.

No one knew who Loyal Heart was, or whence he came; his early years were a mystery.

One day, about fifteen years before, when he was very young, some hunters had met him on the banks of the Arkansas, setting traps for beavers. The few questions put to him concerning his preceding life remained unanswered; and the hunters, people not very talkative by nature, fancying they perceived, from the embarrassment and reticence of the young man, that he had a secret, made a scruple about pressing him further.

At the same time, contrary to other hunters, or trappers of the prairies, who have all one or two companions with whom they associate, and whom they never leave, Loyal Heart lived alone, having no fixed habitation.

Always reserved and melancholy, he avoided the society of his equals, though always ready to render them services, or even to expose his life for them. Then, when they attempted to express their gratitude, he would clap spurs to his horse, and go and set his traps at a distance.

Every year, at the same period, that is to say, about the month of October, Loyal Heart disappeared for several weeks, without any one being able to suspect whither he was gone; and when he returned it was observed that for several days his countenance was more sad than ever.

One day he came back from one of these mysterious expeditions, accompanied by two magnificent young bloodhounds, which had from that time remained with him, and of which he seemed very fond.

Five years before the period at which we resume our narrative, he suddenly perceived the fire of an Indian camp through the trees.

A white youth, scarcely seventeen years of age, was fastened to a stake, and served as mark for the knives of the redskins, who amused themselves with torturing him before they sacrificed him to their sanguinary rage.

Loyal Heart rushed in among the Indians, and placed himself in front of the prisoner, for whom he made a rampart of his body.

These Indians were Comanches. Astonished by this sudden irruption, they remained a few instants motionless, confounded by so much audacity.

Without losing a moment, Loyal Heart cut the bonds of the prisoner, and giving him a knife, they both prepared to sell their lives dearly.

White men inspire Indians with an instinctive terror; the Comanches, however, on recovering from their surprise, showed signs of rushing forward to attack the two men.

But the light of the fire, which fell full upon the face of the hunter, had allowed some of them to recognize him. The redskins drew back with respect.

'Loyal Heart! the great pale-face hunter!'

Eagle Head, for so was the chief of these Indians named, did not know the hunter; it was the first time he had descended into the plains of, the Arkansas, and he could not comprehend the exclamation of his warriors; besides, he cordially detested the pale faces. Enraged at what he considered cowardice on the part of those he commmanded, he advanced alone against Loyal Heart, but then an extraordinary occurrence took place.

The Comanches threw themselves upon their chief, and notwithstanding the respect in which they held him, disarmed him.

Loyal Heart, after thanking them, himself restored his arms to the chief, who received them coldly, casting a sinister glance at his generous adversary.

The hunter, perceiving this feeling, shrugged his shoulders disdainfully, and departed with the prisoner.

Loyal Heart had, in less than ten minutes, made for himself an implacable enemy and a devoted friend.

The history of the prisoner was simple.

Having left Canada with his father, for the purpose of hunting, they had fallen into the hands of the Comanches; after a desperate resistance, his father had fallen covered with wounds. The Indians, irritated at a death which robbed them of a victim, had bestowed the greatest care upon the young man, in order that he might figure at the stake of punishment, and this would inevitably have happened had it not been for the providential intervention of Loyal Heart.

After having heard these particulars, the hunter asked the young man what his intentions were, and whether the rough apprenticeship he had gone through as a wood-ranger had not disgusted him.

'No!' the other replied; 'on the contrary, I feel more determined than ever to follow this career; and, besides, I wish to avenge my father.'

'Quite right,' the hunter observed.

The conversation broke off at this point.

Loyal Heart, having taken the young man to one of his *cachés* (a sort of magazine dug in the earth, in which trappers conceal their wealth), produced the complete equipment of a trapper—gun, knife, pistols, game bags, and traps—and then said, 'Go! and God speed you!'

The other looked at him without replying; he evidently did not understand him.

'You are free,' resumed Loyal Heart; 'here are all the objects necessary for your new trade—I give them to you, the desert is before you. Go.'

The young man shook his head.

'No,' he said, 'I will not leave you unless you drive me from you; I am alone, without family or friends; you have saved my life, and I belong to you.'

'It is not my custom to receive payment for the services I render,' said the hunter.

'You require to be paid for them too dearly,' the other answered warmly, 'since you refused to accept of gratitude. Take back your gifts, they are of no use to me; I am not a mendicant to whom alms can be thrown; I prefer going back and delivering myself up again to the Comanches—adieu!'

And the Canadian resolutely walked away.

Loyal Heart was deeply moved. This young man had so frank, so honest, and so spirited an air, that he felt something in his breast speak strongly in his favor.

'Stop!' he said.

And the other stopped.

'I live alone,' the hunter continued, 'a great grief consumes me; why should you attach yourself to unhappy me?'

'To share your grief, if you think me worthy, and to console you, if that be possible; when man is left alone, he runs the risk of falling into despair; God has ordained that he should seek companions.'

'That is true,' the still undecided hunter murmured.

'Why do you pause?' the young man asked.

Loyal Heart gazed at him for a moment attentively; his eagle eye seemed to seek to penetrate his most secret thoughts; then, doubtless satisfied with his examination, he asked,

'What is your name?'

'Belhumeur,' the other replied; 'or, if you prefer it, George Talbot; but I am generally known by the first name.'

The hunter smiled.

'That is a promising name,' he said, holding out his hand. 'Belhumeur,' he added, 'from this time you are my brother.'

He kissed him above the eyes, as is the custom in the prairies in similar circumstances.

'For life and death,' the Canadian replied.

And this was the way in which Loyal Heart and Belhumeur had become known to each other. During five years not a shadow of a cloud had darkened the friendship which these two superior natures had sworn to each other in the desert. On the contrary, every day seemed to increase it; they had but one heart between them. Completely relying on each other, divining each other's most secret thoughts, these two men had seen their strength augment tenfold, and such was their reciprocal confidence that they doubted nothing, and undertook and carried out the most daring expeditions.

Everything succeeded with them, nothing appeared impossible. It might be said that a charm protected them, and rendered them invulnerable.

Their reputation was thus spread far and near, and those whom their name did not strike with admiration repeated it with terror.

On the day we met them in the prairie, they had been the victims of an audacious robbery, committed by their ancient enemy Eagle

Head, the Comanche chief, whose hatred, instead of being weakened by time, had, on the contrary, only increased.

The Indian, with the characteristic deceit of his race, had dissembled, and devoured in silence the affront he had undergone from his people, and of which the two pale-faced hunters were the direct cause, and awaited patiently the hour of vengeance. He had quietly dug a pit under the feet of his enemies, by prejudicing the redskins by degrees against them, and adroitly spreading calumnies about them. Thanks to this system, he had at length succeeded, or, at least, he thought he had, in making all the individuals dispersed over the prairies, even the white and half-breed hunters, consider these two men as their enemies.

As soon as this result had been obtained, Eagle Head placed himself at the head of thirty warriors; and, anxious to bring about a quarrel that might ruin the men whose death he had sworn to accomplish, he had in one night stolen all their traps, certain that they would not leave such an insult unpunished.

The chief was not deceived in his calculations; all had fallen out just as he had foreseen it would.

In this position he awaited his enemies.

Thinking that they would find no assistance among the Indians or hunters, he flattered himself that with the thirty men he commanded he could easily seize the two hunters, whom he proposed to put to death.

But he had committed the fault of concealing the number of his warriors, in order to inspire more confidence in the hunters.

The latter had only partially been the dupes of this stratagem. Considering themselves sufficiently strong to contend even with twenty Indians, they had claimed the assistance of no one to avenge themselves upon enemies they despised, and had, as we have seen, set out resolutely in pursuit of the Comanches.

THE TRAIL

EAGLE HEAD had not taken any pains to conceal his trail.

It was perfectly visible in the high grass, and if now and then it appeared to be effaced, the hunters had but to turn to one side or the other to regain it.

Never before had a foe been pursued on the prairies in such a fashion. It must have appeared the more singular to Loyal Heart, who, for a long time, had been acquainted with the cunning of the Indians, and knew with what skill, when they judged it necessary, they caused every indication of their passage to disappear.

This facility gave him cause to reflect. As the Comanches had taken no more pains to conceal their track, they must either believe themselves very strong, or else they had prepared an ambush.

The two hunters rode on, casting, from time to time, a look right and left, in order to be sure they were not deceived; but the track still continued in a straight line. It was impossible to meet with greater facilities in a pursuit. Belhumeur himself began to think this very extraordinary.

But if the Comanches had been unwilling to take the pains of concealing their trail, the hunters did not follow their example; they did not advance a step without effacing the trace of their passage.

They arrived thus on the banks of a tolerably broad rivulet, name the Verdigris.

Before crossing this little stream, on the other side of which the hunters would no longer be very far from the Indians, Loyal Heart stopped.

Both dismounted, and sought the shelter of a clump of trees, in order not to be perceived, if some Indian sentinel should be set to watch their approach.

When they were concealed in the thickness of the wood, Loyal

Heart placed a finger on his lip to recommend prudence to his companion, and, approaching his lips to his ear, he said, in a voice low as a breath—

'Before we go any farther, let us consult.'

Belhumeur bent his head in sign of acquiescence.

'I suspect some treachery,' the hunter resumed; 'Indians are too experienced warriors to act in this way without an imperative reason.'

'That is true,' the Canadian replied; 'this trail is too good not to conceal a snare.'

'Yes, but they have been too cunning; their craft has overshot the mark; old hunters, like us, are not to be deceived. We must redouble our prudence, and examine every leaf and blade of grass with care, before we venture nearer the encampment of the redskins.'

'Let us do better,' said Belhumeur; 'let us conceal our horses in a safe place, where we can find them at need, and then reconnoitre on foot the position and the number of our foe.'

'You are right, Belhumeur,' said Loyal Heart; 'your counsel is excellent, we will put it in practice.'

'I think we had better make haste in that case.'

'Why so? On the contrary, do not let us hurry; the Indians, not seeing us appear, will relax in their watchfulness, and we can profit by their negligence to attack them, if we should be forced to have recourse to such extreme measures; besides, it would be better to wait for the night before we commence our expedition.'

'In the first place, let us put our horses in safety.

The hunters left their concealment with the greatest precaution. Instead of crossing the river, they retraced their steps, and then bent a little to the left, and entered a ravine, in which they quickly disappeared among the high grass.

'I leave you to be guide,' said Loyal Heart, 'I really do not know whither you are leading me!'

261

'Leave it to me. I have by chance discovered, within two gunshots of this place, a sort of citadel, where our horses will be safe, and in which, if it should so fall out, we should be able to sustain a regular siege.'

'*Caramba!*' the hunter exclaimed, who, by this oath, which was habitual with him, betrayed his Spanish origin, 'how did you make this precious discovery?'

'Faith!' said Belhumeur, 'in the simplest manner. I had just laid my traps, when, in climbing up the mountain before us in order to shorten my road, at nearly two-thirds of the ascent, I saw, protruding from the bushes the velvety muzzle of a superb bear.'

'Ah! ah! I am pretty well acquainted with that adventure. You brought me that day, if I am not mistaken, not one, but two black bearskins.'

'That is a fact; my fine fellows were two, one male and the other female. You may easily suppose that at the sight of them my hunter's instincts were aroused; forgetful of my fatigue, I cocked my rifle, and set out in pursuit. You will see for yourself what sort of a fortress they had chosen,' he added, as he alighted from his horse.

Before them rose, in the shape of an amphitheater, a mass of rocks, which assumed the most curious and fantastic shapes; thin bushes sprang here and there from the interstices of the stones, climbing plants crowned the summits of the rocks, and gave to this mass, which rose more than six hundred feet above the prairie, the appearance of one of those ancient feudal ruins which are to be met with occasionally on the banks of the great rivers of Europe.

This place was named the White Castle, from the color of the blocks of granite which formed it.

'We shall never be able to get up there with our horses,' said Loyal Heart.

'Let us try, at all events!' said Belhumeur, pulling his horse by the bridle.

The ascent was rough, and any other horses than those of hunters, accustomed to the most difficult roads, would have been unable to accomplish it.

It was necessary to choose with care the spot on which the foot must be placed, and then to spring forward at a bound.

After half an hour of extraordinary difficulties they arrived at a sort of platform, ten yards broad at most.

'Here we are!' said Belhumeur, stopping.

'How here?' Loyal Heart replied, looking around on all sides without perceiving any opening.

'Come this way!' said Belhumeur, smiling.

And dragging his horse after him, he passed behind a block of the rock, the hunter following him.

After walking for five minutes in a sort of trench, at most three feet wide, which seemed to wind round upon itself, the adventurers found themselves suddenly before the yawning mouth of a deep cavern.

This path, formed by one of those convulsions of nature so frequent in these regions, was so well concealed behind the rocks which masked it, that it was impossible to discover it except by chance.

The hunters entered.

Before ascending the mountain, Belhumeur had collected a large provision of candle-wood; he lit two torches, one for himself, and one for his companion.

Then the grotto appeared to them in all its wild majesty.

Its walls were high and covered with brilliant stalactites, which reflected back the light, multiplying it, and forming a fairy-like illumination.

'This cavern,' said Belhumeur, after he had given his friend time to examine it, 'is, I have no doubt, one of the wonders of the prairies; this gallery, which descends in a gentle declivity before us, passes under the Verdigris, and debouches on the other side of the river, at a distance of more than a mile, into the plain. In addition to the gallery by which we entered, and that which is before us, there exist four others, all of which have issues at different places. You see that here we are in no risk of being surrounded.'

Loyal Heart, enchanted with the discovery of this refuge, wished to examine it perfectly, and although he was naturally very silent, the hunter could not always withhold his admiration.

'Why have you never told me of this place before?' he said to Belhumeur.

'I waited for the opportunity,' the latter replied.

The hunters secured their horses, with abundance of provender, in one of the compartments of the grotto, into which the light penetrated by imperceptible fissures; and then, when they were satisfied that the noble animals could want for nothing during their absence, and could not escape, they threw their rifles over their shoulders, whistled to their dogs, and, descended with hasty steps the gallery which passed under the river.

Soon the air became moist around them, a dull, continuous noise was heard above their heads—they were passing under the Verdigris. Thanks to a species of lantern, formed by a hollow rock rising in the middle of the river's course, there was light sufficient to guide them.

After half an hour's walk they debouched in the prairie by an entrance masked by bushes and plants.

They had remained a long time in the grotto. In the first place, they had examined it minutely, like men who foresaw that some day or other they should stand in need of seeking a shelter there; next, they had made a kind of stable for their horses; and lastly, they had snatched a hasty morsel of food, so that the sun was on the point of setting at the moment when they set off.

Then commenced the true Indian pursuit. The two hunters, after having put their bloodhounds on the trail, glided silently in their traces, creeping on their hands and knees through the high grass, the eye on the watch, the ear on the listen, holding their breath, and stopping at intervals to inhale the air, and interrogate those thousand sounds of the prairies which hunters notice with incredible facility.

The desert was plunged in a death-like silence.

At the approach of night in these immense solitudes, nature seems to reflect, and prepare, by religious devotion, for the mysteries of darkness.

All at once the dogs came silently to a stop. The brave animals seemed to comprehend the value of silence in these parts, and that a single cry would cost their masters their lives.

Belhumeur cast a piercing glance around him. His eye flashed, he gathered himself up, and bounding like a panther, he sprang upon an Indian warrior, who, with his body bent forward, and his head down, seemed to know of the approach of an enemy.

The Indian was thrown upon his back, and before he could utter a cry Belhumeur had his throat in his grasp and his knee on his breast.

Then, with the greatest coolness, the hunter unsheathed his knife, and plunged it up to the hilt in the heart of his enemy.

When the savage knew that he was lost, he disdained to attempt any resistance, but fixing upon the Canadian a look of hatred and contempt, an ironical smile curled his lips, and he awaited death with a calm face.

Belhumeur replaced his knife in his belt, and pushing the body on one side, said imperturbably—

'One!'

And he crept on again.

Loyal Heart had watched the movements of his friend with the greatest attention, ready to succor him if it were necessary; when the Indian was dead, he calmly took up the trail again.

Ere long the light of a fire gleamed between the trees, and an odor of roasted meat struck the keen smell of the hunters.

They drew themselves up like two phantoms along an enormous live oak tree, which was within a few paces of them, and embracing the gnarled trunk, concealed themselves among the tufted branches.

Then they found that they were soaring over the camp of the Comanches.

THE TRAVELERS

ABOUT the same hour a rather large party of white travelers halted upon the banks of the great Canadian river and prepared to encamp for the night in a magnificent position.

The hunters and Gambusinos who served as guides to the travellers hastened to unload a dozen mules.

With the bales they made an enclosure of an oval form, in the interior of which they lit a fire; then, without troubling themselves any further about their companions, the guides united together in a little group and prepared their evening repast.

A young officer, about twenty-five years of age, of martial bearing, with delicately-marked features, went up respectfully to a palanquin drawn by two mules and escorted by two horsemen.

'In what place would you wish, senor, the senorita's tent to be pitched?' the young officer asked.

'Where you please, Captain Aguilar, provided it be quickly done; my niece is sinking with fatigue,' the cavalier replied.

He was a man of lofty stature, with hard marked features, and an eagle eye, whose hair was as white as snow, and who, under the large military cloak which he wore, allowed glimpses to appear of the splendid uniform of a Mexican general.

The captain retired, with another bow, and returning to the lanceros, he gave them orders to set up in the middle of the camp-enclosure, a pretty tent, striped rose-color and blue, which was carried across the back of a mule.

Five minutes later, the general offered his hand gallantly to a young female, who sprang lightly from the palanquin, and conducted her to the tent.

Behind the general and his niece, two other persons entered the tent.

One was short and stout with a full, rosy face, green spectacles, and a light-colored wig, who appeared to be choking in the uniform of an army surgeon.

This personage, whose age appeared to be about fifty, was named Jérome Durieux; he was a Frenchman, and a surgeon in the Mexican service.

On alighting from his horse, he had seized and placed under his arm, with every appearance of respect, a large valise fastened to the hinder part of his saddle, and from which he seemed unwilling to part.

The second person was a girl of about fifteen years of age, of a forward and lively mien, with a turn-up nose and a bold look, belonging to the half-breed race, who served as lady's maid to the general's niece.

A superb negro, decorated with the majestic name of Jupiter, hastened, aided by two or three Gambusinos, to prepare the supper.

'Well! doctor,' said the general, smiling, to the fat man, who came in puffing like a bullock, 'how do you find my niece this evening?'

'The senorita is always charming!' the doctor replied gallantly, as he wiped his brow. 'Do you not find the heat very oppressive?'

'Faith! no,' replied the general, 'not more so than usual.'

'Well, it appears so to me!' said the doctor with a sigh. 'What are you laughing at, you little witch?' added he, turning towards the waiting maid.

'Pay no attention to her, doctor; you know she is but a spoilt child,' the young lady said.

'I have always told you, Dona Luz,' persisted the doctor, knitting his large eyebrows, and puffing out his cheeks, 'that that little girl is a demon, to whom you are much too kind, and who will end by playing you an evil turn some of these days.'

'Oh! the wicked picker up of pebbles!' the girl said with a grin, in allusion to the doctor's mania.

'Come, come, peace!' said the general; 'has today's journey fatigued you much, my dear niece?'

'Not exceedingly,' the young lady replied; 'during nearly a month that we have been travelling I have become accustomed to this sort of life, which, I confess, at first I found painful enough.'

The general sighed, but made no reply. The doctor was absorbed by the care with which he was classifying the plants and stones which he had collected.

The half-breed girl flew about the tent like a bird, occupied in putting everything in order that her mistress might want.

We will take advantage of this moment of respite to sketch the portrait of the young lady.

Dona Luz de Bermudez was the daughter of a younger sister of the general.

She was a charming girl of sixteen at most. Her large black eyes, surmounted by eyebrows whose deep color contrasted finely with the whiteness of her fair, pure forehead, were veiled by long velvety lashes, which modestly concealed their splendor; her little mouth was set off by teeth of pearl, edged by lips of coral; her delicate skin wore the down of the ripe peach, and her blue-black hair, when liberated from its bands, formed a veil for her whole person.

Her form was slender and supple, with all the curves of the true line of beauty. She possessed, in an eminent degree, that undulating, gracefully serpentine movement which distinguishes American women; her hands and feet were extremely small, and her step had the careless voluptuousness of the creole, so full of ever-varying attractions.

In short, in the person of this young lady might be said to be combined all the graces and perfections.

Ignorant as most of her compatriots, she was gay and cheerful; amused with the smallest trifle, and knowing nothing of life but the agreeable side.

But this beautiful statue was not animated; it was Pandora before Prometheus had stolen for her fire from heaven; Love had not yet brushed her with his wing, her brow had not yet been contracted by the pressure of thought, her heart had not yet beaten under the influence of passion.

Brought up under the care of the general in the utmost seclusion, she had only quitted it to accompany him in a journey he had undertaken through the prairies.

What was the object of this journey, and why had her uncle so positively insisted upon her making it with him? She knew not.

At the period when we met her, then, Dona Luz was a happy girl, living from day to day, satisfied with the present, and thinking nothing of the future.

Captain Aguilar entered, preceding Jupiter, who brought in the dinner.

The table was laid by Phoebe, the waiting maid.

The repast consisted of preserved meats and a joint of roast venison.

Four persons took their places round the table; the general, his niece, the captain, and the doctor.

Jupiter and Phoebe waited.

Conversation languished at first; but when the appetite of the party was a little abated, the young girl, who delighted in teasing the doctor, said—

'Have you made a rich harvest today, doctor?

'Not too rich, senorita,' he replied.

'Well! but,' she said, laughing, 'there appears to me to be such a lot of stones about, that it only rested with yourself to gather enough to load a mule.'

'You ought to be pleased with your journey,' said the general, 'for it offers you such an opportunity for indulging in your passion for plants of all sorts.'

'Not too great, general, I must confess; the prairie is not so rich as I thought it was; and if it were not for the hope I entertain of discovering one plant, whose qualities may advance science, I should almost regret my little house at Guadeloupe.'

'Bah!' the captain interrupted, 'we are as yet only on the edge of the prairies. You will find, when we have penetrated further, that you will not be able to gather the riches which will spring from under your feet.'

'God grant it may be so,' said the doctor; 'provided I find the plant I seek I shall be satisfied.'

'Is it then such a very valuable plant?' asked Dona Luz.

'What senorita!' cried the doctor, warming with the question. 'A plant which Linnaeus has described and classified, and which no one has since found! a plant that would make my reputation! And you ask me if it is valuable?'

'Of what use is it, then?' the young lady asked.

'None at all, that I am aware of,' the doctor replied ingenuously.

Dona Luz broke into a silvery laugh, whose pearly notes might have made a nightingale jealous.

'And you call it a valuable plant?'

'Yes—if only for its rarity.'

'Ah! that's all.'

'Let us hope you will find it, doctor,' said the general in a conciliatory tone. 'Jupiter, call the chief of the guides hither.'

The negro left the tent, and almost immediately returned, followed by a Gambusino.

The latter was a man of about forty, tall in stature, square-built and muscular. His countenance, though not exactly ugly, had something repulsive in it for which the spectator was at a loss to account; his wild, sinister-looking eyes, buried under their orbits, cast a savage light, which with his low brow, his curly hair, and his coppery complexion, made altogether a not very agreeable whole. He wore the costume of a wood-ranger; he was cold, impassible, of a nature essentially taciturn, and answered to the name of *the Babbler*, which, no doubt, the Indians or his companions had given him by antiphrasis.

'Here, my good fellow,' said the general, handing him a glass filled to the brim with a sort of brandy, called mescal, from the name of the place where it is distilled, 'drink this.'

The hunter bowed, emptied the glass, which contained about a pint, at a draught; then, passing his cuff across his moustache, waited.

'I wish,' said the general, 'to halt for a few days, in some safe position, in order to make certain researches; shall we be secure here?'

'No,' he replied, laconically.

'Why not?'

'Too many Indians and wild beasts.'

'Do you know one more suitable?'

'Yes; about forty miles off.'

'How long will it take us to arrive there?'

'Three days.'

'That will do. Conduct us thither. Tomorrow, at sunrise, we will set forward in our march.'

'Is that all?'

'That is all.'

'Good night.'

And the hunter withdrew.

'What I admire in the Babbler,' said the captain, with a smile, 'is that his conversation never tires you.'

'I should like it much better if he spoke more,' said the doctor, shaking his head. 'I always suspect people who are so afraid of saying too much; they generally have something to conceal.'

The guide, after leaving the tent, joined his companions, with whom he began to talk in a low voice, but in a very animated manner.

The night was magnificent; the travellers, assembled in front of the tent, were chatting together, and smoking their cigars.

Dona Luz was singing one of those charming creole songs, which are so full of sweet melody and expression.

All at once a red-tinted light appeared in the horizon, increasing every instant, and a dull continuous noise, like the growling of distant thunder, was heard.

'What is that?' the general cried, rising hastily.

'The prairie is on fire,' the Babbler replied, quietly.

At this terrible announcement, made so quietly, the camp was all in confusion.

It was necessary to fly instantly, if they did not choose to run the risk of being burnt alive.

One of the Gambusinos, taking advantage of the disorder, glided away among the baggage, and disappeared in the plain, after exchanging a mysterious signal with the Babbler.

THE COMANCHES

THE two hunters, concealed among the branches of the cork tree, were observing the Comanches.

The Indians depended upon the vigilance of their sentinels. Not suspecting their enemies were so near them, and were watching them, they crouched or lay around the fires, eating or smoking carelessly.

These savages, to the number of twenty-five, were dressed in their buffalo robes, and painted in the most varied and fantastic manner. Most of them had their faces covered with vermilion, others were entirely black, with a long white stripe upon each check; they wore their bucklers on their backs, with their bows and arrows, and near them lay their guns.

By the number of wolves' tails fastened to their mocassins, and which dragged on the ground, it was easy to perceive that they were all picked warriors.

At some paces from the group, Eagle Head leant motionless against a tree. With his arms crossed on his breast, and leaning gently forward, he seemed to be listening to to vague sounds.

Eagle Head was an Osage Indian; the Comanches had adopted him when quite young, but he had always preserved the costume and manners of his nation.

He was, at most, twenty-eight years of age, nearly six feet high, and his large limbs, upon which enormous muscles developed themselves, denoted extraordinary strength.

Differing in this respect from his companions, he only wore a blanket fastened round his loins, so as to leave his bust and his arms bare. The expresion of his countenance was handsome and noble; his black, animated eyes, close to his aquiline nose, and his somewhat large mouth, gave him a faint resemblance to a bird of prey. His hair was shaved off, with the exception of a tuft upon the middle of his head, which produced the effect of the crest of a helmet, and a long scalp-lock, in which was fixed a bunch of eagle's feathers, hung down behind him.

His face was painted of four different colors—blue, white, black, and red; the wounds inflicted by him upon his enemies were marked in blue upon his naked breast. Mocassins of untanned deerskin came up above his knees, and numerous wolves' tails were fastened to his heels.

Fortunately for the hunters, the Indians were on the war-path, and had no dogs with them; but for this, they would have been discovered long before, and could not possibly have approached so near the camp.

In spite of his statue-like immobility, the eye of the chief sparkled, his nostrils dilated, and he lifted his right arm mechanically, as if to impose silence upon his warriors.

'We are discovered,' Loyal Heart murmured.

'What is to be done?' Belhumeur replied.

'Act,' said the trapper, laconically.

Both then glided silently from branch to branch, from tree to tree, till they reached the opposite side of the camp, just above the place where the horses of the Comanches were hobbled to graze.

Belhumeur alighted softly, and cut the thongs that held them; the horses, excited by the whips of the hunters, rushed out, neighing and kicking.

The Indians rose in disorder, and hastened, with loud cries, in pursuit of their horses.

Eagle Head alone, as if he had guessed the spot where his enemies were in ambush, directed his steps straight towards them, screening himself as much as possible behind the trees which he passed.

The hunters drew back, looking carefully around, so as not to allow themselves to be encompassed.

The cries of the Indians grew fainter in the distance; they were all in eager pursuit of their horses.

The chief found himself alone in presence of his two enemies.

On arriving at a tree whose enormous trunk appeared to guarantee the desired safety, disdaining to use his gun, and the opportunity seeming favourable, he adjusted an arrow to his bow-string. But whatever might be his prudence and address, he could not make this movement without discovering himself a little. Loyal Heart raised his gun, the trigger was pressed, the ball whizzed, and the chief bounded into the air, uttering a howl of rage, and fell upon the ground.

His arm was broken.

The two hunters were already by his side.

'Not a movement, redskin,' Loyal Heart said to him; 'not a movement, or you are a dead man!'

The Indian remained motionless, apparently stoical.

'I could kill you,' the hunter continued; 'but I will not do so. This is the second time I have given you your life, chief, but it will be the last. Cross my path no more, and, remember, do not steal my traps again.'

'Eagle Head is a chief among the men of his tribe,' the Indian replied; 'he does not fear death; the white hunter may kill him, he will not complain.'

'No, I will not kill you, chief; my God forbids the shedding of human blood unnecessarily.'

'Wah!' said the Indian, with an ironical smile, 'my brother is a missionary.'

'No, I am an honest trapper, and do not wish to be an assassin.'

'My brother speaks the words of old women,' the Indian continued; 'Nehu mutah never pardons.'

'You will do as you please, chief,' the hunter replied; 'I have no intention of trying to change your nature; only remember you are warned—farewell!'

'And the devil take you?' Belhumeur added, giving him a contemptuous shove with his foot.

The chief appeared insensible even to this fresh insult, save that his brows contracted slightly. He did not stir, but followed his enemies with an implacable look, while they, without troubling themselves further about him, plunged into the forest.

'You may say what you like, Loyal Heart,' said Belhumeur, 'you ought to have killed·him.'

'Bah! what for?' the hunter asked, carelessly.

'*Cascaras!* what for? Why, there would have been one head of vermin the less in the prairie.'

'Where there are so many,' said the other, 'one more or less cannot signify.'

'Humph! that's true!' Belhumeur replied, apparently convinced; 'but where are we going now?'

'To look after our traps, *caramba!* Do you think I will lose them?'

'Humph! that's a good thought.'

The hunters advanced in the direction of the camp in the Indian fashion. After progressing in this way for twenty minutes, they arrived at the camp. The Indians had not yet returned; but in all probability, it would not be long before they did so. All their baggage was scattered. Two or three horses, which had not felt disposed to run away, were browsing quietly on the peavines.

Without losing time, the hunters set about collecting their traps, which was soon done. Each loaded himself with five, and, without further delay, they resumed the way to the cavern.

Notwithstanding the tolerably heavy weight they carried on their shoulders, the two men marched lightly, much pleased at having so happily terminated their expedition.

They had gone on thus for some time, and could already hear the murmur of the waters of the river, when the neighing of a horse struck their ears.

'We are pursued,' said Loyal Heart, stopping.

'Hum!' Belhumeur remarked, 'it is, perhaps, a wild horse.'

'No; a wild horse does not neigh in that manner; it is the Comanches; but we can soon know,' he added, as he threw himself down to listen.

'I was sure of it,' he said; 'it is the Comanches; but they are not following a true trail—they are hesitating.'

'Or perhaps their march is retarded by the wound of Eagle Head.'

'That's possible! Oh! oh! do they fancy themselves capable of catching us, if we wished to escape from them?'

'Ah! if we were not loaded, that would soon be done.'

Loyal Heart reflected a minute.

'Come,' he said, 'we have still half an hour, and that is more than we want.'

A rivulet flowed at a short distance from them; the hunter entered its bed with his companion, who followed all his movements.

When he reached the middle of the stream, Loyal Heart carefully wrapped up the traps in a buffalo skin, that no moisture might come to them, and then he allowed them quietly to drop to the bottom of the stream.

This precaution taken, the hunters crossed the rivulet, and made a false trail of about two hundred paces, and afterwards returned cautiously so as not to leave a print that might betray their return. They then re-entered the forest, after having, with a gesture, sent the dogs back. The intelligent animals obeyed, and disappeared.

This resolution to send away the dogs was useful in assisting to throw the Indians off the track, for they could scarcely miss following the traces left by the bloodhounds in the high grass.

Once in the forest, the hunters again climbed up a tree, and began to advance between heaven and earth—a mode of travelling much more frequently used than is believed in Europe, in this country where it is often impossible, on account of the underwood and the trees, to advance without employing an axe to clear a passage.

They advanced in this fashion before their enemies, who drew nearer and nearer, and they soon perceived them under them, marching in Indian file, that is to say, one behind another.

Eagle Head came first, half lying upon his horse, on account of his wound.

When the Comanches passed them, the two trappers gathered themselves up among the leaves, holding their breath. The most trifling circumstance would have sufficed to proclaim their presence.

The Indians passed without seeing them. The hunters resumed their leafy march.

'Ouf!' said Belhumeur, at the end of a minute. 'I think we have got rid of them this time!'

'Do not haloo before you are out of the wood; these demons of red-skins are cunning, they will not long be the dupes of our stratagem.'

'*Sacrebleu!*' the Canadian suddenly exclaimed, 'I have let my knife fall, I don't know where; if these devils find it, we are lost.'

'Most likely,' Loyal Heart murmured; 'the greater reason then for not losing a single minute.'

In the meantime, the forest, which till then had been calm, began all at once to grow excited, the birds flew about uttering cries of terror, and in the thick underwood they could hear the dry branches crack.

'What's going on now?' said Loyal Heart. 'The forest appears to be turned topsy-turvey!'

The hunters sprang up to the top of the tree in which they were, and which happened to be one of the loftiest in the forest.

An immense light tinged the horizon at about a league from the spot. This light increased every minute, and advanced with giant strides.

'Curses on them!' cried Belhumeur, 'the Comanches have fired the prairie.'

'Yes, and I believe this time that, as you said just now, we are lost,' Loyal Heart replied, coolly.

'What's to be done?' said the Canadian; 'in an instant we shall be surrounded.'

Loyal Heart reflected seriously.

At the end of a few seconds he raised his head, and a smile of triumph curled the corners of his mouth.

'They have not got us yet,' he replied; 'follow me, my brother.'

THE PRESERVER

SCARCE had his enemies disappeared among the trees, ere Eagle Head raised himself, bent his body forward, and listened to ascertain if they were really departing. As soon as he had acquired that certainty, he tore off a morsel of his blanket, with which he wrapped up his arm as well as he could, and in spite of the weakness produced by loss of blood, set off resolutely on the trail of the hunters.

He accompanied them, himself unseen, to the limits of the camp. There, concealed behind an ebony tree, he witnessed, without being able to prevent it, the search made by the hunters for their traps, and, at length, their departure after recovering them.

Although the bloodhounds were excellent dogs, trained to scent an Indian from a distance, by a providential chance, which probably saved the life of the Comanche chief, they had fallen upon the remains of the repast of the redskins, and their masters, not dreaming that they were watched, did not think of commanding their vigilance.

The Comanches at length regained their camp, after catching their horses.

The sight of their wounded chief caused them great surprise, and still greater anger, of which Eagle Head took advantage to send them all off again in pursuit of the hunters, who, retarded by the traps they carried, could not be far off.

They had been but for an instant the dupes of the stratagem invented by Loyal Heart, and had not been long in recognizing traces of the passage of their enemies.

At this moment Eagle Head, ashamed of being thus held in check by two determined men, whose cunning deceived all his calculation, resolved to put an end to them at once, by carrying into execution the diabolical project of setting fire to the forest.

In consequence, dispersing his warriors in various directions, so as to form a vast circle, he ordered the high grass to be set on fire in various places simultaneously.

The idea, though barbarous and worthy of the savage warriors who employed it, was a good one. The hunters, after having vainly endeavoured to escape from the network of flame which encompassed them on all sides, would be obliged, in spite of themselves, to surrender quietly to their ferocious enemies.

Eagle Head had calculated and foreseen everything, except the most easy and most simple thing, the only chance of safety that would be left to Loyal Heart and his companion.

As we have said, at the command of their chief the warriors had dispersed, and had lighted the conflagration at several points simultaneously.

At this advanced season of the year the plants and grass, parched by the incandescent rays of the summer's sun, were immediately in a blaze, and the fire extended in all directions with frightful rapidity.

Not, however, so quickly as not to allow a certain time to elapse before it united.

Loyal Heart had not hesitated. Whilst the Indians were running like demons around the barrier of flame they had just opposed to their enemies, and were uttering yells of joy, the hunter, followed by his friend, had rushed at full speed between two walls of fire, which from right and left advanced upon him, hissing, and threatening to unite at once above his head and beneath his feet. Amidst calcined trees which fell with a crash, blinded by clouds of thick smoke which stopped their respiration, burnt by showers of sparks which poured upon them from all parts, following boldly their course beneath a vault of flame, the intrepid adventurers had cleared, at the cost of a few trifling burns, the accursed enclosure in which the Indians had thought to bury them for ever, and were already far from the enemies who were congratulating themselves upon the success of their artful and barbarous plan.

The conflagration, meantime, assumed formidable proportions; the forest shrivelled up under the fire; the prairie was but one sheet of flame, in the midst of which wild animals, driven from their dens and lairs by this unexpected catastrophe, ran about, mad with terror.

The sky gleamed with blood-red reflections, and an impetuous wind swept before it both flames and smoke.

The Indians were terrified at their own handiwork, on seeing around them entire mountains lighted up like beacons; the earth became hot, and immense herds of buffaloes made the ground tremble in their furious course, while they uttered those bellowings which fill with terror the hearts of the bravest men.

In the camp of the Mexicans everything was in the greatest disorder; all was noise and frightful confusion. The horses had broken away, and fled in all directions; the men seized their arms and ammunition; others carried the saddles and packages.

Every one was screaming, swearing, commanding—all were running about the camp as if they had been struck with madness.

The fire continued to advance, swallowing up everything in its passage, preceded by a countless number of animals of all kinds, who bounded along with howls of fear, pursued by the scourge.

A thick smoke, laden with sparks, was already passing over the camp of the Mexicans; twenty minutes more and all would be over with them.

The general, pressing his niece in his arms, in vain demanded of the guides the best means of avoiding the immense peril which threatened them.

But these men, terrified by the imminence of the peril, had lost all self-possession. And then what remedy could be employed?

The strong breeze, however, which up to that moment had kept alive the conflagration, by lending it wings, sank all at once.

There was not a breath of air. The progress of the fire slackened.

Providence granted these unhappy creatures a few minutes more. At this moment the camp presented a strange aspect.

All the men, struck with terror, had lost the sense even of self-preservation.

The *lanceros* confessed to each other.

The guides were plunged in gloomy despair.

The general accused Heaven of his misfortune.

As for the doctor, he only regretted the plant he could not discover; with him every other consideration yielded to that.

Dona Luz, with her hands clasped, and her knees on the ground, was praying fervently.

The fire continued to approach, with its vanguard of wild beasts.

'Oh!' cried the general, shaking the arm of the guide violently, 'will you leave us to be burnt thus?'

'What can be done against the will of God?' the Babbler replied, stoically.

'Are there no means of escaping death?'

'None!'

'There is one!' a man cried, who, with a scorched face, and half-burnt hair, rushed forward, followed by another individual.

'Who are you?' the general exclaimed.

'That is of little consequence,' the stranger replied, drily; 'I come to save you! my companion and I were out of danger; to succor you we have braved unheard-of perils. Your safety is in your own hands; you have only to will it.'

'Command!' the general replied, 'I will be the first to give you the example of obedience.'

'Have you no guides with you, then?'

'Certainly we have,' said the general.

'Then they are traitors, for the means I am about to employ are known to everybody in the prairie.'

The general darted a glance of mistrust at the Babbler, who was not able to suppress an appearance of surprise at the sudden coming of the two strangers.

'Well,' said the hunter, 'that is an account you can settle with them hereafter; we have something else to think of now.'

The Mexicans, at the sight of this determined man, with his sharp impressive language, had instinctively recognized a preserver; they felt their courage revive with hope, and held themselves ready to execute his orders.

'Be quick!' said the hunter, 'and pull up all the grass that surrounds the camp.'

Every one set to work at once.

'For our part,' the stranger continued, addressing the general, 'we will take wetted blankets, and spread them in front of the baggage.'

The general, the captain, and the doctor, under the directions of the hunter, did as he desired, whilst his companion lassoed the horses and the mules.

'Be quick! be quick!' the hunter cried incessantly, 'the fire gains upon us!'

Every one redoubled his exertions, and in a short time a large space was cleared.

Dona Luz gazed with admiration at this stranger, who had suddenly appeared among them in such a providential manner, and who, amidst the horrible danger that enveloped them, was as calm and self-possessed as if he had had the power to command the awful scourge which continued to advance upon them with giant strides.

The maiden could not take her eyes off him; in spite of herself, she felt attracted towards this unknown preserver.

When the grass and herbs had been pulled up with that feverish rapidity which men in fear of death display in all they do, the hunter smiled calmly.

'Now,' he said, addressing the Mexicans, 'the rest concerns myself and my friend; leave us to act; wrap yourselves carefully in damp blankets.'

Every one followed his directions.

The stranger cast a glance around him, and then after making a sign to his friend, walked straight towards the fire.

'I shall not quit you,' the general said, earnestly.

'Come on, then,' the stranger replied, laconically.

When they reached the extremity of the space where the grass had been pulled up, the hunter piled up a heap of plants and dry wood with his feet, and scattering a little gunpowder over it, he set fire to the mass.

'What are you doing?' the general exclaimed.

'As you see, I make fire fight against fire,' the hunter replied, quietly.

His companion had acted in the same manner in an opposite direction.

A curtain of flames arose rapidly around them, and, for some minutes, the camp was almost concealed beneath a vault of fire.

A quarter of an hour of terrible anxiety and intense expectation ensued.

By degrees the flames became less fierce, the air more pure; the smoke dispersed, the roarings of the conflagration diminished.

At length they were able to recognize each other in this horrible chaos.

A sigh of relief burst from every breast.

The camp was saved!

The conflagration, whose roaring became gradually more dull, conquered by the hunter, went to convey destruction in other directions.

'You have saved the life of my niece,' said the general warmly: 'how shall I discharge my debt?'

'You owe me nothing, sir,' the hunter replied, with noble

simplicity; 'in the prairie all men are brothers; I have only performed my duty.'

As soon as the first moments of joy were passed, and the camp had been put in a little order, every one felt the necessity for repose.

The two strangers, who had constantly repulsed modestly, but firmly, the advances the general had made in the warmth of his gratitude, threw themselves carelessly on the baggage for a few hours' rest.

A little before dawn they arose.

'The earth must be cool by this time,' said the hunter: 'let us be gone before these people wake.'

'Let us be gone!' the other replied laconically.

At the moment he was about to pass out of the camp, a hand was laid lightly upon the shoulder of the elder. He turned, and Dona Luz was before him.

The two men stopped and bowed respectfully to the young lady.

'Are you going to leave us?' she asked in a soft and melodious voice.

'We must, senorita,' the hunter replied.

'I understand,' she said with a charming smile; 'now that, thanks to you, we are saved, you have nothing more to do here—is it not so?'

The two men bowed without replying.

'Grant me a favor,' she said.

'Name it, senorita.'

She took from her neck a little diamond cross.

'Keep this, in remembrance of me.'

The hunter hesitated.

'I beg you to do so,' she murmured in an agitated voice.

'I accept it, senorita,' the hunter said; 'I shall have another talisman to add to that which my mother gave me.'

'Thank you,' the girl replied joyfully; 'one word more.'

'Speak it, lady.'

'What are your names?'

'My companion is called Belhumeur.'

'But yourself?'

'Loyal Heart.'

And bowing a second time, in sign of farewell, the two hunters departed at a quick pace, and soon disappeared in the darkness.

Dona Luz looked after them as long as she could perceive them, and then returned slowly and pensively towards her tent, repeating to herself—

'Loyal Heart! Oh! I shall remember that name.'

THE SURPRISE

A FEW days after the events we have related in our preceding chapter, a strange scene was passing in a settlement built scarcely two years before, upon the banks of the great Canadian river, in a beautiful position at the foot of a verdant hill.

This settlement consisted of about a hundred cabins, grouped capriciously near each other, and protected by a little fort, armed with four small cannon which commanded the course of the river.

The village, though so young, had already, thanks to American activity, acquired all the importance of a city. Two taverns overflowed with tipplers, and three temples of different sects served to gather together the faithful.

The inhabitants moved about here and there with the preoccupation of people who work seriously and look sharply after their affairs.

Numerous canoes ploughed the river, and carts loaded with merchandise passed about in all directions.

Nevertheless, in spite of all this movement, it was easy to observe that a certain uneasiness prevailed.

The inhabitants questioned each other, groups were formed upon the steps of doors, and several men, mounted upon powerful horses, rode rapidly away, as scouts, in all directions. after taking their orders from the captain commanding the fort, who, dressed in uniform, with a telescope in his hand, was walking backwards and forwards with hasty steps, upon the glacis of the little fort.

By degrees, the canoes regained the shore, the carts were unteamed, the beasts of burden were collected in the home pastures, and the entire population assembled upon the square of the village.

The sun was sinking rapidly towards the horizon, night would soon be upon them, and the horsemen sent to the environs had all returned.

'You see,' said the captain, 'that we have nothing to fear, it was only a false alarm; you may return peaceably to your dwellings, no trace of Indians can be found for twenty miles round.'

'Hum!' said an old half-breed hunter, 'Indians are not long in travelling twenty miles!'

'That is possible, White Eyes,' the commandant replied, 'but be convinced that if I have acted as I have done, it has been simply with the view of reassuring the people; the Indians will not dare to avenge themselves.'

'Indians always avenge themselves, captain.'

You have drunk too much whisky, White Eyes; you are dreaming, with your eyes open.'

'God grant you may be right, captain! but I have passed all my life in the clearings, and know the manners of the redskins, while you have only been on the frontiers two years.'

'That is quite as long as is necessary,' the captain interrupted, peremptorily.

'Nevertheless, with your permission, Indians are men, and the two Comanches, who were treacherously assassinated here, in contempt of the laws of nations, were warriors renowned in their tribes.'

'White Eyes, you are of mixed breed, you lean a little too much to the red race,' said the captain.

'The red race,' the hunter replied, proudly, 'are loyal; they do not assassinate for the pleasure of shedding blood, as you yourself did, four days ago, in killing those two warriors who were passing inoffensively in their canoe, under the pretence of trying a new gun.'

'Well, well! that's enough! Spare me your comments, White Eyes.'

The hunger bowed awkwardly, threw his gun upon his shoulder and retired grumbling.

'Blood cries for vengeance; the redskins are men, and will not leave the crime unpunished.'

The captain retired into the fort, much annoyed by what the half-breed had said to him. Gradually the inhabitants dispersed and closed their dwellings with that listlessness peculiar to men accustomed to risk their lives every minute.

An hour later night had completely set in, thick darkness enveloped the village, and the inhabitants, fatigued with the rude labors of the day, were reposing in profound security.

The scouts sent out by the captain towards the decline of day had badly performed their duty.

Scarcely a mile from the village, concealed by the thick bushes and intertwining trees of a virgin forest, of which the nearest part had already fallen under the indefatigable axe of the clearers, two hundred warriors of the tribe of the Serpent, guided by several renowned chiefs, among whom was Eagle Head, who, although wounded, insisted upon joining the expedition, were waiting, with that Indian patience which nothing can foil, the propitious moment.

Several hours passed thus, and the silence of night was not disturbed by any noise whatever.

The Indians, motionless as bronze statues, waited without displaying the slightest impatience.

Towards eleven o'clock the moon rose.

At the same instant the distant howling of a dog was repeated twice.

Eagle Head then left the tree behind which he had been screened, and began to creep with extreme address and velocity, in the direction of the village.

On reaching the skirts of the forest he stopped; then he imitated the neighing of a horse with such perfection that two horses of the village immediately replied.

After waiting for a few seconds, the practised ear of the chief perceived an almost insensible noise among the leaves; the bellowing of an ox was heard a short distance away; then the chief arose and waited.

Two seconds later a man joined him.

This man was White Eyes, the old hunter.

A sinister smile curled the corners of his thin lips.

'What are the white men doing?' the chief asked.

'They are asleep,' the half-breed answered.

'Will my brother give them up to me?'

'For a fair exchange.'

'A chief has but one word. The pale woman and the grey-head?'

'Are here.'

'Shall they belong to me?'

'All the inhabitants of the village shall be placed in the hands of my brethren.'

'Och! Has not the hunter come?'

'Not yet.'

'He will come presently?'

'Probably he will.'

'What does my brother say now?'

'Where is that which I demanded of the chief?'

'The skins, the guns, and the powder, are in the rear, guarded by my young men.'

'I trust to you, chief,' the hunter replied, 'but if you deceive me—'

'An Indian has but one word.'

'That is good! Whenever you please, then.'

Ten minutes later the Indians were masters of the village, all the inhabitants of which, roused one after the other, were made prisoners without a struggle.

The fort was surrounded by the Comanches, who, after heaping up at the foot of the walls trunks of trees, carts, furniture, and all the farming implements of the colonists, only waited for a signal from their chief to commence the attack.

All at once a vague form stood out from the top of the fort, and the cry of the sparrow-hawk echoed through the air.

The Indians set fire to the kind of pyre they had raised and rushed towards the palisades, uttering altogether their horrible and piercing war cry, which, on the frontiers, is always the signal for a massacre.

INDIAN VENGEANCE

THE position of the Americans was most critical.

The captain, surprised by the silent attack of the Comanches, had been suddenly awakened by the frightful war cry they uttered, as soon as they had set fire to the materials heaped up on front of the fort.

Springing out of bed, the brave officer half-dressed himself, and, sabre in hand, rushed towards the side where the garrison reposed; they had already taken the alarm, and were hastening to their posts with that careless bravery which distinguishes the Yankees.

The garrison amounted, captain included, to twelve men.

How, with so weak a force, could they resist the Indians, whose diabolical profiles they saw lit up in the sinister reflections of the conflagration?

In the incessant combats fought on the Indian frontiers, the laws of civilized warfare are completely unknown.

The *vae victis* reigns in the full acceptation of the term.

Inveterate enemies, who fight one against another with all the refinements of barbarity, never ask or give quarter.

Every conflict, then, is a question of life and death.

Such is the custom.

The captain knew this well, therefore he did not indulge in the least illusion as to the fate that awaited him if he fell into the hands of the Comanches.

He had committed the fault of allowing himself to be surprised by the redskins, and he must undergo the consequence of his imprudence.

But the captain was a brave soldier; certain of not being able to retreat safe and sound from the trap into which he had fallen, he wished to succumb with honor.

The soldiers had no need to be excited to do their duty; they knew as well as their captain that they had no chance of safety left.

The defenders of the fort, therefore, placed themselves resolutely behind the barricades, and began to fire upon the Indians with a precision that speedily caused them a heavy loss.

The first person the captain saw, on mounting the platform of the little fort, was White Eyes.

'Ah, ah!' murmured the officer to himself, 'what is this fellow doing here?'

Drawing a pistol from his belt, he walked straight up to the half-breed, and, seizing him by the throat, clapped the barrel of his pistol to his breast, saying to him with that coolness which the Americans inherit from the English—

'In what fashion did you introduce yourself into the fort, you old screech owl?'

'Why, by the gate seemingly,' the other replied, unmoved.

'You must be a sorcerer, then!'

'Perhaps I am.'

'A truce with your jokes, mixed-blood: you have sold us to your brothers the redskins.'

A sinister smile passed over the countenance of the half-breed; the captain perceived it.

'But your treachery shall not profit you, you miserable scoundrel!' he said, in a voice of thunder.

The hunter disengaged himself by a quick, unexpected movement; then, with a spring backwards, and clapping his gun to his shoulder, he said—

'We shall see,' with a sneer.

These two men, placed face to face upon that narrow platform, lighted by the sinister reflection of the fire, the intensity of which increased every minute, would have had a terrific expression for the spectator who was able to contemplate them coolly.

Each of them personified in himself those two races, whose struggle will only finish by the complete extinction of the one, to the profit of the other.

At their feet the combat was taking the gigantic proportions of an epic.

The Indians rushed with rage against the intrenchments, where the Americans received them with musket shots or at the point of the bayonet.

But the fire continued to increase, the soldiers fell one after another; all promised soon to be over.

To the menace of White Eyes, the captain had replied by a smile of contempt.

Quick as lightning he discharged his pistol at the hunter; the latter let his gun droop.

The captain sprang upon him with a shout of joy.

The half-breed was knocked down by this shock.

Then his enemy placing his knee upon his breast, and looking at him for an instant, said, with a laugh—

'Well! was I mistaken?'

'No,' the half-breed replied in a firm tone; 'I am a fool—my life belongs to you—kill me!'

'Be satisfied I shall reserve you for an Indian death.'

'You must be quick, then, if you wish to avenge yourself,' the half-breed said, ironically, 'for it will soon be too late.'

'I have time enough. Why did you betray us, you miserble wretch?'

'Of what consequence is that to you?'

'I wish to know.'

'Well then, be satisfied,' the hunter said: 'the white men, your brothers, were the murderers of all my family, and I wished to avenge them.'

'But we had done nothing to you, had we?'

'Are you not white men? Kill me, and put an end to all this, I can die joyfully, for numbers of victims will follow me to the tomb.'

'Well, since it is so,' said the captain, with a sinister smile, 'I will send you to join your brothers.'

Then pressing his knees strongly on the chest of the hunter, to prevent his escape from the punishment he reserved for him, he cried—

'In the Indian fashion!'

And taking his knife, he seized with his left hand the half-breed's thick and tangled head of hair, and with the greatest dexterity scalped him.

The hunter could not restrain a cry of frightful agony at this unexpected mutilation. The blood flowed in torrents from his bare skull.

'Kill me!' he said; 'this is horrible!'

'Do you find it so?' said the captain.

'Oh! kill me! kill me!'

'What,' said the captain, 'do you take me for? No, I will restore you to your worthy friends.'

He then took the hunter by the legs, and dragging him to the edge of the platform, pushed him with his foot.

The miserable creature instinctively endeavored to hold himself up by seizing, with his left hand, the extremity of a post which projected outward.

For an instant he remained suspended in space.

He was hideous to behold; his denuded skull, his face, over which streams of black blood continued flowing, contracted by pain and terror; his whole body, agitated by convulsive movements, inspired horror and disgust.

'Pity! pity!' he murmured.

The captain surveyed him with a bitter smile.

But the exhausted nerves of the hunter could sustain him no longer; his clenched fingers relaxed their hold of the post he had seized with the energy of despair.

'Hangman! be for ever accursed!' he cried.

And he fell.

'A good journey to you!' said the captain.

An immense clamor arose from the gates of the fort.

The captain rushed to the assistance of his people.

The Comanches had gained the barricades.

They rushed in a crowd into the interior of the fort, massacring and scalping their enemies.

Four American soldiers only were left standing. The captain entrenched himself in the middle of the staircase which led to the platform.

'My friends,' he said to his comrades, 'die without regret, for I have killed the man who betrayed us.'

The soldiers replied by a shout of joy to this novel consolation, and prepared to sell their lives dearly.

But at this moment the cries of the Indians ceased, as if by enchantment.

The attack was suspended.

'What are they about now?' the captain muttered; 'what new devil's trick have these demons invented?'

Once master of all the approaches to the fort, Eagle Head ordered the fight to cease.

The colonists who were made prisoners in the village were brought, one after another, into his presence: there were twelve of them, and four were women.

When these twelve unfortunates stood before him, Eagle Head commanded the women to be set apart.

Ordering the men to pass one by one before him, he looked at them attentively, and then made a sign to the warriors standing by his side.

The latter instantly seized the Americans, chopped off their hands at the wrists with their knives, and, after having scalped them, pushed them into the fort.

Seven colonists underwent this atrocious torture, and there remained but one.

He was an old man of lofty stature, thin, but still active; his hair, white as snow, fell on his shoulders; his black eyes flashed, but his features remained unmoved; he waited, apparently impassible, till Eagle Head should decide his fate.

But the chief continued to survey him attentively.

At length the features of the savage expanded, a smile played upon his lips, and he held out his hand—

'*Usted no conocer amigo?*' (No you know friend?) he said to him in Spanish, with the guttural accent of his race.

'Oh!' said the old man, 'El Gallo!' (the Cock).

'Wah!' replied the chief, 'I am a friend of the grey-head; redskins have not two hearts; my father saved my life—my father shall come to my hut.'

'Thanks, chief! I accept your offer,' said the old man, warmly pressing the hand the Indian held out.

And he hastily placed himself by a woman of middle age, with a noble countenance, whose features, though faded by grief, still preserved traces of great beauty.

'God be praised!' she said, with great emotion, when the old man rejoined her.

'God never abandons those who place their trust in Him,' he replied.

During this time the redskins were preparing the last scenes of the terrible drama.

When all the colonists were shut up in the fort, the fire was revived with all the materials the Indians could find; a barrier of flames for ever separated the unfortunate Americans from the world.

The fort soon became one immense funeral pyre, from which escaped cries of pain, mingled at intervals with the report of fire-arms.

The Comanches, motionless, watched at a distance the progress of the fire, and laughed like demons at the spectacle of their vengeance.

The flames, which had seized upon the whole building, mounted with fearful rapidity, throwing their light over the desert like a dismal beacon.

On the top of the fort some individuals were seen rushing about in despair, while others, on their knees, seemed to be imploring divine mercy.

Suddenly a horrible crackling was heard, a cry of extreme agony rose towards heaven, and the fort crumbled down into the burning pile which consumed it, throwing up millions of sparks.

All the Americans had perished.

The Comanches planted an enormous mast on the spot where the square had been. This mast, to which were nailed the hands of the colonists, was surmounted by a hatchet, the iron of which was stained with blood.

Then, after setting fire to the few cabins that were left standing, Eagle Head gave orders for departure.

The women and the old man, the sole survivors of the population of the settlement, followed the Comanches.

THE PHANTOM

IT was about eight o'clock in the morning, a cheering autumn sun lit up the prairie splendidly.

Birds flew hither and thither, uttering strange cries, whilst others, concealed under the thickest of the foliage, poured forth melodious concerts. Now and then a deer raised its timid head above the tall grass, and then disappeared with a bound.

Two horsemen, clothed in the costume of wood-rangers, mounted upon magnificent half-wild horses, were following, at a brisk trot, the left bank of the great Canadian river, whilst several bloodhounds, with glossy black skins, and eyes and chests stained with red, ran and gambolled around them; they were Loyal Heart and Belhumeur.

Contrary to his usual deportment, Loyal Heart seemed affected by the most lively joy, his countenance beamed with cheerfulness, and he looked around him with complacency. Sometimes he would stop, and looked out ahead, appearing anxiously to seek in the horizon some object he could not yet discern. Then, with an expression of vexation, he resumed his journey, to repeat a hundred paces further on the same manoeuvre.

'Ah, parbleu!' said Belhumeur, laughing, 'we shall get there in good time. Be quiet, do!'

'*Eh, caramba!* I know that well enough; but I long to be there! For me, the only hours of happiness that God grants me, are passed with her whom we are going to see—my mother, my beloved mother! who gave up everything for me, abandoned all without regret, without hesitation. Oh, what happiness it is to have a mother! to possess one heart which understands yours, which makes a complete abnegation of self to absorb itself in you; which lives in your existence, rejoices in your joys, sorrows in your sorrows; which divides your life into two parts, reserving to itself the heaviest and leaving you the lightest and the most easy. Shall we never get there?'

'Well! here we are at the ford.'

'I don't know why, but a secret fear has suddenly fallen upon my spirits.'

'Oh, nonsense! In a few minutes we shall be with your mother.'

'That is true! And yet I don't know whether I am mistaken, but it seems to me as if the country does not wear its usual aspect; this silence which reigns around us does not appear to be natural. We are close to the village, we ought already to hear the barking of the dogs, the crowing of the cocks, and the thousand noises that proclaim inhabited places.'

'Well,' said Belhumeur, with vague uneasiness, 'I must confess that everything seems strangely silent.'

The travellers came to a spot where the river makes a sharp curve; being deeply embanked, and skirted by immense blocks of rock and thick copse wood, it did not allow any extensive view.

The village towards which the travellers were directing their course, was scarcely a gun shot from the ford where they were preparing to cross the river, but it was completely invisible, owing to the peculiar nature of the country.

At the moment the horses placed their feet in the water, they made a sudden movement backwards, and the bloodhounds uttered one of those plaintive howlings peculiar to their race, which freeze the bravest man with terror.

'What does this mean?' Loyal Heart exclaimed, turning pale as death.

'Look!' said Belhumeur, pointing with his finger to several dead bodies which the river was carrying away.

'Oh!' cried Loyal Heart, 'something terrible has taken place here. My mother! my mother!'

'Do not alarm yourself so,' said Belhumeur; 'no doubt she is in safety.'

Without listening to the consolations his friend poured out, though he did not believe in them himself, Loyal Heart drove the spurs into his horse's flanks, and sprang into the water.

They soon gained the opposite bank, and there all was explained. They had before them the most awful scene that can possibly be imagined. The village and the fort were a heap of ruins. A black, thick, sickening smoke ascended in long wreaths towards the heavens.

In the centre of what had been the village, arose a mast against which were nailed human fragments, for which *urubus* were contending with loud cries.

Here and there lay bodies half-devoured by wild beasts.

No living being appeared.

Nothing remained intact—everything was either broken, displaced, or overthrown. It was evident, at the first glance, that the Indians had passed there. Their steps were deeply imprinted in letters of fire and blood.

'Oh!' the hunter cried shuddering, 'my presentiments were a warning from Heaven—my mother! my mother!'

Loyal Heart fell upon the ground in utter despair; he concealed his face in his hands and wept.

His sobs were like roarings, they rent his breast.

Belhumeur respected the grief of his friend—indeed what consolation could he offer him? It was better to allow his tears to flow, and give the first paroxysm of despair time to calm itself; certain that his unyielding nature could not long be cast down, and that a reaction would soon come, which would permit him to act.

Still, with that instinct innate to hunters, he began to look about in the hope of finding some indication which might serve to direct their researches.

After wandering for a long time about the ruins, he was suddenly attracted towards a large bush at a little distance from him by barkings which he thought he recognized.

He advanced towards it precipitately; a bloodhound like their own jumped up joyfully upon him, and covered him with wild caresses.

'Oh, oh!' said the hunter, 'what does this mean? Who has tied poor Trim up in this fashion?'

He cut the rope which fastened the animal, and, in doing so, perceived that a piece of carefully folded paper was tied to its neck.

He seized it, and running to Loyal Heart, exclaimed—

'Brother! brother! Hope! hope!'

The hunter knew his brother was not a man to waste vulgar consolations upon him; he raised his tear-bathed face towards him.

As soon as it was free, the dog fled away with incredible velocity, baying with the dull, short yelps of a bloodhound following the scent.

Belhumeur, who had foreseen this flight, had hastened to tie his cravat round the animal's neck.

'No one knows what may happen,' murmured the hunter, on seeing the dog disappear.

'What is the matter?' Loyal Heart asked.

'Read!' Belhumeur quietly replied.

The hunter seized the paper, which he read eagerly. It contained only these few words—

'We are prisoners of the red-skins. Courage! Nothing bad has happened to your mother.'

'God be praised!' said Loyal Heart with great emotion, kissing the paper. 'My mother still lives! Oh, I shall find her again!'

'Of course,' said Belhumeur in a tone of conviction.

A complete change, as if by enchantment, had taken place in the mind of the hunter; he drew himself up to his full height, his face beaming with pleasure.

'Let us search,' he said; 'perhaps one of the unfortunate inhabitants has escaped death, and we may learn from him what has taken place.'

'That's well,' said Belhumeur joyfully; 'that's the way. Let us search.'

The dogs were scratching furiously among the ruins of the fort.

Both set to work to clear away the rubbish. They worked with an ardor incomprehensible to themselves. At the end of twenty minutes they discovered a sort of trap-door, and heard weak and inarticulate cries arise from beneath it.

'They are here,' said Belhumeur.

'God grant we may be in time to save them.'

It was not till after a length of time, and with infinite trouble that they succeeded in raising the trap, and then a horrid spectacle presented itself.

In a cellar exhaling a fetid odor, a score of individuals were literally piled up one upon another.

Of all these men, one alone showed signs of life; all the rest were dead.

They dragged him out, laid him gently on a heap of dry leaves, and gave him every assistance in their power.

At the end of a few minutes the man made a slight movement, opened his eyes several times, and then breathed a profound sigh.

Belhumeur introduced between his clenched teeth the mouth of a leathern bottle filled with rum, and obliged him to swallow a few drops of the liquor.

'He is very bad,' said the hunter.

'He is past recovery,' Loyal Heart replied.

Nevetheless the wounded man revived a little.

'My God,' said he, 'I am dying!'

'Hope!' said Belhumeur, kindly.

A fugitive tinge passed across the pale cheeks of the wounded man, and a sad smile curled his lips.

'Why should I live?' he murmured. 'The Indians have massacred all my companions, after having horribly mutilated them. Life would be too heavy a burden for me.'

'If, before you die, you wish anything to be done that is in our power to do, speak, and we will do it.'

The eyes of the dying man flashed faintly.

'Your gourd,' he said to Belhumeur.

The latter gave it to him, and he drank greedily. His brow was covered with a moist perspiration, and a feverish redness inflamed his countenance, which assumed a frightful expression.

'Listen,' said he, in a hoarse and broken voice. 'I was commander here; the Indians, aided by a wretched half-breed, who sold us to them, surprised the village.'

'The name of that man?' the hunter said, eagerly.

'He is dead—I killed him!' the captain replied, with an inexpressible accent of hatred and joy. 'The Indians endeavored to gain possession of the fort; the contest was terrible. We were twelve man against four hundred savages; what could we do? Fight to the death—that was what we resolved on doing. The Indians, finding the impossibility of taking us alive, cast the colonists of the village in among us, after cutting off their hands and scalping them, and then set fire to the fort.'

The wounded man, whose voice grew weaker and weaker, and whose words were becoming unintelligible, swallowed a few more drops of the liquor, and then continued his recital.

'A cave, which served as a cellar, extended under the ditches of the fort. When I knew that all means of safety had escaped, and that flight was impossible, I led my unfortunate companions into this cave, hoping that God would permit us to be thus saved. A few minutes after, the fort fell down over us! No one can imagine the tortures we have suffered in this infected hole, without air or light. The cries of the wounded—and we were all so, more or less— screaming for water, and the rattle of the dying, formed a terrible concert that no pen can describe. How long did it last? I cannot tell. I was already sensible that the death which had carried off all my companions was about to take possession of me, when you came to retard it for a few minutes. God be praised! I shall not die without vengeance.'

After these words, pronounced in a scarcely articulate voice, there was silence among these men—interrupted only by the dull rattle in the throat of the dying man, whose agony had begun.

All at once the captain made an effort; he raised himself, and fixing his eyes upon the hunters, said—

'The savages who attacked me belong to the Comanches; their chief is named Eagle Head; swear to avenge me.'

'We swear to do so,' the two men cried.

'Thanks,' the captain murmured, and falling back, was dead.

His distorted features and his open eyes still preserved the expression of hatred and despair which had animated him to the last.

The hunters surveyed him for an instant, and then, shaking off this painful impression, they set about the duty of paying the last honors to the remains of the unfortunate victims of Indian rage.

By the last rays of the setting sun, they completed the melancholy task.

After a short rest, Loyal Heart arose, and saddling his horse, said—

'Now, brother, let us start on the trail of Eagle Head.'

'Come on,' the hunter replied.

The two men cast around them a farewell glance, and whistling their dogs, boldly entered the forest where the Comanches had disappeared.

At this moment the moon arose amidst an ocean of vapor, and profusely scattered her melancholy beams upon the ruins of the American village, in which solitude and death were doomed to reign for ever.

THE ENTRENCHED CAMP

A FEW minutes after the two men had quitted the camp of the Mexicans, the general left his tent, and whilst casting an investigating look around him, and inhaling the fresh air of the morning, he began to walk about in a preoccupied manner.

The events of the night had produced a strong impression upon the old soldier.

For the first time, perhaps, since he had undertaken this expedition, he began to see it in its true light. He asked himself if he had really the right to associate with him in this life of continual perils and ambushes a girl of the age of his niece, whose existence up to that time had been an uninterrupted series of mild and peaceful emotions.

His perplexity was great. He adored his niece; she was his only object of love, his only consolation. For her he would, without regret or hesitation, a thousand times sacrifice all he possessed; but, on the other side, the reasons which had obliged him to undertake this perilous journey were of such importance that he trembled at the thought of renouncing it.

'What is to be done?' he said to himself. 'What is to be done?'

Dona Luz, who was in her turn leaving her tent, perceived her uncle, whose reflective walk still continued, and, running towards him, threw her arms affectionately round his neck.

'Good day, uncle,' she said, kissing him.

'Good day, my daughter,' the general replied. He was accustomed to call her so. 'Eh! eh! my child, you are very gay this morning.'

And he returned the caresses she had lavished on him.

'Why should I not be gay, uncle? Thanks to God, we have just escaped a great peril; everything in nature seems to smile, the birds are singing upon every branch, the sun inundates us with warm rays; we should be ungrateful towards the Creator if we remained insensible to these manifestations of His goodness.'

'Then the perils of last night have left no distressing impression upon your mind, my dear child?'

'None at all, uncle, except a deep sense of gratitude for the benefits God has favored us with.'

'That is well, my daughter,' the general replied, joyfully. 'I am happy to hear you speak thus.'

'All the better, if it please you, uncle.'

'Then,' the general continued, 'the life we are now leading is not fatiguing to you?'

'Oh, not at all; on the contrary, I find it very agreeable,' she said, with a smile.

'Yes,' the general continued; 'but,' he added, 'I think we are too forgetful of our liberators.'

'They are gone,' Dona Luz replied.

'Gone?' the general said, with great surprise.

'Full an hour ago.'

'How do you know that, my child?'

'Very simply, they bade me adieu before they left.'

'That is not right,' the general murmured in a tone of vexation; 'a service is as binding upon those who bestow it as upon those who receive it; they should not have left us thus without bidding me farewell, without telling us whether we should ever see them again, and leaving us even unacquainted with their names.'

'I know them.'

'You know them, my daughter?' the general said.

'Yes, uncle; before they went they told me.'

'And—what are they?' the general asked, eagerly.

'The younger is named Belhumeur.'

'And the elder?'

'Loyal Heart.'

'Oh! I must find these two men again,' the general said, with an emotion he could not account for.

'Who knows?' the young girl replied, 'perhaps at the first danger that threatens us they will make their appearance.'

'God grant we may not owe their return among us to a similar cause.'

The captain came up to pay the compliments of the morning.

'Well, captain,' said the general, with a smile, 'have you recovered from the effects of your alarm?'

'Perfectly, general,' the young man replied, 'and quite ready, whenever you please to give the order.'

'After breakfast we will strike our tents; have the goodness to give the necessary orders to the lancers, and send the Babbler to me.'

The captain bowed and retired.

'On your part, niece,' the general continued, addressing Dona Luz, 'superintend the preparations for breakfast, if you please, whilst I talk to our guide.'

The young lady tripped away, and the Babbler entered. His air was dull, and his manner more reserved than usual.

The general took no notice of this.

'You remember,' he said, 'that you yesterday manifested an intention of finding a spot where we might conveniently encamp for a few days?'

'Yes, general.'

'You told me you were acquainted with a situation that would perfectly suit our purpose?'

'Yes, general.'

'What time will it require to gain this spot?'

'Two days.'

'Very well. We will set out, then, immediately after breakfast.'

The Babbler bowed without reply.

'By the way,' the general said, with feigned indifference, 'one of your men seems to be missing.'

'Yes.'

'What is become of him?'

'I do not know.'

'How! you do not know?' said the general.

'No; as soon as he saw the fire, terror seized him, and he escaped.'

'Very well!'

'He is most probably the victim of his cowardice.'

'What do you mean by that?'

'The fire, most likely, has devoured him.'

'Poor devil!'

A sardonic smile curled the lips of the guide.

'Have you anything more to say to me, general?'

'No—but stop.'

'I attend your orders.'

'Do you know the two hunters who rendered us such timely service?'

'We all know each other in the prairie.'

'What are those men?'

'Hunters and trappers.'

'That is not what I ask you.'

'What then?'

'I mean as to their character.'

'Oh!' said the guide, with an appearance of displeasure.

'Yes, their moral character.'

'I don't know anything much about them.'

'What are their names?'

'Belhumeur and Loyal Heart.'

'And you know nothing of their lives?'

'Nothing.'

'That will do—you may retire.'

The guide bowed, and rejoined his companions.

'Hum!' the general murmured, as he looked after him, 'I must keep a watch upon that fellow; there is something sinister in his manner.'

After this aside, the general entered his tent, where the doctor, the captain, and Dona Luz were waiting breakfast for him.

Half an hour later the caravan was pursuing its journey under the direction of the Babbler, who rode about twenty paces in advance of the troop.

The aspect of the prairie was much changed since the preceding evening.

The black, burnt earth was covered in places with heaps of smoking ashes; here and there charred trees, still standing, displayed their saddening skeletons; the fire still roared at a distance, and clouds of coppery smoke obscured the horizon.

The horses advanced with precaution over this uneven ground, where they constantly stumbled over the bones of animals that had fallen victims to the terrible embraces of the flames.

A melancholy sadness, much increased by the sight of the prospect unfolded before them, had taken possession of the travellers; they journeyed on, close to each other, without speaking, buried in their own reflections.

The day passed away thus, and excepting the fatigue which oppressed them, the monotony of the journey was not broken by any incident.

In the evening they encamped in a plain absolutely bare, but in the horizon they could perceive an appearance of verdure, which afforded them great consolation—they were about, at last, to enter a zone spared by the conflagration.

The next morning, two hours before sunrise, the Babbler gave orders to prepare for departure.

The day proved more fatiguing than the last; the travellers were literally worn out when they encamped.

The Babbler had not deceived the general. The site was admirably chosen to repel an attack of the Indians. It was the spot on which we met with the hunters, when they appeared on the scene for the first time.

The general, after casting around him the infallible glance of the experienced soldier, could not help manifesting his satisfaction.

'Bravo!' he said to the guide; 'if we have had almost insurmountable difficulties to encounter in getting here, we could at least, if things should so fall out, sustain a siege on this spot.'

The guide made no reply; he bowed with an equivocal smile, and retired.

'It is surprising,' the general murmured to himself, 'that although that man's conduct may be in appearance loyal, and however impossible it may be to reproach him with the least thing—in spite of all that, I cannot divest myself of the presentiment that he is deceiving us.'

The general was an old soldier of considerable experience, who would never leave anything to chance.

Notwithstanding the fatigue of his people, he would not lose a moment; aided by the captain, he had an enormous number of trees cut down, to form a solid entrenchment, protected by *chevaux de frise*. Behind this intrenchment the lancers dug a wide ditch, of which they threw out the earth on the side of the camp; and then, behind this second intrenchment the baggage was piled up, to make a third and last enclosure.

The tent was pitched in the center of the camp, the sentinels were posted, and every one else went to seek that repose of which they stood so much in need.

The general, who intended sojourning on this spot for some time, wished, as far as it could be possible, to assure the safety of his companions.

For two days the travelers had been marching along execrable roads, almost without sleep, only stopping to snatch a morsel of food; they were quite worn out with fatigue. Notwithstanding, then, their desire to keep awake, the sentinels could not resist the sleep which overpowered them, and were soon in as complete forgetfulness as their companions.

Towards midnight, at the moment when every one in the camp was plunged in sleep, a man rose softly, and creeping along in the shade, with the quickness of a reptile, but with extreme precaution, glided out of the barricades and intrenchments.

He then went down upon the ground, and by degrees, in a manner almost insensibly, directed his course, upon his hands and knees, through the high grass towards a forest which covered the first ascent of the hill, and extended some way into the prairie.

When he had gone a certain distance, and was safe from discovery, he rose. A moonbeam threw a light upon his countenance.

That man was the Babbler.

He looked round anxiously, listened attentively, and then, with incredible perfection, imitated the cry of the prairie dog.

Almost instantly the same cry was repeated, and a man rose up, within at most ten paces of the Babbler.

This man was the guide who, three days before, had escaped from the camp.

THE BARGAIN

INDIANS and wood-rangers have two languages, of which they make use by turns—spoken language, and the language of gestures.

Like the spoken language, the language of signs has infinite fluctuations; every one, so to say, invents his own. It is a compound of strange and mysterious gestures, a kind of masonic telegraph, the signs of which are only comprehensible to a small number.

The Babbler and his companion were conversing in signs.

This singular conversation lasted nearly an hour; it appeared to interest the speakers warmly; so warmly, indeed, that they did not remark, in spite of all the precautions they had taken not to be surprised, two fiery eyes that, from the middle of a tuft of underwood, were fixed upon them with strange intenseness.

At length the Babbler, risking the utterance of a few words, said, 'I await your good pleasure.'

'And you shall not wait it long,' the other replied.

'I depend upon you, Kennedy; for my part, I have fulfilled my promise.'

'That's well! We don't require many words to come to an understanding,' said Kennedy, 'only you need not have conducted them to so strong a position—it will not be very easy to surprise them.'

'That's your concern,' said the Babbler.

His companion looked at him for a moment with great attention.

'Hum!' said he; 'beware, *compadre*; it is almost always awkward to play a double game with men like us.'

'I am playing no double game; but I think you and I have known each other a pretty considerable time, Kennedy, have we not?'

'What follows?'

'What follows? Well! I am not disposed that a thing should happen that has happened before.'

'Do you draw back, or are you thinking about betraying us?'

'I do not draw back, and I have not the least intention of betraying you, only—'

'Only?' the other repeated.

'This time I will not give up to you what I have promised till my conditions have been agreed to pretty plainly; if not, no—'

'Well, at least that's frank.'

'People should speak plainly in business affairs,' the Babbler observed, shaking his head.

'That's true! Well, come, repeat the conditions; I will see if we can accept them.'

'What's the good of that? You are not the principal chief, are you?'

'No—but—yet—'

'You could pledge yourself to nothing—so it's of no use. If Waktehno—he who kills—were here now, it would be quite another thing. He and I should soon understand one another.'

'Speak then, he is listening to you,' said a strong, sonorous voice.

There was a movement in the bushes, and the personage who, up to that moment, had remained an invisible hearer of the conversation of the two men, judged, without doubt, that the time to take a part in it was arrived, for, with a bound, he sprang out of the bushes that had concealed him, and placed himself between the speakers.

'Oh! oh! you were listening to us, Captain Waktehno, were you?' said the Babbler.

'Is that unpleasant to you?' the new comer asked, with an ironical smile.

'Oh! not the least in the world.'

'Continue, then, my worthy friend—I am all ears.'

'Well,' said the guide, 'it will, perhaps, be better so.'

'Go on, then—speak; I attend to you.'

The personage to whom the Babbler gave the terrible Indian

name of Waktehno was a man of pure white race, thirty years of age, of lofty stature, and well proportioned, handsome in appearance, and wearing with a certain dashing carelessness the picturesque costume of the wood-rangers. His features were noble, strongly marked, and impressed with that loyal and haughty expression so often met with among men accustomed to the rude, free life of the prairies.

He fixed his large, black, brilliant eyes upon the Babbler, a smile curled his lips, and he leant carelessly upon his rifle whilst listening to the guide.

'If I cause the people I am paid to escort and conduct to fall into your hands, you may depend upon it I will not do so unless I am amply recompensed,' said the bandit.

'That is but fair,' Kennedy remarked; 'and the captain is ready to assure your being so recompensed.'

'Yes,' said the other, nodding his head.

'Very well,' the guide resumed. 'But what will be my recompense?'

'What do you ask?' the captain said. 'We must know what your conditions are before we agree to satisfy them.'

'Oh! my terms are very moderate.'

'Well, but what are they?'

The guide hesitated, or, rather, he calculated mentally the chances of gain and loss the affair offered.

'These Mexicans are very rich.'

'Probably,' said the captain.

'Therefore it appears to me—'

'Speak without tergiversation, Babbler; we have no time to listen to your circumlocutions. Like all half-bloods, the Indian nature always prevails in you, and you never come frankly to the purpose.'

'Well, then,' the guide bluntly replied, 'I will have five thousand duros, or nothing shall be done.'

'For once you speak out; now we know what we have to trust to;

you demand five thousand dollars?'

'I do.'

'And for that sum you agree to deliver up to us, the general, his niece, and all the individuals who accompany them.'

'At your first signal.'

'Very well! Now listen to what I am going to say to you. You know dependance is to be placed upon my word?'

'It is as good as gold.'

'That's well. If you loyally fulfil the engagements you freely make with me, that is to say, deliver up to me, not all the Mexicans who comprise your caravan—very respectable people no doubt, but for whom I care very little—but only the girl called, I think, Dona Luz, I will not give you five thousand dollars as you ask, but eight thousand—you understand me, do you not?'

The eyes of the guide sparkled with greediness.

'Yes!' he said emphatically. 'But it will be a difficult matter to draw her out of the camp alone.'

'That's your affair.'

'I should prefer giving them all up in a lump.'

'Go to the devil! What could I do with them?'

'Hum! what will the general say?'

'What he likes; that is nothing to me. Yes or no—do you accept the offer I make you?'

'Oh! I accept it.'

'Well, I give you nine days; that is to say, on the eve of their departure the young girl must be given up to me.'

'Oh! in that way—'

'Then that arrangement suits you?'

'It could not be better.'

'Is it agreed?'

'Irrevocably.'

'Here, then, Babbler," said the captain, giving the guide a

magnificent diamond pin, 'here is my earnest.'

'Oh!' the bandit exclaimed, seizing the jewel joyfully.

'That pin,' said the captain, 'is a present I make you in addition to the eight thousand dollars I will hand over to you on receiving Dona Luz.'

'You are noble and generous, captain,' said the guide; 'it is a pleasure to serve you.'

'Still,' the captain rejoined, in a rough voice, 'I would have you remember I am called He Who Kills; and that if you deceive me, there does not exist in the prairie a place sufficiently strong or sufficiently remote to protect you from the terrible effects of my vengeance.'

'I know that, captain,' said the half-breed; 'you may be quite satisfied I will not deceive.'

'I hope you will not! Now let us separate. In nine days I shall be here.'

'In nine days I will place the girl in your hands.'

After these words the guide returned to the camp, which he entered without being seen.

As soon as they were alone, the two men with whom the Babbler had just made this hideous and strange bargain retreated silently among the underwood, through which they crawled like serpents.

They soon reached the banks of a little rivulet which ran, unperceived and unknown, through the forest. Kennedy whistled in a certain fashion twice.

A slight noise was heard, and a horseman, holding two horses, appeared at a few paces.

'Come on, Frank,' said Kennedy, 'you may approach without fear.'

The horseman immediately advanced.

'What is there new?' Kennedy asked.

'Nothing very important,' the horseman replied. 'I have discovered an Indian trail.'

'In what direction?'

'It cuts the prairie from east to west.'

'Well done, Frank; and who are these Indians?'

'As well as I can make out, they are Comanches.'

'Frank and you, Kennedy,' said the captain, at the expiration of a minute, 'will go to the passage of the Buffalo, and encamp in the grotto which is there; carefully watching the movements of the Mexicans, but in such a manner as not to be discovered.'

'Be satisfied of that, captain.'

'Oh; I know you are very adroit and devoted comrades, therefore I perfectly rely upon you. Watch the Babbler, likewise; that half-breed only inspires me with moderate confidence.'

'That shall be done!'

'Farewell, then, till we meet again. You shall soon hear of me.'

Notwithstanding the darkness, the three men set off at a gallop in two different directions.

PSYCHOLOGICAL

THE general had kept the causes which made him undertake a journey into the prairies so profound a secret, that the persons who accompanied him had not even a suspicion of them.

Several times already, at his command, and without any apparent reason, the caravan had encamped in regions completely desert, where he had passed a week, and sometimes a fortnight, without any apparent motive for such a halt.

On these various occasions the general would set out every morning, attended by one of the guides, and not return till evening.

What was he doing during the long hours of his absence? With what object were these explorations made, at the end of which a greater degree of sadness darkened his countenance? No one knew.

During these excursions, Dona Luz led a sufficiently monotonous life, isolated among the rude people who surrounded her. She passed whole days seated sadly in front of her tent, or, mounted on horseback, escorted by Captain Aguilar, or the fat doctor, took rides near the camp, without object or interest.

It happened this time again, exactly as it had happened at the preceding stations of the caravan.

The young girl, abandoned by her uncle, and even by the doctor, who was pursuing, with increasing ardor, the great search for his fantastic plant, and set out resolutely every morning herbalising, was reduced to the company of Captain Aguilar.

But Captain Aguilar was, although young, elegant, and endowed with some intelligence, not a very amusing companion.

A brave soldier, with the courage of a lion, entirely devoted to the general, to whom he owed everything, the captain entertained for the niece of his chief great attachment and respect; he watched with the utmost care over her safety, but he was completely unacquainted with the means of rendering the time shorter by those attentions and that pleasant chat which are so agreeable to girls.

Dona Luz was not so *ennuyée* as usual. Since that terrible night—from the time that, like one of those fabulous heroes whose history and incredible feats she had so often read, Loyal Heart had appeared to her to save her and those who accompanied her—a new sentiment, which she had not even thought of analysing, had germinated in her maiden heart, had grown by degrees, and in a very few days had taken possession of her whole being.

The image of the hunter was incessantly present to her thought, encircled with that glory which is won by the energy of the man who struggles, with some immense danger, and forces it to acknowledge his superiority. She took delight in recalling to her mind the different scenes of that tragedy of a few hours, in which the hunter had played the principle character.

Her memory, like that of all pure young girls, retraced with incredible fidelity the smallest details.

In a word she reconstructed in her thoughts the series of events in which the hunter had mingled, and in which he had, thanks to his indomitable courage and presence of mind, extricated in so happy a fashion those he had suddenly come to succor, at the instant when they were without hope.

The hurried manner in which the hunter had left them, disdaining the most simple thanks, and appearing even unconcerned for those he had saved, had vexed the girl; she was piqued more than can be imagined by this real or affected indifference; And, consequently, she continually revolved means to make her preserver, if possible, repent that indifference.

It is a well-known paradox, that from hatred, or, at least, from curiosity to love, there is but one step, and Dona Luz passed it at full speed.

Dona Luz had been educated in a convent, at the gates of which the sounds of the world died away. Her youth had passed calm and colorless, in the religious, or, rather, superstitious practices, upon which in Mexico religion is built. When her uncle took her from the convent to take her with him through the journey he meditated into the prairies, the girl was ignorant of the most simple exigencies of life, and had no more idea of the outward world, in which she was so suddenly cast, than a blind man has of the splendor of the sun's beams.

This ignorance, which suited the projects of the uncle, was for the niece a stumbling-block against which she twenty times a day came into collision.

But, thanks to the care with which the general surrounded her, the few weeks which passed away before their departure from Mexico had been spent without too much pain by the young girl.

We feel called upon, however, to notice here an incident, trifling in appearance, but which left too deep a trace in the mind of Dona Luz not to be related.

The general was actively employed in getting together the people he wanted, and was obliged to neglect his niece more than he would have wished.

As he, however, feared that the young girl would be unhappy at being left so much alone with an old duenna in the palace he occupied, in the Calle de los Plateros, he sent her frequently to spend her evenings at the house of a female relation who received a select society.

Now one evening, when the assembly had been more numerous than usual, it did not break up till late.

At the first stroke of eleven, sounded by the ancient clock of the convent of the Merced, Dona Luz and her duenna, preceded by a peon carrying a torch, set off on their return home, casting anxious looks right and left. They had but a short distance to go, when all at once, on turning the corner of the Calle San Agustin to enter that of Plateros, four or five men of evil appearance seemed to rise from the earth, and surrounded the two women, after having previously, by a vigorous blow, extinguished the torch carried by the peon.

To express the terror of the young lady at this unexpected apparition is impossible.

She was so frightened that, without having the strength to utter a cry, she fell on her knees, with her hands clasped, before the bandits.

The duenna, on the contrary, sent forth deafening screams.

The Mexican bandits, all very expeditious men, had, in the shortest time possible, reduced the duenna to silence, by gagging her with her own rebozo; then, with all the calmness which these worthies bring to the exercise of their functions, assured of impunity by that justice with which they generally go halves, proceeded to plunder their victims.

The operation was shortened by the latter, for, so far from offering any resistance, they tore off their jewels in the greatest haste, and the bandits pocketed them with grins of satisfaction.

But suddenly a sword gleamed over their heads, and two of the bandits fell to the ground, swearing and howling.

Those who were left standing, enraged at this unaccustomed attack, turned to avenge their companions, and rushed all together upon the aggressor.

The latter, heedless of their number, made a step backwards, and placed himself on guard.

But, with the change in his position, the moonlight fell upon his face. The bandits instantly drew back in terror, and promptly sheathed their machetes.

'Ah, ah!' said the stranger, with a smile of contempt, as he advanced towards them, 'you recognize me, my masters, do you? By the Virgin ! I am sorry for it—I was preparing to give you a rather sharp lesson. Is this the manner in which you execute my orders?'

The bandits remained silent, contrite and repentant, in appearance at least.

'Come, empty your pockets, you paltry thieves, and restore to these ladies what you have taken!'

Without a moment's delay, the thieves unbandaged the duenna, and restored the booty, which, an instant before, they had so joyfully appropriated.

Dona Luz could not overcome her astonishment, she looked with the greatest surprise at this strange man, who possessed such authority over bandits acknowledging neither faith nor law.

'Is this really all?' he said, addressing the young lady; 'are you sure you miss nothing, senora?'

'Nothing—nothing, sir!' she replied.

'Now, then, begone, you scoundrels,' the stranger continued; 'I will take upon myself to be the escort of these ladies.'

The bandits did not require to be twice told; they disappeared, carrying off the wounded.

As soon as he was left alone with the two women, the stranger turned towrds Dona Luz—

'Permit me, senorita,' he said, with refined courtesy of manner, 'to offer you my arm as far as your palace; the fright you have just experienced must render your steps uncertain.'

Mechanically, and without reply, the young girl placed her hand within the arm so courteously offered.

When they arrived at the palace, the stranger knocked at the door, and then taking off his hat, said—

'Senorita, I am happy that chance has enabled me to render you a slight service. I shall have the honor of seeing you again. I have already, for a long time, followed your steps like your shadow. God, who has granted me the favor of an opportunity of speaking with you once, will, I feel assured, grant me a second, although, in a few days, you are to set out on a long journey. Permit me then to say not *adieu*, but *au revoir*.'

After bowing humbly and gracefully to the young lady, he departed at a rapid pace.

A fortnight after this strange adventure, of which she did not speak to her uncle, Dona Luz quitted Mexico, without having again seen the unknown. Only, on the eve of her departure, when retiring to her bed-chamber, she found a folded note, written in an elegant hand—

'You are going, Dona Luz! Remember that I told you I should see you again.

'Your preserver of the Calle de los Plateros.'

For a long time this strange meeting strongly occupied the mind of the young girl; for an instant, she had even believed that Loyal Heart and her unknown preserver were the same man; but what probability was there in it? Would Loyal Heart, after having saved her, so quickly have departed?

But, by one of those strange consequences of the human mind, in proportion as the affair of Mexico was effaced from her thoughts, that of Loyal Heart became more prominent.

She longed to see the hunter and talk with him.

Why? She did not herself know. To see him—to hear his voice—to meet his look, at once so soft and so proud—nothing else; all maidens are the same.

In reply to the question 'How to see him again?' arose an impossibility, before which the poor girl dropped her head with discouragement.

And yet something at the bottom of her heart, perhaps that voice divine which in the secret depths of their hearts whispers of love to young girls, told her that her wish would soon be accomplished.

She hoped, then, for some unforeseen incident—some terrible danger—which might reunite them.

True love may doubt sometimes, but it never despairs.

Four days after the establishment of the camp upon the hill, in the evening, when retiring to her tent, Dona Luz smiled inwardly as she looked at her uncle, who was pensively preparing to go to rest.

She had at length thought of a means of going in search of Loyal Heart.

THE BEE-HUNT

THE sun was scarcely above the horizon, when the general, whose horse was already saddled, left the reed cabin which served him as a sleeping apartment, and prepared to set out on his usual daily ride. As he was putting his foot in the stirrup, a little hand lifted the curtain of the tent, and Dona Luz appeared.

'Oh! oh! what, up already!' said the general, smiling. 'So much the better, dear child. I shall be able to have a kiss before I set out; and that perhaps may bring me good luck,' he added, stifling a sigh.

'You will not go thus, uncle,' she replied, presenting her cheek, upon which he placed a kiss.

'Why not, fair lady?' he asked gaily.

'Because I wish you to partake of something I have prepared for you; you cannot refuse me, can you, dear uncle?' she said, with that coaxing smile which delights the hearts of old men.

'Certainly not, dear child, upon condition that the breakfast you offer me be not delayed. I am in a hurry.'

'I only ask for a few minutes,' she replied, returning to the tent.

'For a few minutes be it then,' said he, following her.

The young girl clapped her hands with joy.

In the twinkling of an eye, the breakfast was ready, and the general at table with his niece. Whilst assisting her uncle, and taking great care that he wanted for nothing, the young girl looked at him from time to time in an embarrassed manner, and did it so evidently, that the old soldier ended by observing it.

'It is my opinion,' he said, laying down his knife and fork, 'that you have something to ask me, Lucita; you know very well that I am not accustomed to refuse you anything.'

'That is true, dear uncle; but this time, I am afraid, you will be more difficult to be prevailed upon.'

'Ah! ah!' the general said, gaily; 'it must be something serious, then!'

'Quite the contrary, uncle; and yet, I confess, I am afraid you will refuse me.'

'Speak, notwithstanding, my child,' said the old soldier; 'speak without fear; when you have told me what this mighty affair is, I will soon answer you.'

'Well, uncle,' the girl said, blushing, but determined on her purpose, 'I am compelled to say that the residence in the camp is very dull.'

'I can conceive that, my child; but what do you wish me to do to make it otherwise?'

'If you were always here, dear uncle, it would not be dull; I should have your company.'

'What you say is very amiable; but, as you know I am absent every morning, I cannot be here, and—'

'But, if you were willing, it could be easily removed.'

'Well, I don't see too clearly how, unless I remained always with you, and that is impossible.'

'Oh; there are other means that would arrange the whole affair.'

'Well, then, darling, what are these means?'

'That you should take me with you every morning.'

'Oh! oh!' said the general frowning; 'do you know what you ask me, my dear child?'

'Why, a very natural thing, uncle, as I think.'

The general made no reply; he reflected. The girl watched anxiously the fugitive traces of his thoughts.

At the end of a few instants, he raised his head.

'Well, perhaps it would be better so;' and fixing a piercing look upon his niece, he said, 'it would give you pleasure, then, to accompany me?'

'Yes, uncle, yes!' she replied.

'Well, then, get ready, my dear child; henceforth you shall accompany me in my excursions.'

She arose from her seat with a bound, kissed her uncle warmly, and ordered her horse.

A quarter of an hour later, Dona Luz and her uncle, preceded by the Babbler, and followed by two lanceros, quitted the camp, and plunged into the forest.

'Which way would you wish to direct your course today, general?' the guide asked.

'Conduct me to the huts of those trappers you spoke of yesterday.'

The guide bowed in sign of obedience. The little party advanced slowly and with some difficulty along a scarcely-traced path, where, at every step, the horses became entangled in the creeping plants, or stumbled over the roots of trees above the level of the ground.

Dona Luz was gay and happy. Perhaps in these excursions she might meet with Loyal Heart.

The Babbler, who was a few paces in advance, suddenly uttered a cry.

'Eh!' said the general, 'what extraordinary thing has happened, Master Babbler, to induce you to speak?'

'The bees, senor.'

'What! bees! are there bees here?'

'Yes; but lately only.'

'How only lately?'

'Why, you know, of course, that bees were brought into America by the whites.'

'That I know. How is it, then, they are met with here?'

'The bees are simply the advanced sentinels of the whites. In proportion as the whites penetrate into the interior of America, the bees go forward to trace the route for them, and point out the clearings. Their appearance in an uninhabited country always presages the arrival of a colony of pioneers or squatters.'

'This is strange,' the general murmured; 'are you sure of what you are telling me?'

'Oh! quite sure, senor; the fact is well known to all Indians: they are not mistaken in it, be assured; for as soon as they see the bees arrive, they retreat.'

'That is truly singular.'

'The honey must be very good,' said Dona Luz.

'Excellent, senorita, and if you wish for it, nothing is more easy than to get it.'

'Get some, then,' said the general.

The guide, who some moments before had placed a bait for the bees upon the bushes, to which, with his piercing sight, he had already seen several bees attracted, made a sign to those behind him to stop.

The bees had, in fact, lighted upon the bait, and were examining it all over; when they had extracted what they needed, they rose very high into the air, and took flight in a direct line with the velocity of a cannon ball.

The guide carefully watched the direction they took, and making a sign to the general, he sprang after them, followed by the whole party, clearing themselves a way through interlaced roots, fallen trees, bushes and briars, their eyes directed all the while towards the sky.

In this fashion they never lost sight of the bees, and after a difficult pursuit of an hour, they saw them arrive at their nest, constructed in the hollow of a dead ebony tree; after buzzing for a moment, they entered a hole situated at more than eighty feet from the ground.

Then the guide, after having warned his companions to keep at a respectful distance, in order to be out of the way of the falling tree and the vengeance of its inhabitants, seized his axe and attacked the ebony vigorously near the base.

The bees did not seem at all alarmed by the stroke of the axe; they continued going in and out, carrying on their industrial labors in full security. A violent cracking even, which announced the splitting of the trunk, did not divert them from their occupations.

At length the tree fell, with a horrible crash, opening the whole of its length, and leaving the accumulated treasures of the community exposed to view.

The guide immediately seized a bundle of hay which he had prepared, and to which he set fire to defend himself; but they attacked nobody; they did not seek to avenge themselves. The poor creatures were stupefied; they flew in all directions round their destroyed empire, without thinking of anything but how to account for this unlooked-for catastrophe.

Then the men set to work with spoons and knives to get out the comb and fill the wine-skins.

Some of the comb was of a deep brown, and of ancient date, other parts were of a beautiful white; the honey in the cells was almost limpid.

Whilst they were hastening to get possession of the best combs, they saw arrive on the wing from all points of the horizon numberless swarms of honey bees, who, plunging into the broken cells, loaded themselves, while the ex-proprietors of the hive, dull and stupefied, looked on, without seeking to save the least morsel, at the robbery of their honey.

It is impossible to describe the astonishment of the bees that were absent at the moment of the catastrophe, as they arrived at their late home with their cargoes; they described circles in the air round the place the tree had occupied, astonished to find it empty; at length, however, they seemed to comprehend their disaster, and collected in groups upon the dried branch of a neighboring tree, appearing to contemplate thence the fallen ruin.

'Let us go,' said Dona Luz, affected in spite of herself; 'I repent of having wished for honey; my greediness has made too many unhappy.'

'Let us be gone,' said the general, smiling; 'leave them these few combs.'

'Oh!' said the guide, shrugging his shoulders, 'they will soon be carried away by the vermin.'

'The vermin! What vermin do you mean?'

'Oh! the racoons, the opossums, but particularly the bears.'

'The bears?' said Dona Luz.

'Oh, senorita!' the guide replied, 'they are the cleverest vermin in the world in discovering a tree of bees, and getting their share of the honey.'

'Do they like honey, then?' said the lady.

'Why, they are mad after it, senorita,' the guide, who really seemed to relax of his cynical humor, rejoined. 'Imagine how greedy they are after it, when they will gnaw a tree for weeks, until they succeed in making a hole large enough to put their paws in, and then they carry off honey and bees.'

'Now,' said the general, 'let us resume our route, and seek the residence of the trappers.'

'We shall soon be there, senor,' replied the guide; 'yonder is the great Canadian river, and trappers are established all along the stream.'

The little party proceeded on their way again.

The bee-hunt had left an impression of sadness on the mind of the young lady, which she could not overcome. Those poor little creatures, so gentle and so industrious, attacked! and ruined for a caprice, grieved her, and made her thoughtful.

Her uncle perceived this disposition of her mind.

'Dear child!' he said, 'what is passing in your head? You are no longer so gay as when we set out.'

'Do not let that disturb you, uncle; I am, like other young girls, rather wild and whimsical; this bee-hunt, from which I promised myself so much pleasure, has left a sadness behind it I cannot get rid of.'

'Happy child!' the general murmured, 'whom so futile a cause has still the power to trouble. God grant, darling, that you may continue long in that disposition, and that greater and more real troubles may never reach you!'

'My kind uncle, shall I not always be happy while near you?'

'Alas! my child, who knows whether God may permit me to watch over you long!'

'Do not say so, uncle; I hope we have many years to pass together.'

The general was preparing to answer her, when the guide,

suddenly coming up to them, made a sign to command silence, by saying, in a voice as low as a breath—

'A man!'

BLACK ELK

IN the desert, this word man almost always means an enemy. Man in the prairies is more dreaded by his fellow than the most ferocious wild beast. A man is a rival, a forced associate, who, by the right of being the stronger, comes to share with the first occupant, and often, if we may not say always, strives to deprive him of the fruits of his thankless labor.

Thus, whites, Indians, or half-breeds, when they meet in the prairies, salute each other with eye on the watch, ears open, and the finger on the trigger.

At this cry of a man, the general and the lanceros, at all hazards, prepared against a sudden attack by cocking their guns, and concealing themselves as much as possible behind the bushes.

At fifty paces before them stood an individual, who, his two hands leaning on the barrel of a long rifle, was observing them attentively.

He was a man of lofty stature, energetic features, and a frank, determined look. His long hair, arranged with care, was plaited, mingled with otter skins and ribbons of various colors. A hunting-blouse of ornamented leather fell to his knees; gaiters of a singular cut, with strings, fringes, and a profusion of little bells covered his legs; his shoes consisted of a pair of superb mocassins, embroidered with false pearls.

A scarlet blanket hung from his shoulders, and was fastened round his middle by a red belt, through which were passed two pistols, a knife, and an Indian pipe.

His rifle was profusely decorated with vermilion and little copper nails.

At a few paces from him his horse was browsing on the mast of the trees.

Like its master, it was equipped in the most fantastic manner, spotted and striped with vermilion, the reins and crupper ornamented with beads and bunches of ribbon, while its head, mane, and tail, were abundantly decorated with eagle's feathers floating in the wind.

At sight of this personage the general could not restrain a cry of surprise.

'To what Indian tribe does this man belong?' he asked the guide.

'To none,' he replied; 'he is a white trapper.'

'And so dressed?'

The guide shrugged his shoulders.

'We are in the prairies,' he said.

'That is true,' the general murmured.

In the meantime, the individual we have described, tired, no doubt, of the hesitation of the little party before him, and wishing to know what their disposition was, resolutely accosted them.

'Eh! eh!' he said in English. 'Who the devil are you—and what do you want here?'

'*Caramba!*' the general replied, throwing his gun behind him, and ordering his people to do the same; 'we are travellers, fatigued with a long journey; the sun is hot, and we ask permission to rest a short time in your rancho.'

These words being spoken in Spanish, the trapper replied in the same language—

'Approach without fear; Black Elk is a good sort of fellow when people no not thwart him; you can share the little he possesses, and much good may it do you.'

At the name of Black Elk the guide could not repress a movement of terror; he wished even to say a few words, but he had not time, for the hunter, throwing his gun upon his shoulder, and leaping into his saddle with a bound, advanced towards the Mexicans.

'My rancho is a few paces from this spot,' said he; 'if the senorita is inclined to taste a well-seasoned hump of buffalo, I am in a position to offer it to her.'

'I thank you, caballero,' the young lady replied, with a smile; 'but I confess that at this moment I stand in more need of repose than anything else.'

'Everything will come in its time,' the trapper said sententiously. 'Permit me, for a few moments, to take the place of your guide.'

'We are at your orders,' said the general.

'Forward! then,' said the trapper, placing himself at the head of the little troop.

At this moment his eyes fell upon the guide—his eyebrows contracted. 'Hum!' he muttered to himself, 'what does this mean? We shall see,' he added.

And without taking further notice of the man, without appearing to recognise him, he gave the signal for departure.

After riding for some time silently along the banks of a moderately wide rivulet the trapper made a sharp turn, and plunged again into the forest.

'I crave your pardon,' he said, 'for making you turn out of your way; but this is a beaver pond, and I do not wish to frighten them.'

'Oh!' the young lady cried, 'how delighted I should be to see those industrious animals at work!'

'Nothing more easy, senorita,' said the trapper, 'if you will follow me, while your companions remain here, and wait for us.'

'Yes, yes!' Dona Luz replied eagerly; then checking herself, added, 'Oh, pardon me, dear uncle.'

The general cast a look at the trapper.

'Go, my child,' he said, 'we will wait for you here.'

'Thank you, uncle,' the young girl remarked joyfully, as she leaped from her horse.

'I will be answerable for her,' the trapper said frankly; 'fear nothing.'

'I fear nothing when trusting her to your care, my friend,' the general replied.

'Thanks!' And making a sign to Dona Luz, Black Elk disappeared with her among the bushes.

When they had gone some distance, the trapper stopped. After listening and looking around him on all sides, he stooped towards the young girl, and laying his hand lightly on her right arm, said—

'Listen!'

Dona Luz stood still, uneasy and trembling.

The trapper perceived her agitation.

'Be not afraid,' he rejoined; 'I am an honest man; you are in as much safety here alone with me in this desert as if you were in the Cathedral of Mexico, at the foot of the high altar.'

The young girl cast a furtive glance at the trapper. In spite of his singular costume, his face wore such an expression of frankness, his eye was so soft and limpid, that she felt completely reassured.

'Speak!' she said.

'You belong,' the trapper resumed, 'I perceive, to that party of strangers who, for some days past, have been exploring the prairies in every direction.'

'Yes.'

Among you is a sort of madman, who wears blue spectacles and a white wig, and who amuses himself—for what purpose I cannot tell—with making a provision of herbs and stones, instead of trying, like a brave hunter, to trap a beaver, or knock over a deer.'

'I know the man you speak of; he is a very learned physician.'

'I know he is; he told me so himself. He often comes this way. We are very good friends. By means of a powder, which he persuaded me to take, he completely checked a fever which had tormented me two months, and of which I could not get rid.'

'Indeed! I am happy to hear of such a result.'

'I should like to do something for you, to show my gratitude for that service.'

'I thank you, my friend, but I cannot see anything in which you can be useful to me, unless it be in showing me the beavers.'

The trapper shook his head.

'Perhaps in something else,' he said, 'and that much sooner than you may fancy. Listen to me attentively, senorita. I am but a poor man; but here in the prairie, we know many things that God reveals to us, because we live face to face with Him. I will give you a piece of good advice. That man who serves you as a guide is an arrant scoundrel. I am very much deceived if he will not lead you into some ambush. There is no lack here of plenty of rogues with whom he may lay plans to destroy you, or at least rob you.'

'Are you sure of what you say?' the girl exclaimed, terrified at words which coincided so strangely with what Loyal Heart had said to her.

'I am as sure as a man can be; that is to say, after the antecedents of the Babbler, everything of the sort must be expected from him. Believe me, if he has not already betrayed you, it will not be long before he will.'

'Good God! I will go and warn my uncle.'

'Beware of doing that! that would ruin all. The people with whom your guide will soon be in collusion, if he be not so already, are numerous, determined, and thoroughly acquainted with the prairie.'

'What is to be done, then?' the young lady asked.

'Nothing. Wait; and, without appearing to do so, carefully watch all your guide's proceedings.'

'But—'

'You must be sure,' the trapper interrupted, 'that if I lead you to mistrust him, it is not with a view of deserting you when the right moment comes.'

dam; but very shortly five others appeared, carrying pieces of wood, mud, and bushes. They then all directed their course towards a part of the barrier which, as the lady could perceive, needed repair. They deposited their load on the broken part, and plunged into the water, but only to reappear almost instantly on the surface.

Each brought up a certain quantity of slimy mud, which they employed as mortar to join and render firm the pieces of wood and the bushes; they went away and returned again with more wood and mud; in short, this work of masonry was carried on till the breach had entirely disappeared.

As soon as all was in order, the industrious animals enjoyed a moment's recreation; they pursued each other in the pond, plunged to the bottom of the water, or sported on the surface, striking the water noisily with their tails.

Whilst the first were amusing themselves thus, two other members of the community appeared. For some time they looked gravely on at the sports of their companions, without showing any inclination to join them; then climbing up the steep bank not far from the spot where the trapper and the young girl were watching, they seated themselves upon their hind paws, leaning the fore ones upon a young pine, and beginning to gnaw the bark of it. Sometimes they detached a small piece, and held it between their paws, still remaining seated; they nibbled it with contortions and grimaces pretty much resembling those of a monkey shelling a walnut.

The evident object of these beavers was to cut down the tree, and they labored at it earnestly. It was a young pine of about eighteen inches in diameter at the part where they attacked it, as straight as an arrow, and of considerable height. No doubt they would soon have succeeded in cutting it through; but the general, uneasy at the prolonged absence of his niece, made up his mind to go in search of her, and the beavers, terrified at the noise of the horses, dived into the water and disappeared.

The general reproached his niece gently for her long absence; but she, delighted with what she had seen, did not heed him, and promised herself often to be a spectator of the proceedings of the beavers.

The little party, under the direction of the trapper, directed their course towards the rancho, in which he had offered them shelter from the burning rays of the sun, which was now at its zenith.

The travellers soon reached a miserable hut, made of interlaced branches of trees, scarcely capable of sheltering them from the rays of the sun, and in every respect resembling, as regarded convenience, those of other trappers of the prairies, who are men that trouble themselves the least about the comforts of life.

Nevertheless, such as it was, Black Elk did the honors of it very warmly to the strangers.

A second trapper was squatting before the hut, occupied in watching the roasting of the buffalo's hump which Black Elk had promised his guests.

This man, whose costume was in all respects like that of Black Elk, was scarcely forty years old; but the fatigue and miseries of his hard profession had dug upon his face such a network of inextricable wrinkles as made him look older than he was.

In fact, there does not exist in the world a more dangerous, more painful, or less profitble trade than that of a trapper. These poor people are often, whether by Indians or hunters, robbed of their hardly-earned gains, scalped, and massacred, and no one troubles himself to learn what has become of them.

'Take your place, senorita; and you also, gentlemen,' said Black Elk, politely. 'However poor my hut may be, it is large enough to contain you all.'

The travellers cheerfully accepted his invitation; they alighted from their horses, and were soon stretched comfortably upon beds of dry leaves, covered with the skins of bears, elks, and buffaloes.

The repast—truly a hunter's repast—was washed down with some cups of excellent mezcal which the general always carried with him on his expeditions, and which the trappers appreciated as it deserved.

Whilst Dona Luz and the others took a siesta till the heat of the sun's rays should be a little abated, the general, begging Black Elk to follow him, went out of the hut.

As soon as they were at a sufficient distance, the general seated himself at the foot of an ebony-tree, motioning for his companion to follow his example.

After a moment's silence—

'Allow me, in the first place,' the general said, 'to thank you for your frank hospitality. That duty performed, I wish to put a few questions.'

'Caballero!' the trapper replied, 'you know what the redskins say: between every word smoke your calumet, in order to weigh your words well.'

'You speak like a sensible man; but be satisfied that I have no intention of putting questions to you that concern your profession, or any object that can affect you personally.'

'If I am able to answer you, caballero, be assured I will not hesitate to satisfy you.'

'Thank you, friend, I expected no less from you. How long have you been an inhabitant of the prairies?'

'Ten years, already, sir; and God grant I may remain here as many more.'

'This sort of life pleases you then?'

'More than I can tell you. A man must, as I have done, begin it almost as a boy, undergo all the trials, endure all the sufferings, partake all its hazards, in order to understand all the intoxicating charms it procures, the celestial joy it gives, and the unknown pleasures into which it plunges us! In the desert, in the prairie, face to face with God, his ideas enlarge, his spirit grows, and he becomes really what the Supreme Being meant to make him; that is to say, the king of the creation.'

The general sighed deeply as he spoke, a furtive tear trickled over his grey moustache.

'That's true,' he said, sadly; 'this life has strange charms for the man who has tasted it, and they attach him by bonds nothing can break. Have you many Mexicans among your companions?'

'Many.'

'I should like to obtain some information respecting them.'

'There is only one man who could give you any, sir; and that man is not at this moment here.'

'And he is called?'

'Loyal Heart.'

'Loyal Heart!' the general replied, warmly; 'surely I know that man.'

'Yes, you do.'

'Good heavens! what a fatality!'

'Perhaps it will be more easy than you suppose to meet with him again, if you really wish to see him.'

'I have an immense interest in wishing it.'

'Then make your mind easy; you will soon see him.'

'How so?'

'Oh! very simply. Loyal Heart lays his traps near me; at the present time I am watching them; but it cannot be long before he returns.'

'God grant it may be so!' said the general.

'As soon as he comes I will send you word, if you have not quitted your camp.'

'Do you know where my troop is encamped?'

'We know everything in the desert,' the trapper said, with a smile.

At that moment Dona Luz came out of the hut. The travelers remounted their horses, and after thanking the trappers for their cordial hospitality, they again took the road to the camp.

TREACHERY

The return was dull; the general was plunged in profound reflections, caused by his conversation with the trapper. Dona Luz was thinking of the warning that had been given her; the guide embarrassed by the two conversations of Black Elk with the lady and the general, had a secret presentiment, which told him to keep on his guard. The two lanceros alone rode on carelessly, thinking, only of one thing – the repose which awaited them on regaining the camp.

The Babbler incessantly cast anxious looks around him, appearing to seek for auxiliaries amidst the thickets which the little party passed silently through.

Day was drawing to a close; it would not be long before the sun disappeared, and already the mysterious denizens of the forests at intervals sent forth dull roarings.

'Are we far from the camp?' the general asked.

'No ,' the guide replied; 'scarcely an hour's ride.'

'Let us mend our speed then; I should not like to be surprised by the night in this woody country.'

The troop fell into a quick trot, which, in less than half an hour, brought them home.

Captain Aguilar and the doctor came to receive the travelers on their arrival, and they seated themselves at table.

But the sadness which for some time past seemed to have taken possession of the general and his niece increased instead of diminishing. It had its effect upon the repast; all swallowed their food hastily, without exchanging a word. As soon as they had finished, under pretext of the fatigues of the journey, they separated, ostensibly to seek repose, but, in reality, for the sake of being alone.

On his part, the guide was not at his ease, a bad conscience, a sage has said, is the most annoying night companion a man can have. As Babbler possessed the worst of all bad consciences, he had no inclination to sleep. He walked about the camp, harassed by anxiety and perhaps remorse, seeking for some means of getting out of the scrape in which he found himself. But it was in vain for him to put his mind to the rack: nothing suggested itself to calm his apprehensions.

In the meantime night was advancing, the moon had disappeared, and a thick darkness hovered over all.

Everyone was asleep, or appearing to sleep; the guide alone, who had taken upon himself the first watch, was seated on a bale, with his arms crossed upon his breast, and his eyes fixed upon vacancy.

All at once a hand was placed upon his shoulder, and a voice murmured in his ear the single word -

'Kennedy!'

The guide, with that presence of mind, and that imperturbable phlegm which never abandons the Indian or the half-breed, cast a timid glance around him, to assure himself that he was alone; then he seized the hand which had remained resting upon his shoulder, and dragged the man who had spoken to him, and who followed him without resistance, to a retired spot, where he thought he was certain of being overheard by nobody.

As the two men passed by the tent, the curtains opened, and a shadow glided silently after them.

When they were concealed amidst the packages, and standing near enough to each other to speak in a voice as low as a breath, the guide muttered -

'God be praised! I have been expecting your visit with impatience, Kennedy.'

'Did you know that I was about to come?' the latter remarked, suspiciously.

and the captain will come up with the rest of the troop. Then he may arrange his matters with the girl as well as he is able; that is his concern; my task will be accomplished.'

'Capital.'

'In this fashion we shall avoid bloodshed and blows, for which I have not great fancy.'

'We know your prudence in that respect.'

'Zounds! my dear fellow, when we have affairs like this on hand, which, when they succeed, present great advantages, we should always endeavor so to arrange matters as to have all the chances in our favor.'

'Perfectly well reasoned; besides which, your idea pleases me much, and, without delay, I will put it into execution; but, in the first place, let us make things clear, to avoid misunderstandings, which are always disagreeable.'

'Very well.'

'If, as I believe he will, the captain finds your plan good, and very likely to succeed, as soon as we are at the foot of the hill, I will come up with six resolute fellows, whom I will pick out myself. On which side must we introduce ourselves into the camp?'

'The devil! why, on the side you have already entered; you ought to know it.'

'And you, where will you be?'

'At the spot where you enter, ready to assist you.'

'That's well. Now all is agreed and understood, and I am off.'

'The sooner the better.'

'You are always right. Guide me to the place I am to go out at; it is so cursedly dark, that I may lose my way, and tumble over some sleeping soldier, and that would not help our business at all.'

'Give me your hand.'

'Here it is.'

The two men rose, and prepared to proceed to the place where the

344

captain's emissary was to leave the camp; but, at the same moment a shadow interposed itself between them, and a firm voice said –

'You are traitors, and shall die!'

In spite of their self-possession, the two men remained for an instant stupefied. Without giving them time to recover their presence of mind, the person who had spoken discharged two pistols, point blank at them.

The miserable wretches uttered a loud cry. One fell, but the other, bounding like a tiger-cat, scrambled over the intrenchments and disappeared before a second shot could be fired at him.

At the double report and the cry uttered by the bandits, the whole camp was roused, and all rushed to the barricades.

The general and Captain Aguilar were the first to arrive at the spot. They found Dona Luz, with two smoking pistols in her hands, whilst, at her feet, a man was writhing in agonies of death.

'What does all this mean, niece? What has happened, in the name of Heaven? Are you wounded?' the terrified general asked.

'Be at ease, dear uncle, on my account,' the young lady replied. 'I have only punished a traitor. Two wretches were plotting in the dark against our common safety; one of them has escaped, but I believe the other is at least seriously wounded.'

The general eagerly examined the dying man. By the light of the torch he held in his hand he at once recognized Kennedy, the guide whom the Babbler pretended had been burnt alive in the conflagration of the prairie.

'Oh, oh!' he said, 'what does all this mean?'

'It means, uncle, the girl replied, 'that if God had not come to my aid, we should have been this very night surprised by a troop of bandits, lying in ambush close to us.'

'Let us lose no time, then!'

And the general, assisted by Captain Aguilar, hastened to prepare everything for a vigorous resistance.

The Babbler had fled, but a large track of blood proved that he was seriously wounded. If it had been light enough, they would have attempted to pursue him, and, perhaps, might have taken him; but, in the midst of darkness, and suspecting that their enemies were in ambush in the neighborhood, the general was not willing to risk his soldier out of the camp.

As to Kennedy, he was dead.

The first moment of excitement past, Dona Luz, no longer sustained by the danger of her situation, began to feel she was a woman. Her energy disappeared, her eyes closed, a convulsive trembling shook her whole frame; she fainted, and would have fallen, if the doctor, who was watching her, had not caught her in his arms.

He carried her in that state into the tent, and lavished upon her all the remedies usual in such cases.

The young lady gradually recovered: her spirits were calmed, and order was re-established in her ideas.

The advice given her that very day by Black Elk then naturally recurred to her mind; she deemed the moment was coming for claiming the execution of his promise, and she made a sign to the doctor.

'My dear doctor,' she said, in a sweet but weak voice, 'are you willing to render me a great service?'

'Dispose of me as you please, senorita.'

'Do you know a trapper named Black Elk?'

'Yes; he has a hut not a great way from us, near a beaver pond.'

'That is the person, my good doctor. Well, as soon as it is light, you must go to him from me.'

'For what purpose, senorita?'

'Because I ask you,' she said, in a calm tone.

'Oh! then you may be at ease; I will go,' he replied.

'Thank you, doctor.'

'What shall I say to him?'

346

'You will give him an account of what has taken place here tonight.'

'The deuce!'

'And then you will add – retain my exact words, you must repeat them to him to the very letter.'

'I listen with all my ears, and will engrave them on my memory.'

'"Black Elk, the hour is come!" You understand that, do you not?'

'Perfectly, senorita.'

'You swear to do what I ask of you?'

'I swear it, he said, in a solemn voice. 'At sunrise, I will go to the trapper; I will give him an account of the events of the night, and will add – "Black Elk, the hour is come." That is all?'

'Yes, all, my kind doctor.'

'Well, then, now get a little sleep, senorita; I swear to you that what you wish shall be done.'

'Again, thank you!' the young girl murmured, with a sweet smile, and pressing his hand.

Then, quite broken down by the terrible emotions of the night, she sank back upon her bed, where she soon fell into a calm, refreshing sleep.

At daybreak, in spite of the observations of the general, who in vain endeavored to prevent his leaving the camp, by recounting to him all the dangers he was needlessly going to expose himself to, the worthy doctor, who had shaken his head at all that his friend said to him, persisted, without giving any reason, in going out, and set off down the hill at a sharp trot.

When once in the forest, he put spurs to his horse, and galloped towards the hut of Black Elk.